Dalit Policies, Politics and Parliament

Narender Kumar

SHIPRA

ISBN: 81-7541-152-X

First Published in India in 2004

Dalit Policies, Politics and Parliament

Published by:
SHIPRA PUBLICATIONS
115-A, Shakarpur, Vikas Marg
Delhi-110092, INDIA
Phone: 22458662, 22500954
Fax: 91-11-22458662
E-mail: siprapub@satyam.net.in
www.shiprapublications.com

Laser typesetting by:
Kumar DTP Systems
Delhi-110091

Printed at:
Choudhary Offset Process
Delhi-110051

Preface

Dalits have become a force to reckon with during recent years because they have emerged as a leading protest group against subordination based on evil social beliefs and misguiding customs. Attempts by various radical social reformers and the constitutional measures have forced others to listen them attentively.

Public policies (of which Dalit policies are part) as constitutional measures have come under detailed scrutiny in recent years, thus shifting the focus on alternative policy formulation. The concern today is not just for alternative policies but also to create new structures and processes for their formulation and implementation. And it is in this context that political dynamics and the role of Indian Parliament becomes relevant with regard to the policy formulation for Dalits. Special representation for Dalits in Lok Sabha has been a historic phenomenon and it has not got its due attention from academicians, intellectuals and research scholars as it should have.

The present study examines the role of Parliament in policy formulation for Dalits. The study goes beyond analyzing the various processes and procedures of parliamentary control over the administrative machinery or its activities with regard to Dalit policies and programs, or merely studying the socio-economic background of the Dalit representatives in the Lower House of the Parliament, i.e. the Lok Sabha.

Our concern is to study the impact of parliamentary debates and questions on the policies meant for Dalits and examine the role of Dalit representatives in the formulation of such policies. This study has been undertaken against the backdrop of the growing disenchantment with the Legislature in policy formulation. Studies on Dalits and reserved constituencies have shown that Dalit issues are not taken seriously. Moreover, with the liberalization of the economy from the 1990s, the role of the State- on whom Dalits have been dependent - is declining in developmental activities. Thus, we thought it to be an urgent need to examine how Parliament has responded to the Dalit aspirations at various crucial junctures.

I extend my heartfelt thanks to Prof. Kuldeep Mathur of Centre for Political Studies, Jawaharlal Nehru University for his valuable guidance and constant encouragement with critical and constructive comments. My sincerest thanks to Prof. C.P. Bhambhari, Prof. Gopal Guru and Prof. S. K. Thorat for their valuable suggestions.My thanks to Mr. Waman Meshram, President, BAMCEF, who has been source of inspiration. I am obliged to Dr.R.M. Pal, Y.S.Alone, V.Rajashekhar and friends for their constant support.

My family members, particularly my life-partner Anju and colleagues in the Motilal Nehru College kept encouraging me to complete the work, I express my gratitude to them.

Contents

Abbreviation

BJP	Bhartiya Janata Party
BSP	Bahujan Samaj Party
CAD	Constituent Assembly Debates
CAG	Comptroller and Auditor General
Cong.	Indian National Congress
CSCT	Commissioner for Scheduled Caste and Scheduled Tribes
DOPT	Department of Personnel and Training
IRDP	Integrated Rural Development Programme
ITDP	Integrated Tribal Development Programme
JD	Janata Dal
LSD	Lok Sabha Debates
MHA	Ministry of Home Affairs
MP	Member of Parliament
MW	Ministry of Welfare
NCSCT	National Commission for Scheduled Castes and Scheduled Tribes
PAA	Prevention of Atrocities Act
PAB	Prevention of Atrocities Bill
PCRA	Protection of Civil Rights Act
PWSCT	Parliamentary Committee on the Welfare of Scheduled Castes and Scheduled Tribes
SC	Scheduled Caste
SCP	Special Component Plan
SCSTFDC	Scheduled Castes and Scheduled Tribes Financial Development Corporation
SRD	Special Recruitment Drive
ST	Scheduled Tribe
TSP	Tribal Sub-Plan
UPSC	Union Public Service Commission

1

Introduction

> If we wish to preserve the Constitution in which we have sought to enshrine the principle of Government of the people, for the people and by the people, let us resolve not to be tardy in the recognition of the evils that lie across our path and which induce people to prefer Government for the people to Government by the people, nor to be weak in our initiative to remove them.
>
> —*Dr. B.R. Ambedkar*
>
> (Concluding remarks in the Constituent Assembly)

The *Varna* and the Caste systems have been the basic features of the Indian society. The *Varna* system includes the four categories of Hindus, *viz. Brahmin, Kshatriya, Vaishya* and *Shudra.* However, it has always been debated whether the untouchables and the tribals come under this system or not. In spite of this debate the fact remains that the untouchables have been residing on the 'periphery' of the areas dominated by the Hindus, as a distinct and independent social group, whereas the tribals remained completely isolated from the Hindu society.

The subjugation of millions of people through the ideology of Caste system has been a part of Indian social history for centuries. Untouchables having been at the margins of Indian society always remained at the receiving end. Robert Deliege pointing towards this states "... in the Indian social system everyone is to some extent impure, and that impurity is a relative concept. But the impurity of untouchables is peculiar to them, in that it is indelible and unreversible." (Deliege 1999:50). The social conditions of the untouchables were such that they were not merely ritually assailable but vulnerable in several other ways, as explained by various social scientists. The deprivation of the untouchables has largely been three-fold: low ritual status, wretched economic conditions, and lack of access to political power (Oomen 1984:46).

Caste system found critics both within India as well as outside. Efforts have been made from time to time both by the untouchables and the non-untouchables alike to ameliorate the wretched conditions of the untouchables. During the medieval period, saints like Ravidas, Tukaram, Kabirdas etc. addressed the issue and in the 19th and 20th centuries Jotiba Phuley, Sahu Maharaj, the Britishers, Hindu social reformers, and Dr. Ambedkar tried to bring about certain degree of equality in the Indian society.

Ambedkar's role in addressing the question has been seen differently because he raised his voice for the social, economic, and political rights of the untouchables and fought for these rights politically. This was not often the case with other advocates. Whether during the *Mahad Satyagraha* or the Round Table Conferences (RTCs) or the Poona Pact or the Constituent Assembly, his objective and demand was, for equality and the empowerment of the deprived communities. His strategy was usually political in nature. Thus the role of Dr. Ambedkar remained crucial in the process. His emphasis on the political rights of Depressed Classes (DCs) has to be understood in the light of special representation in separate electorates that was demanded during RTCs by him, and its culmination into the Poona Pact between caste-Hindus and DCs in 1932. The Poona Pact reserved constituencies with joint electorates for DCs, where not only they but others could also vote to elect candidates from amongst them. Without a proper representation to DCs in the form of separate electorates, Ambedkar was apprehensive of the consequences of a Constituent Assembly that was to be dominated by caste-Hindus, and where the representatives of DCs would be reduced to mere tools in their hands (Moon 1991). Later on elections were held to the Constituent Assembly according to joint electorates and Ambedkar also became its member and worked for the development of the deprived.

Ambedkar is the architect of the special provisions towards Scheduled Castes and Scheduled Tribes (SC/STs) laid down in the Indian Constitution. This is a distinguishing feature of the Constitution. His zeal for the removal of inequality and establishing a just social order through the Constitution can be understood through his concluding remarks in the Constituent Assembly. Here he thundered, that in politics, we may have introduced, equality through 'one man one vote' but the question is how to remove inequality prevalent in the social and economic life. The contradiction between political equality and socio-economic inequality remains un-addressed in concrete terms. He further stated:

> We must remove this contradiction at the earliest possible moment or else those who suffer from inequality will blow up the structure of political democracy which this assembly has so laboriously built up (Govt. of India 1992, *Ambedkar and Social Justice*, Vol II:190).

Ambedkar's role as a Chairperson of the Drafting Committee in the Constituent Assembly was quite effective and dominating. The result was the framing of several laws and provisions for the oppressed. He must have expected a similar role from the SC/ST (Dalit)[1] representatives who later came to constitute a good number in the Lok Sabha *i.e.*, the lower house of Union Legislature that has been bestowed upon with the power of formulating laws for diverse sections of the Indian society. Through his dynamic leadership and a proper understanding of the socio-political conditions of Dalits, Ambedkar not only argued but also convinced others to take a special care of Dalits through constitutional measures.

Policy Formulation

Policies are formulated with an aim to address the present issues which confront the political demands of the society and the need to foster desirable changes according to those demands. Public policies have been defined as guidelines for public action, prescribing in general terms, the means for moving towards a desired course of events or outcome (Poister 1978:1). Public policy may have broader goals like socio-economic development, liberty, and equality as its objective, or narrower goals which are more tangible, concrete, and immediate such as educational development or family planning. A policy can be for a larger section of the society or for smaller sections. Thus public policy indicates a deliberative choice of collective goals and their implementation through decision-making. These decisions, once enacted, are considered authoritatively binding upon all members of the society (Michels 1969:391). Decision-making is an integral part of policy-making, but every decision may not constitute a policy. While formulating policies, policy-makers keep eliminating policy options until the final selection. Elimination of policy options involves recognition of limitations which reveals what is not feasible, and by

---

1 From now onwards, we shall also use Dalit as a substitute for the SC/ST. In popular language Dalit has come to identify the SC/ST category, through connovation of both deprivation and oppression. The term Dalit has come to be used interchangeably with the SC/ST.

implication, what is feasible under the given circumstances (Howlett *et. al.* 1995:123).

Policy-making in a democratic system is almost always entrusted to the elected representatives. The elected representatives debate and discuss various measures in the interest of society. In a country like India, the Legislature occupies a central role in the enactment of laws and policies. Parliament being the supreme law-making body performs a major function of ensuring 'social justice' to the disadvantaged sections of the Indian society. The expectations of the under privileged sections have increased over the years due to welfare policies adopted to uplift the Backward Castes, Minorities, Women, and Dalits in the last five decades. In a society dominated by caste, class, gender, religion, and regionalism, it is the Parliament that can work as a catalytic agency for social change and social justice.

Laws help in the governance of a country. The Rule of Law has become fundamental to the modern day systems of governance. Legislative bodies make laws and the Executive regulates the affairs of the society as per the law. Legislative bodies are made up of the representatives elected by the people. Thus, theoretically, the elected house represents the will of the people. Since people elect the representatives who are expected to guard people's interests, legislative bodies can no longer remain indifferent to people's needs. This system of governance created the necessary conditions whereby the modern State evolved into a welfare State. This value system of the modern State-system can be recognised as the universal characteristic of democracy.

However, public policies have come under considerable and microscopic scrutiny in recent years. Consequently there has been a shift towards the focus on alternative policy formulations. Now the concern is not just a search for alternative policies and making minor changes in existing policies, but also to create new structures and processes for their formulation and implementation (Mathur 1997). And it is in this context that the role of Parliament assumes significance.

In the case of a parliamentary form of government, as in India, two integrated concepts are in evidence - first, the supremacy of the Parliament and second, the prerogative of the Executive to take the initiative in formulating and implementing decisions regarding policies. On several occasions the Executive has taken the initiative and formulated policies and the Legislature deliberated upon them and ultimately approved or disapproved of such decisions. Thus the

Executive's accountability or responsiveness to the Legislature is a major feature of parliamentary democracy.

The parliamentary system of governance had been in existence in ancient India as well. Indicating this system Ambedkar affirms,

> "if you go through the *'Suktas'* of *Mahaparinirvana*, you will find ample evidences in support of my point (parliamentary government). In those suktas, it is stated that while *Bhagwan Buddha* was dying at *Kusinara (Kusinagara)*, message to this effect was sent to the *Mallas* who were sitting in session at that time... they decided that they should not close the session but would carry on with their work and go to Kusinara after finishing the business of the parliament" (Ahir 1977:81).

And the notion of accountability to the citizens either directly or indirectly through their elected representatives, is a crucial aspect of the parliamentary system of governance. The Indian parliamentary system, wherein elected representatives of the citizens make the policies, has been adopted from its British counterpart. Although unlike the British Parliament, the Indian Parliament is subject to limitations as posed by the 'Judicial Review' as per our Constitution.[2]

The historical antecedents of the modern Indian Parliament can be found in the Government of India Acts of 1909, 1919, and 1935 and some other rulings of British rule in the post 1857 period.[3] The principle of parliamentary supremacy as in the British model has been modified in India according to its specialities. However, the combination of the parliamentary system and the federal structure has led to the division of powers between the Union Parliament and the State Legislatures. The Fundamental Rights of the citizens, Directive Principles of State Policy and Judicial Review that impose limitations on the power of the parliament in India, are non-existent in Britain. Thus, the Parliament of India has been considered neither sovereign nor supreme (Delhi Laws Act. 1912 A.I.R., 1951:332)

In terms of the legislative-executive relationship, the Indian Parliament like its counterpart in Britain, presents a fusion rather than a separation of powers as existent in United States of America. In spite of

---

2 The laws passed by the Parliament in India can be examined by the High Courts and the Supreme Court for constitutionality.

3 For historical sketch of constitutional reforms in British India, see Subhash C. Kashyap (1992).

fusion of powers, the two are distinct bodies in terms of functions and powers as mentioned in the Article 75 of the Constitution. The Executive governs the country and the Parliament legislates, advises, ventilates public grievances, and also critically analyses the executive. The Executive has almost unlimited power, to initiate and formulate legislative and financial proposals, unfettered and unhindered by the Parliament. Similarly, the Parliament has unlimited power to ask for information, to discuss and debate, to scrutinise the policies, and to put the seal of popular approval on the proposals made by the Executive (Kashyap: 1987).

In practice, the actual policy formulation is undertaken by the experts working under the Cabinet and only a few modifications take place on the floor of the Parliament – in India as well as in Britain. Thus the well-known observation of Ramsay Muir apply to both the Indian as well as the British parliamentary systems. He states:

> Parliamentary system of government has changed into Prime-Ministerial form of government diminishing the power and prestige of Parliament, making it to appear as maintaining and criticising the Cabinet.

Nonetheless, the significance of the Indian Parliament lies in the fact that the discussions on the Bills on the floor of the House and in the Parliamentary Committees can force the Cabinet to change, over-rule, or simplify the decisions of the Judiciary according to the suggestions of the Members. The three stages which every legislation has to pass through also influence the policy formulation.

The Process of Policy-Making

The process by which a proposal is translated into public policy is often a complex and lengthy one. Public policy involves deliberate choice of collective goals and the implementation of public decisions. When enacted, such decisions are considered authoritatively binding upon all members of the society. In the formation of public policies, four principal stages can be identified. They are: initiation, formulation, deliberation and approval, and implementation (Norton 1993:53).

Initiation and formulation or drafting of policy is undertaken by the Executive, as it has legal and constitutional experts at its disposal. These experts render their services on demand, and draft the proposals of the Cabinet to put before the Parliament. Though there is also a provision for Private Member's Bill in the parliamentary system, but in practice such bills are rarely approved. Even if approved, the technicalities are furnished by the experts and only then such proposals are legislated. The MPs lack the resources and the time inside the Parliament to initiate a policy on regular basis. Moreover, the Private Member's Bill though initiated by 'back benchers', cannot make a charge on the public revenue, putting a limitation on it (Norton 1993:68).

It would be misleading to suggest that the Parliament is concerned only with the deliberation and approval of policy. It has the power of initiation and formulation of a policy on the one hand, and implementation of it on the other. Apart from the parliamentary and post enactment stages, the Parliament's role in the preparatory stage of a bill could be significant, as legislation is influenced by various sources that may bear influence on the proposed legislation. The Parliament may also be involved in the post-enactment stage by way of reviewing where the legislative shoe pinches (Rush 1976:84).

Legislation is normally the product of a complex and long-drawn process – the stages of which can be easily described theoretically, but difficult to unravel practically. This applies more to the preparatory stage as it takes place in private. It may be possible to discover who did what, how, and when, but answering 'why' is a formidable task. Pressure groups and back benchers in particular may be consulted by the Treasury benches but it is seldom acknowledged that their decisions have been influenced by them. Apart from the pressure group, and back benchers, Cabinet colleagues, the party in power, the government's priorities, the attitude of the opposition, the socio-economic situation etc., could also influence a legislation. However, to give each factor its due, for arriving at a rational conclusion in influencing a decision is probably impossible. One may argue that each decision has an element of uniqueness.

The second stage *i.e.*, the parliamentary stage may take a long time and result in various substantial changes in the original bill, but may not alter its fundamental purpose. A study conducted by J.A.G. Griffith on British Parliament showed that of the forty-eight government bills passed during 1967-68, 12 per cent were substantially amended, 39 per cent were slightly amended, another 39 per cent were negligibly amended, leaving 10 per cent of legislation with the substance of the bill left intact. This provides conclusive evidence of the limited number of changes made to government bills by parliament (Quoted by Rush 1976:87)

The post-enactment stage of a legislation to implement the provisions of an Act could alter the legislations. During this stage, several statutory bodies in implementing the legislations may suggest modifications in the original enactment. The parliamentary questions and other means of scrutinising the bills are also effective in the post-enactment stage. The most important means, and one on which the greatest hopes have been pinned by the advocates of reforms in parliamentary procedures, are the Select Committees.

The Legislature, both inside the Parliament house and in the committees has been envisaged essentially as 'demand input processor' and legislative policy decisions are generally termed as 'policy output', but the linkage between policy demands and policy output is much more complex and circuitous than it appears or is thought to be (Wahlke 1978:151-52).

Policy output has been classified in terms of "distributive", "regulatory", and "redistributive" policies. This suggests that the arena of power or focus of decision-making varies from policy to policy. And on the other hand, "area policies" affect the total population, while the "segmental policies" are for specific sections of the population (Quoted by Eulau *et. al.* 1978:165).

If we look at the policies for Dalits then these policies can be 'regulatory', 'distributive' and 'redistributive'. But all said and done these are essentially "segmental policies" meant for a particular section of the population. When these are "segmental policies" then the policy output in the Parliament needs to be understood in distinct terms because they have special representatives in the Lok Sabha to address their concerns.

Does Parliament Matter?

In the light of the above discussion, it may be concluded that the Parliament, due to its limited role, is of little significance in formulating the public policies. But the issue does not end here. Instead, it questions the significance of the Parliament itself as an institution and also whether it is a living institution which caters to the Indian situation.

Analysing the significance of British Parliament, Richardson and Jordan observed that the significance of Parliament lies in its very insignificance (Richardson *et. al.* 1979:121). One must bear in mind that the Parliament may not be the central actor in the determination of public policy but it does not mean that the Parliament does not matter (Norton 1993:202). Thus the issue turns the other way round. To be precise, "the insignificance of Parliament lies in its significance in terms of its relationship with the government in formation and the conduct of government and its relationship with the citizens" (*Ibid.*). Can we think of the Indian polity without the Parliament, or to be more precise, without the Lok Sabha? In order to answer this question satisfactorily, one has to turn towards the functions of Parliament and the role played by it in choosing the government, representing the citizens, legitimising and monitoring the actions of people's representatives, and most importantly, representing the interests of diverse social groups in the country. One may argue that the media, courts, opinion polls, debates on television, and referendums, etc., can substantiate the role played by the Indian Parliament. However, even then the significance of Parliament would not be ruled out. Norton has put it very rightly: "What makes Parliament distinct and indispensable is the fact that it alone enjoys the popularity as well as the formal legitimacy to undertake all these tasks" (*ibid*).

Parliament, Constitution, and Policy Initiatives

Parliament may concern itself with policy matters on various occasions. Apart from basic constitutional policies mentioned in the Preamble, Fundamental Rights and the Directive Principles of State Policy, at times the political vision of the party at the helm of affairs also provide a framework for government policies. The ascending to power of a political party is considered to be the result of an endorsement of the policy perspectives made known to the people through its statements and party manifestos, etc.

The legislative control over policy concerns, starts with the opening of the first session of the parliament after the elections or in the new session annually, with the President's Address. Further, Question Hour, debate on proposed legislations, Motions, Resolutions, and various Parliamentary Committee reports are the instruments to give rise to occasions for extending parliamentary influence over the activities of the government. On some occasions such as levying or modifying taxes, voting on grants, etc., Parliament asserts its power to make Executive accountable to the masses.

The Questions Hour is basically to seek information from the ministers, but if utilised properly, it could force the government to rethink on a particular policy. As a follow up to an incomplete answer to a Question, the Members may demand half-an-hour discussion at the end of the day. The proposed legislations by the government invite a detailed debate and discussion where MPs may assume significant role.

Under a 'Call Attention' notice, a Member may, with the prior permission of the Speaker, ask for the attention of a Minister to any matter of urgent public importance and force the Minister to make a statement on the subject. Once a Calling Attention Notice has been admitted by the Speaker, the Minister cannot refuse to make a statement. Various reports of Commissions such as the NCSCT are not only tabled on the floor of the House but a full-fledged discussion also takes place where the policies of the government come under detailed scrutiny. Finally, the Parliament appoints committees to look into various aspects of the government. Often discussions in these committees enable the government to strengthen or change the existing policies. The discussions are important as they indicate parliamentary mood and bring the impact of public thinking on the administrative apparatus, which may otherwise remain immune to public sentiments and feelings. Parliamentary debates serve to remind the administration and the government of their duties and obligations, affecting their way of thinking. Administrative accountability is laid down during discussions. After the parliament approves the policies, the onus of execution and implementation rests on the administration that has the complete freedom to implement them. But they are nevertheless guided by the various viewpoints expressed on the floor of the House (Shakdher 1977:180-84).

To check the decline of legislative powers, legislative committees "meant to provide a balancing factor in a system that is otherwise geared to the hegemony of the Executive" have been formed (*Parliamentary Committees in India* 1973. New Delhi: Institute of Constitutional and Parliamentary Studies).

Though the Article 105 of the Indian Constitution makes provisions for legislative committees, it was only in 1954 that Consultative Committees were established. A consistent demand was put to the government to revise Standing Committees by the parliamentarians but it was only in 1993 that 17 Standing Committees were established to review and report on laws, programmes, and policy objectives and implementation. These are called subject-based Standing Committees, and relate to subjects like, agriculture, commerce, defence, etc. Prior to these subject-based Standing Committees, there have been other Select Committees such as Public Accounts Committee, Committee on the Welfare of SC/STs, etc.

Due to the enormous territorial area and the diverse cultural character of Indian society, and the federal system, the Cabinet/Executive cannot formulate and decide the course of action on any given issue arbitrarily. The complexity of issues involved in the Indian socio-political system has perhaps been the reason behind the frequent assertion by Indian Parliament of its share of power in the process of legislation (Jain 1985:241).

A number of instruments in the hands of Parliament may make one believe that it has got tremendous powers to formulate policies and keep check on the Executive. But there has been a demand for parliamentary reforms for a long time. And scholars have been arguing for strengthening the institution of Parliament (Surya Prakash 1995).

Though, Parliament has various instruments to make the government accountable to the citizens but questions have been raised over the adequacy of these measures due to its declining role in the policy formulation process. James Margach (1981) puts it directly when he states that "the modern Parliament has become in practice a central registry for recording votes and giving effect to decisions taken elsewhere in the Cabinet and in Government Departments". Another study by J.A.G. Griffith (1974) argues that governments hardly yield before the Parliament and even if they do so, it is on their own terms and very rarely, when opposition to their proposals is strong and widespread. It is not only true regarding the British Parliament but also the Indian Parliament, which has inadequate powers to control the Executive. Subhash Kashyap (1987) reaffirms that "the operative reality of politics today is that the real power resides in the Prime Minister and his or her Cabinet and not in Parliament". Thus the Prime Minister and the Cabinet control not only the government but also the legislative functions due to its extensive power to take and implement decisions.

These studies on the lack of governmental accountability towards Parliament make us believe that the Parliament does not possess adequate instruments to scrutinise the governmental activities. A study by Rubinoff (1995) analysed the workings of subject-based Standing Committees (formed on March 31, 1993 to examine the policies and demands for grants of the various governmental departments) in making the Executive accountable and for strengthening the Parliament. He argues that such committees can only counter-balance a strong Executive and make the Parliament effective.

One may argue that Select Committees have existed for a long time to scrutinise the Bills which become major policies of the government, but their role has not strengthened the Parliament. And if some more reforms take place, it will be possible for Parliament to strengthen itself. But there is certainly a ray of hope in strengthening the resources at the Parliament's disposal and political will to do so. Norton (1993) correctly states that the "members alone can determine whether parliament jumps into the twenty-first century or enters it as a body more responsive than ever before to the demands of changing society". There is a need to interlink the issue of inadequate role of Parliament on the one hand, and provide it with a greater role in making the executive more accountable to it, on the other. There may be limitations of the Parliament to play a significant role, but its significance in the overall policy making process cannot be ignored and specially in the context of national policies for Dalits, who have both special representatives in Lok Sabha and a sizeable population in India.

The Indian Constitution states basic policy concerns with regard to the citizens in general and Dalits in particular. Any policy is a collective's response to conditions of the political, economic, and social environment. Changes in policy may occur with alteration in the socio-political environment. Consider this:

> policy functions as a response to environmental conditions, both physical and social, that has built into it an anticipation of a future state of affairs... a change in policy is both causal and purposive: it is "caused" by environmental stimuli, but it is also directed towards a goal and shaped for a purpose. The tension arising out of the simultaneity of causal and purposive forcing is a basic property of policy (Eulau 1978:179).

Thus the Parliament, could be seen as an institution which is meant to respond to the changing demands that function not only at policy initiatives level but also for policy-making.

Representation in Parliament

A 'representative' is to protect and advance the interests of the individuals or the group who s/he is representing. The central idea of representation rests on whether or not the representative is able to co-ordinate between the constituents on whose behalf s/he is supposed to act. It also includes the institution of Legislature. The composition of the Legislature is expected to determine the activities of different groups represented in it and there is need for a high co-relation of the characteristics of the Legislatures with their constituents.

In the liberal democratic framework, responsibility and representation are closely linked. The relation between legislative behaviour and representation is quite complex. And the search is for responsible and representative government under this framework. If one looks at Edmund Burk's notion of virtual and actual representation, one finds how representation is not merely concerned with *what* decisions are made but 'how they are made'. Explaining three forms of role-orientations - trustee, politico, and delegate of the legislator, Eulau observes:

> The trustee claims to rely on his conscience or what he thinks right, or on his considered judgement of the facts involved in the issue which he has to decide. The delegate claims that he seeks and follows instructions from his constituents or other clienteles. The politico claims that he will adopt one or other orientation as conditions call for, and he must balance one against the other. Under modern conditions the trustee orientation is probably more realistic. Given the complexity of governmental problems on the one hand and the difficulty of finding out what clienteles may want the delegate orientation is probably the least functional from the point of view of effective representation (*Ibid*: 286).

The underlying concept of representation is the similarities between the representative and those represented. A basic task of Political Science is to understand the behaviours of important political actors – in our case the MPs in the Parliament. To influence policy is one of the legislator's defining characteristics and tasks. The response of its Members to the institution's policy is of fundamental significance. While legislators are ubiquitous, their influence in policy formulation process varies greatly across political systems, both in quantity and in quality (Polsby 1975, Norton 1984). The cross sectional comparisons seeking to investigate the connection between legislative power and the behaviour of the legislators, confront inevitable problems. Participation is active involvement in the legislative process and the policy influence of a legislator is his/her ability to not only initiate legislation, but also to amend, delay, or even reject legislation proposed by the Executive (Blondel 1970).

The representational consequences of special interests may be understood with the help of two basic approaches - descriptive representation and substantive representation. The former relates to the societal relationship with the constituents of the representative in the physical world and the latter moves beyond appearances to the specific question of how the representative serve the interests of the constituents whom s/he is supposedly representing (Canon 1999:351-55).

Given the distinctive nature of special interests such as the Blacks in America and the Dalits in India, and such other similar social representations, questions have been raised about, (a) how should these interests be represented, (b) whether other representations can represent such interest, and (c) what impact special representation may have on the nature of representation, accountability, legitimacy, and equality, etc.

Representation in Legislatures through Reservations

Special interests have been understood in terms of the "politics of difference" versus the "politics of commonality" (Connely 1991, Young 1993). The recognition of community based identities have led to special representation so that the representatives and those represented share common aspects of socio-economic life. The choice of the legislator among Dalits obviously reflects the similar socio-economic characteristics within the Dalit community at large. Thus while providing reservations in legislatures, it was believed that a Dalit representative would be in a better position to comprehend the problems faced by his/her community than a non-SC/ST legislator. The seats have been reserved in the Lok Sabha with joint electorates, wherein Dalit as well as non-Dalit voters participate in the election process to choose a Dalit candidate. It obviously does not accept separate electorates—giving voting rights exclusively to the Dalit community.[4]

In this work, taking the functional view of representation, the legislators' behaviour with special reference to SC/ST representatives, as well as their counterparts is analysed, with relation to the policies for Dalits in the Lower House of the Union Legislature *i.e.*, the Lok Sabha.

The period for the study is 1985-95. It was a time where two significant developments were taking place. At one level there was an upsurge in the consciousness among deprived sections as well as their

---

4 Initially, a system of 'certified candidate' for the representation of Dalits was introduced by the British government. Accordingly, the Governor of the province was entitled to nominate a "depressed classes" candidate to the legislature. But Rao Bahadur Srinivasan, a prominent leader of untouchables at that time, deplored this and stated: "If the Governor who had to certify happened to be a Hindu, he could use this power in the interest of a party instead of the interests of the Depressed Classes" (Speech at the Round Table Conference Session, 30th November 1931:165).

increased participation in the electoral politics. Two, the period witnessed the State withdrawing from the public arena in terms of mass welfare programmes and the liberalisation of the economy, that finally led to increasing privatisation and globalisation. The 1990s in particular, saw an expanding base of electoral democracy, that was a fallout of witnessing greater participation and more intense politicisation than before, among the marginal social groups (Yadav 1999:2393-99). The liberalisation of the economy "was a conscious decision to substantially reduce the role of the State in the process of economic development and rely far more on the market", where "long-term development objectives such as education, human resource development, or the acquisition of technological and managerial capabilities, are simply neglected" (Nayyar 1998:3127-3128). This reflects the unfolding of the contradiction between the logic of political equality and that of social inequality that was warned against by Ambedkar in the Constituent Assembly. Policy functions as a response to physical and social environment, and a change in policy is both causal and purposive, as it is not only caused by environmental stimuli but also directed towards a goal and shaped by a purpose (Eulau 1978:179). Thus, our study becomes more relevant when we examine and develop a relationship among special representations, politico-socio-economic environment in the late 1980s and early 1990s on the one hand, and the role of Parliament on the other, *vis-à-vis* the Dalits.

The role played by the legislators themselves in influencing changing/ rejecting/ modifying/accepting policies for Dalits, constitute the subject matter of the present research. Their response towards the Reports of NCSCT and their initiative to get its recommendations implemented and translated into policy through Bills, participation in debate and discussions, and their performance during Question Hour in Lok Sabha have been analysed in the light of the fact that they are representatives of Dalit masses. Whether various parliamentary procedures like Question Hour, No Confidence Motion, Calling Attention Notice, etc., are utilised or not by these Members deserve special attention for such analysis.

On the composition of the joint electorates under the Poona Pact, Ambedkar questioned "will the Scheduled Castes be able to elect a Scheduled Caste candidate who has their confidence to the seat reserved for them or will the Hindus be able to elect a Scheduled Caste Candidate who is their tool and who has no confidence of the Scheduled Castes?" (Moon 1991:154).

Analysing the results of 1937 election, Ambedkar re-affirmed his stand and did not term the representatives coming from the joint electorates as true representatives of the DCs . He observed that "an untouchable candidate whose majority is the result of split in the camp of his opponents and who, if there had been no split, would have lost, cannot be taken as the real representative of the untouchables" (Moon 1991:157).

The question again came up for discussion in the Constituent Assembly and demand for separate electorates was once again raised by Ambedkar. But finally the Constituent Assembly rejected this demand and adopted in principle the system of joint electorates with reserved seats as per the Poona Pact (Rao 1967:93-96).

Thus, Dalits were given special representation, not as minorities but as a special social class to help them revert the history of their political and social subjugation for centuries together. And this provision was stated to be purely temporary, which would span a period of ten years. Ambedkar himself moved an amendment in the Constituent Assembly that the reservation of seats for the SCs and STs would come to an end after completion of ten years and it was accepted and adopted (CAD Vol. IX August 1949:674). But it is being continuously extended even after the completion of five decades.

National Commission for Scheduled Castes and Scheduled Tribes (NCSCT) and Parliamentary Committee on the Welfare of SC/STs (PCWSCT) are two major institutional mechanism, to look into the implementation and formulation of Dalit policies. The former functions outside the Parliament and the latter within parliamentary system of governance. We look into their evolution in this chapter and later on to their role in policy making.

National Commission for Scheduled Castes and Scheduled Tribes

The NCSCT owes its origin to the Article 338 of the Indian Constitution that provides for the Special Officer for SC/STs. The first appointment to this office was made on November 18, 1950. The office was designated as 'Commissioner for Scheduled Castes and Scheduled Tribes' (CSCT). The appointee's tenure was fixed at three years. It was subsequently raisea to five years, on the recommendation of the PCWSCT in 1970. The CSCT had a two-fold thrust: (i) to monitor the functioning of the constitutional safeguards for SC and STs, and ii) to look into the working of the welfare measures for Dalits. At that stage it had no role in the formulation of policies for these sections. But 1954 onwards it associated itself with the examination of schemes for grants-in-aid received by the state governments and non-governmental agencies for the development of Scheduled Castes and Tribal areas. The CSCT's organisation also helped the state governments in the formulation of their schemes and their proper implementation (PCWSCT 1969:10-11).[5]

Recognising the increasing importance of the role of the CSCT, the Estimates Committee (IInd Lok Sabha) in its 48th Report on the "Ministry of Home Affairs: Scheduled Castes, Scheduled Tribes, and Other Background Classes" recommended assignment of some more functions to the CSCT. But, in 1967 it was decided that the CSCT should be relieved from the functions of formulation of schemes for SC/STs (PCWSCT 1971:2).

This was a regressive measure as it did not allow the CSCT to address the grievances of Dalits adequately. To fill up the gap, the Ministry of Home Affairs (MHA) came out with a resolution dated 21 July 1978 which asked for the constitution of a Commission for SC/STs in addition to the appointment of the CSCT. This Commission was to consist of a Chairman and four members including the CSCT . It was to share the CSCT's burden in various ways. But in its report for the term 1979-81, it observed that the establishment of the Commission has not materially changed the situation with regard to his office (CSCT 1979-81:51). Commenting on the present functioning, it observed:

> There appears to be only two options open: (i) either to amend article 338 of the Constitution and replace the Commissioner for Scheduled Castes and Scheduled Tribes by a multi-member Commission or (ii) to retain both the offices of Commissioner as well as that of Commission, with distinctly drawn up functions and status. In the case of the latter option being accepted: it would be desirable appropriately to revise the functions assigned to the Commission so that these do not overlap with the functions assigned to the Commissioner under the Constitution. And there is a revision in view of the magnitude of the problems relating to the Scheduled Castes and Scheduled Tribes (*Ibid*).

---

5 During the period of our study, three statutory and constitutional bodies, *viz.*, Commissioner for SC/STs, Commission for SC/STs and the National Commission for SC/STs have been in existence, it has been used as Commissioner or CSCT, Commission and NCSCT or National Commission respectively, now onwards.

Interestingly, the above observation came after the Government of India introduced the Constitution (46th Amendment) Bill 1978 that could not be passed during the Winter Session of the Parliament. Yet again in 1979 the same Bill was brought up as the 51st Amendment Bill, 1979. It was debated on the floor of the Lok Sabha on 16 May 1979 but during the voting on the next day, it could not be passed for want of requisite majority (NCSCT 1992-3:10).

Under these circumstances, the two agencies, namely the CSCT and Commission for SC/STs co-existed, till March 11, 1992. At last a fresh legislation called the Constitution (65th Amendment) Act 1990 was passed by the Parliament to constitute a National Commission for Scheduled Castes and Scheduled Tribes. It came into force on March 12, 1992.

The reports of the NCSCT are supposed to be tabled on the floor of Parliament and the Government need to come out with the Action Taken Report on its recommendations. It is to be noted that during the period of our study NCSCT submitted three Reports, but no discussion had taken place on these reports.

Committee on the Welfare of Scheduled Castes and Scheduled Tribes

The Parliament is not capable to deliberate upon each and every issue that comes before it. A study conducted to ascertain the Indian Parliament's capability to check Executive power states that "the systems that are in vogue are wholly inadequate and the accountability of the Executive is still a far cry". (Surya Prakash 1995:310). A ray of hope has been envisaged in the proper functioning of the Standing Committees and strengthening the supervisory role of the MPs constituting these. It is true that the Parliament has been relegated to a position of minor importance and has become increasingly incapable of having a check on the government. A detailed investigation by the Committees could become the best means of redressing the balance. But providing wide ranging powers to Parliament could mean "seriously undermining the functions of the Executive, leading to parliamentary government, not government through Parliament but government by Parliament" (Rush 1976:104). So the question is not whether the Parliament decides, but how it influences the policies and carries public opinion to the government regarding the realisation of policies of mass welfare and the empowerment of the people. In this context, the role of PCWSCT becomes significant. (PCWSCT was instituted in 1968 on the suggestion of the Lok Sabha members, during the course of discussion on the Fourteenth and Fifteenth reports of the CSCT). The PCWSCT consists of 30 Members - 20 elected by the Lok Sabha and 10 by the Rajya Sabha from amongst the MPs in accordance with the system of proportional representation by means of single transferable vote. The Chairperson of the committee is appointed by the Speaker of the Lok Sabha from amongst the members of the Committee. And the term of the Committee is usually one year.

The Committee has been submitting its reports since 1969 and its first report was on 'the Reorganisation of the Office of the Commissioner for Scheduled Castes and Scheduled Tribes and Director General, Backward Class welfare.[6] During the period of our study, the Committee submitted ninety-three reports (22 reports in the 8th Lok Sabha, 6 in the 9th Lok Sabha and 65 reports in the 10th Lok Sabha), on the various aspects of the Dalit policy paradigm ranging from the issue of atrocities to the issue of development.

Overview of Literature

After the adoption of the Constitution, various aspects of Dalit policies have been studied and analysed by scholars, both within India and outside.

Lelah Dushkin (1961) in her articles outlined the polices and programmes for Dalits in three areas - education, services and politics. The major themes covered by her studies relate to the future of the policy and the alternatives to it. S.M. Chitinis (1972) points to the fact that scholarships for Dalit students had not been optimally and equitably used by them with the consequence that there was creation of new inequalities. Karuna Ahmed (1978) in her study on the consequences of protective discrimination argues for the need of an integrated programme for the dispersal of benefits to the Dalits.

With regard to the legal implications of Dalit policies, Marc Galanter (1972) points out the role of the law in the abolition of untouchability and other disabilities. In yet another paper (1979) he studies the impact of compensatory discrimination in political representation. Here, he analyses the costs and benefits of the policy of reserved seats.

Barbara R. Joshi (1982) in her work, deals with the political reservation for Dalits and argues that the policy of political reservation

6 First Report of Parliamentary Committee on the Welfare of Scheduled Castes and Scheduled Tribes, Lok Sabha Secretariat, New Delhi 1969.

has proved to be supportive for the untouchables' developmental programmes in the event of increasing violent opposition against the mobilising untouchables. She concludes that the policy has made the Dalit legislators assertive on socio-economic issues concerning Dalit masses. Her work points out that the political reservation has accelerated and helped social mobility of Dalits. Another major aspect on which she throws light, is the importance of reserved constituencies where political parties cannot afford to ignore Dalits completely. The caste-Hindu politicians consider the Dalits as a potential factor in the struggle for gaining power. The factional politics within a party also increases the importance of Dalit politicians and in turn they get benefited through party tickets and funds for election campaigns. The low educational and economic status leaves Dalit legislators in hardship. She argues that the institution of reserved constituencies can reduce the political problems of Dalits but cannot completely compensate for them. Joshi avers that the lack of art of political skill as well as the experience and knowledge of political power – which are a part of the legacy of the past – have not been eliminated in the case of Dalit legislators. So they are frequently forced to depend on caste-Hindus regarding their own issues.

Satish Saberwal (1972) while summarising the problems of political reservations argues that the Dalit representatives lack political socialisation and thus avoid assuming militant political postures. They do not understand the potentiality of the large system, to generate effective social, political, and economic equality. Moreover, they are not able to generate a new social philosophy or new legislative postures but adopt the same politically mediatory benefits that are available to others. He also concludes that in spite of all such restraints, the Dalits access to the political arena and to various elite settings would decline without a political reservation for them.

Gopal Guru (1986) in his study points out that the belief among the academics that the reservation policy in general and the reserved constituency in particular owes its origin to the British policy of 'divide and rule' needs to be analysed from a much more comprehensive and critical angle. In his final conclusions, he argues that the provision of reserved constituency for Dalits does not necessarily lead to the creation of a clout for the political development of the Dalit community as a whole. It helps a few Dalit legislators to get political benefits which is not sufficient to encourage an institutionalised political participation among Dalits. Yet again this provision is very much subservient to the political interests of the political parties dominated by the elite of the dominant castes having sufficient socio-economic resources. And the elite are found using these constituencies as an institutional device to protect their interests and not the interests of the Dalit community.

G. Narayana (1980) analysed the changing socio-economic characteristics of the Dalit MPs of the 3rd, 4th and 5th Lok Sabha during 1962-71. The changing recruitment patterns of key position holders in the political power structure has been drawn here. Among various variables examined are age, educational background, occupation, place of residence, and previous experience as Members of Lok Sabha. A comparison with non-Dalit Members reveals that the SC Members were younger then the general Members, but interestingly the other variables show much more similarities between the two.

In yet another similar study, D.N.S. Chauhan and S.L. Chopra (1969) compared the socio-economic background of the SC Members in the Lok Sabha with general Members. On the educational and occupational front, differences between the SC and non-SC Members as well as similarities within the SC community as a whole are noted and evaluated.

A recent study by Mendelsohn and Vicziany (1998) quite categorically states that the preferential treatment policies have not been of much significance for Dalits. Rather it is the overall developmental process that has benefited them, as the health and literacy indicators show in the case of Kerala. The anti-discriminatory policies of the State, particularly the court enforcement of those legislations, have been very dismal. The section on Dalit representatives show the silver lining in the case of the increasing vote capacity of the Dalit masses which would help to grow an interest in supporting their people as representatives.

Demolishing the theory of *Harijan* elite, mainly propounded by Sachchidananda (1977), Mandelsohn and Vicziany (1998) see little merit in the proposition, that reservations have created a particularly selfish and uncaring community of Dalit politicians. The hereditary character of culture and its hierarchised advantages, lead to the tendency of the concentration of benefits in a few hands, which may also be true for the future in the case of Dalits. But today, the reality is different. Parliamentary reservation is seen as the most problematic aspect of compensatory discrimination. As a case in point, the authors observe that Kanshi Ram and the like argue that Dalits will learn to struggle when they no longer have any institutional guarantees. The greatest manifestation of Dalit power is seen in their freedom to vote in elections rather than in the number of their 'representatives' in the Parliament. And this capacity to vote with free will has the potential to create new conditions which would give rise to the possibility of parliamentarians taking bold steps for the masses, in the times to come.

Objectives of the Study

The present study goes beyond analysing the various processes and procedures of parliamentary control over the administrative machinery or its activities with regard to Dalit policies and programmes, or merely studying the socio-economic background of the Dalit representatives in the Lower House of the Parliament, *i.e.* the Lok Sabha. Such studies already exist in one form or the other. The purpose of the present work is to look into some select issues of Dalit policy paradigm with a view to analyse the impact of parliamentary involvement in these areas and also the role of Dalit representatives in influencing the policies that are likely to have a bearing on their constituents, *i.e.*, the Dalit masses.

Our concern is to study the impact of parliamentary debates and questions on the policies meant for Dalits and examine the role of Dalit representatives in the formulation of such policies. This study has been undertaken against the backdrop of the growing disenchantment with the Legislature in policy formulation. Studies on Dalits and reserved constituencies have shown that Dalit issues are not taken seriously. However, in the post-Mandal period Dalits have become more politically conscious and active in electoral politics. Notwithstanding this, it needs to be tested how far their active participation in electoral politics has altered the role of the Parliament in policy decisions and how far Dalit MPs consider their accountability as obligatory to the Dalit masses. With the liberalisation of the economy from the 1990s, the role of the State - on whom Dalits have been dependent – is declining in developmental activities. Thus it becomes an urgent need to examine how Parliament has responded to the Dalit aspirations at various crucial junctures. Although the focus of the study remains on the Dalit parliamentarians; the role of their counterparts in Dalit policy formulation forms only an incidental and critical reference point.

Studies have demonstrated that the Dalit representative's role as spokespersons of Dalit masses is far from satisfactory. However, such studies basically belong to times when Dalit masses were hardly conscious and assertive against the State or societal injustices inflicted upon them. Here, we have attempted to cover a relatively more conscious and assertive phase where it is expected that the Dalit representatives would be more vocal and instrumental, if not in deciding the policies, at least in influencing them, for those whom they socio-politically represent.

In this work, the role of Dalit representatives in the Parliament at various junctures has been analysed. The impact of their deliberations on the Bills, Statements, and the reply of Ministers with regard to the presentation of the Reports of CSCT and NCSCT get special attention.

The 8th, 9th and 10th Lok Sabhas, marked by the pre-Mandal and post-Mandal phases of Indian politics have been covered here. During this period the backward classes asserted to capture not only the political institutions but also to get their share in administrative and educational fields.

Although the term Dalit is used both broadly and in the narrow sense but in this study both the SCs and the STs, have been included among 'Dalits'.

Policy-making is a complex and difficult task. This work has been undertaken to study the role of Lok Sabha in general and the Dalit representatives in particular in policy formulation for the upliftment of the deprived (SC/STs) sections. Their role in Lok Sabha for Dalit constituents apparently depends upon the perceptions adopted and demands pursued by them. These perceptions and demands are reflected while discussing Dalit issues in the Lok Sabha. Thus examining their contributions to policy making - either for continuation of the present Dalit policy paradigm or to alter it - becomes central to the present study.

- Study the role of Parliament in policy formulation for Dalits, through Lok Sabha debates and questions.
- Examine, whether the Lok Sabha is able to bring any shift in the Dalit policy paradigm or it works merely as per constitutional safeguards.
- Evaluate the impact of the Reports of the CSCT and the NCSCT on the policies meant for Dalits.
- Examine the socio-political background of those participating frequently on Dalit issues.
- Finally, study the rejection of Dalit policies formulated by the government and rejected by the House.

The Dalit problem being embedded in the social structure is not an area specific issue but is general in nature. The political representation of SC/STs in the Lok Sabha raises higher expectations among Dalit masses, more so after getting conscious of their low socio-economic status and the existence of laws to ameliorate these hardships. In this context the following pertinent questions need to be examined:

— How does the Parliament put Dalit issues on the policy formulation agenda and identify the concerns of the MPs?
— How these concerns reflect the long-term interests of Dalit masses?
— Are the proposals of Dalit MPs withdrawn after discussion?
— How effectively does the Government handle the proposals?

Scope

Public policies have come under detailed scrutiny in recent years, thus shifting the focus on alternative policy formulations. The concern today is not just a search for alternative policies but also to create new structures and processes for their formulation and implementation. And it is in this context that the role of the Indian Parliament becomes relevant with regard to the policy formulation for Dalits, who have started asserting their rights and establishing their own political parties. The role of the Indian Parliament in policy formulation has hardly been a concern of the researchers except a few. Moreover, there is a dearth of literature on the role of Dalit parliamentarians in the recent past. Special representation for Dalits in legislatures has been a historic phenomenon. The impact of special representation on policy outputs in Parliament has drawn least attention from academics, intellectuals, and research scholars. In this sense the present work becomes relevant. Moreover, in the present socio-political environment where demands are being raised for special representation for women and other under privileged sections, the usefulness of existing special representation in changing policies for such sections could be ascertained.

This study examines the debates and questions regarding social and economic upliftment of the Dalits. Only those discussions of the Lok Sabha have been examined which concern the majority of Dalit population. Thus, the Bills for including new communities in the list for SC/STs do not find mention because these do not have an impact on Dalit policy paradigm except conferment of the safeguard to few others. Endorsing extensions of political reservations in the Lok Sabha and the State Assemblies is also a routine function of Parliament. So this is not included within the ambit of this study.

Similarly, instead of analysing all the questions during 1985-95, a sample of four-year questions have been selected, *viz*., 1985, 1990, 1991 and 1995. These provide representation to all the three Lok Sabhas, *i.e.*, the 8th, 9th and 10th. During this period, PCWSCT produced ninety-three reports. But only those reports have been discussed which relate to policy formulation. Though reports of the NCSCT were not discussed in the Lok Sabha, but summarised them as these are supposed to provide a framework for the development of Dalit policies.

Methodology

The study undertaken is partly empirical and partly analytical. The data/information has been collected basically from primary sources like Government Reports, Lok Sabha Debates, Reports of the National Commission for SC &STs and CSCT, etc. To ascertain the contributions of the MPs during the Lok Sabha debates, their contributions have been classified into two ways, *i.e.*, phenomenal representation and enduring representation, where the former relates to short-terms concerns and the latter to long-term policy objectives. Similarly the MPs' reactions to the Government Bills have been looked into as: one, enduring representation of customary character and two, enduring representation of specific character. Here the former relates to the simple debate and discussion, whereas, the latter to the amendments proposed by the MPs to alter the themes of the proposed legislations. The secondary sources include books, journals, and newspaper reports.

2

Genesis of Dalit Policy Paradigm: Reports of the Commissioner and National Commission for SC/STs

Dalit Policy Initiatives

The Britishers are largely considered to be the formal initiators of policies for Dalits in modern India. Initially, they did not take measures, construed as a confrontationist with the caste-based Hindu society. But as the days rolled by, the administrative compusions and pressures from Hindu social reformers forced the Britishers to take steps that 'opened' the 'closed' Hindu society (Chatterjee 1996:139).

The Britishers opened the doors of education to all sections of society, introduced Western system of education, paved the way for urbanisation and industrialisation, established networks of communication like the railways and roadways, enacted social legislation's like prohibition of *sati*, child-marriage, and conferred limited franchise, etc. Initially, the British wanted to sustain traditional Hindu and Muslim laws but in 1864 a new policy was adopted and the British courts started administering a uniform criminal law. It removed from the purview of caste *panchayats*, several matters and issues that used to be previously adjudicated by it. Previously the cases of assault, adultery, rape, and the like were taken to the caste councils but gradually they started losing their importance even matters of civil laws such as marriage, divorce, were taken to the British Courts. Though the avowed intention of the British was to be guided by the caste customs, slowly but surely various decisions of the High Courts practically set aside the authority of caste (Ghure 1990:271). To remove the inherent inequalities, the Disabilities Removal Act was introduced in 1850. It was the first major blow to the integrity of caste. It facilitated conversion from one religion to another and similarly admission into another caste. Setting aside the custom of disinheriting a person for changing caste or religion, the Act Provided that a person does not forfeit his ordinary rights of property by loss of caste or change of religion (Lathe 1924:373).

Caste as a social reality was being accepted by the government. Now not only Acts were passed acknowledging it but arguments to mention caste in the census were produced.

Finally, to know different castes and their people, the Census Commission of 1881 recommended that the lists of caste and their occupations should be prepared (Census 1951, West Bengal, The Tribes and Castes of West Bengal 1953:1).

Occupational Mobility among Untouchables in British India

The untouchables were traditionally engaged in menial jobs like scavenging, removing dead cattle, working as village watchmen, etc. From the late 18th century, mahars (one of the untouchables group) were recruited into the Bombay army of the East India Company. Cohen estimates that they constituted nearly one-sixth of the army upto 1857(Cohen 1987:455). Similarly in Bihar *dusadhs* and *chamars* and in Madras *Paraiyas* were recruited into the army.[1] The experience of army life under the British had a transformative impact on the outlook of many of the untouchables.

Around the same period, industrialisation commenced in India. Being traditionally associated with hard and uncongenial labour, untouchables were naturally slotted into the least attractive positions in the industrial sector (Mendelsohn and Vicziany 1998:89). Thus the untouchables began experiencing new opportunities, although lower in the strata. In western India, they moved into the textile mills established by the British, concentrated in the *Vidarbha* region, especially in Nagpur and Bombay (Mumbai). The 1921 Census states that they comprised 12% of the workforce in the Bombay mills (Moris 1965:75).

The untouchable communities in various parts of India were traditionally associated with the work of cleaning of public space and disposal of waste material. In western India, *Bhangis* functioned traditionally, though not exclusively as sweepers and scavengers of human waste. Thus the most prominent new employment for these sections within the organised sector of colonial India was that of the sweepers (Mendelsohn and Vicziany 1998:89). The Mahars of Western

---

1 Army service was not unknown to them as prior to the British, Shivaji's army also had untouchables in it but they were not able to rise above the meanest rank of foot soldier (Cadell 1938:12).

India, the Malas of Telugu country and the Holeyas of the Kannada speaking region are the three major examples in this category.

Yet some others migrating from rural to urban areas found employment as butlers and maids to British families and clubs (Robertson 1938:4). Thus, during the British period, industrialisation, jobs in the army, and migration from rural to urban areas paved the way for limited occupational mobility for the untouchables.

Introduction to Education

In the pre-British Indian society, education was the privilege of the upper strata of the society such as *Brahmins*, *Kshatriyas* and *Vaishyas*. But the British rule in India established Western system of education based on the theory of equality and universalistic criteria of admittance, opening the doors of education to all irrespective of caste, class, sex, or religion.

The British officers, who by nature were averse to discrimination on the basis of caste sympathised with, and encouraged the deprived sections of the Indian society to seek education and employment under their supervision. In a court case of 1856, where a boy from the depressed class was refused admission on the ground of alienating caste-Hindu, the Court of Directors quashed the order and opined that "all schools maintained at the sole cost of the Government shall be open to all classes of its subjects without distinctions" (Sinha 1986:42). Referring to caste prejudice among caste-Hindus regarding education for untouchables, it was observed in 1920 that "both teacher and pupils make it most difficult for low caste boys to sit in class rooms" (*Ibid*).

Education, as a channel of mobility, had a very limited significance for the lower income groups. Moreover, the untouchables being at the lowest rung of the society in economic terms were unable to afford higher education. Realising this, in 1885, the education department of the Government of Bombay proposed to reserve fifty per cent of free scholarships for Muslims and backward Hindu castes, since the Britishers felt that scholarship based on merit would 'perpetuate the *Brahmin* monopoly'.

Job Reservations

With the education development came the demand for government services that was regarded as a status symbol. Once competition for the position of power and status became stiff, protection and security acquired a new dimension in the backward class movements like, non-Brahmin and self-respect movements in South India (Chatterjee

1996:180). The claim for representation of backward classes in the State services was voiced in the South Indian states. In Mysore, a system of communal rotation was introduced and strict instructions were issued in 1895 that certain reservation of posts should be earmarked for all communities except *Brahmins* (*Ibid*). Due to problems of implementation, the Government evolved a policy which would give representation to all communities, but accord representation to the unrepresented first, the under-represented next, and the represented last. The Governments of Travancore and Cochin states followed the policy of representation to the various communities in their states based on proportional representation (First Backward Classes Commission Report 1955:129).

Political Representation for Depressed Classes

Edwin S. Montague, the then Secretary of State for India, announced a new policy for India, in the House of Commons on August 20, 1917. Around the same time two major meetings of the DCs were held in the city to "grant the untouchables their own representation in the various legislative bodies to ensure them their civil and political rights" (Ambedkar 1970:15).

> "...the depressed classes must be abolished or rather they should be raised socially and economically so that they may take their proper place in the community. The only effective way to do this is to give them educational and other facilities for their advancement and remove all the obstacles in the way of their advance" (Indian Quarterly Register 1923:30).

Initially a report called Mont-Fort Report was submitted to the Government of India but it provided no representation to the DCs. Later on in its decision of April 23, 1919, the Government of India suggested that in each council there should be enough representatives of these classes to save them from being entirely submerged. The Report pointed out that "we intend to make the best arrangement that we can for their representation, in order that they too may learn ultimately the lesson of self-protection" (Report on Indian Constitutional Reforms 1918:155). While framing the details of the Constitution they were granted representation by nomination. In 1924, the Reform Enquiry Committee was constituted under the Chairmanship of Home Member Alexander Muddiman. It had eight other members. The Committee in its report observed that

> So far as the depressed classes are concerned, we consider that unless in any particular case a local government is prepared to recommend a system of election, the representation by nomination becomes necessary in the provisions of the Act, which place a minimum limit upon the proportion of elected members in each legislative body and in certain cases require amendment
>
> (Report of Reforms Enquiry Committee 1924:55-56).

It was the beginning of a new era in Indian politics that accorded legitimacy to the claims of the DCs for separate representation in the legislature.

Depressed Classes under the Government of India Act 1919

The Government of India Act 1919 stands out as the first major step towards the way of developing Dalit leadership in the legislatures. It provided 13 seats for DCs in provincial legislative council to be filled on the basis of nomination. Accordingly, Madras was to send 5 members; Bihar, Orissa and Central Provinces 2 each; and, Assam and Bengal one each. Finally the Muddiman Committee Report recommended 20 seats for DCs which was accepted by the British government. Thus 10 seats were reserved in Madras, 2 in Bombay, 4 in Central Provinces and one each in Bengal, Bihar, Orissa, and the United Provinces (Report of the Indian Statutory Commission 1, Survey Appendix III :144-5). However, no seats were reserved for the DCs of Punjab and Assam in the Provincial Legislative Councils (Gupta 1985:204). Commenting on this, Dr. Ambedkar stated that the right of the depressed classed to special representation in the legislature had become a principle which was not only accepted but adopted in the Constitution of 1919. So well was this principle recognised that in 1919 it was extended even to District and Local Boards, School Boards, and Municipalities. It become a right which had been perfected by the representatives of Depressed classes and that could not be disputed by anybody (Moon 1989:312)

A provision was made that after the expiry of ten years from the passing of the Act, a commission will be formed for the purpose of inquiry into the working of the system of government set up under the Act, and suggest desirable constitutional changes. On the same line on November 8, 1927 a statutory commission was announced consisting of five members of British Parliament with Sir John Simon as its head. Most of the Indian political parties at that time protested against it but the commission and sixteen of them asked for separate electorates for untouchables (Zelliot 1972:45)., The Commission submitted its report to the British Government. In the meantime, the Labour Government came to power kin Britain, and in May 1929 it announced its willingness to confer Dominion status to India and invited representatives of different interest groups from India for a conference to discuss the British India and All-India problems (India Quarterly Register 1923:139).

Round Table Conferences and Dalit Question

Soon after the Commission's report, different interest groups became active to mobilise support for themselves and organised meetings and conferences. In a similar exercise, the All-India Depressed Classes Conference was held at Nagpur in 1930. At the session Ambedkar remarked:

> I agree with the Congressmen that no country is good enough to rule over another. But I must also take the liberty to tell them point-back that the proposition does not end there and that it is equally true that no class is good enough to rule over another class. It is only in the Swaraj constitution that you stand any chance of getting the political power into your own hands without which you cannot bring salvation to your people (Indian Quarterly Register 1930:367-74).

The first Round Table Conference (RTC) began on November 12, 1930. Dr. Ambedkar and Rao Bahadur Srinivasan presented a joint memorandum that constituted a chapter of demands for the untouchables. It included a demand for untouchables to elect their representatives through adult suffrage and separate electorates for the first ten years. It also demanded joint electorates with reserved seats but with the consent of the concerned groups. The prominent demands mentioned in the Memorandum were: equal citizenship, equal opportunity, ban on social boycott, establishment of law, sanitation, creation of special department (in charge of a Minister for the purpose) and representation in the Cabinet. (Proceeding of Sub-committee vol. II sub-committee No. II Minorities, India Round Table Conference 1930-31:77-78).

Though the first RTC was adjourned without any decision, the representatives of the DCs did succeed in convincing the conference that they were entitled to recognition as a separate entity for political and constitutional purposes (Chatterjee 1996:235).

The Congress abstained from the first RTC. But at the second RTC, Gandhi represented the Congress, and expressed his strong opposition for separate electorates. He stated:

> The Congress has reconciled itself to special treatment of the Hindu-Muslim, Sikh tangle. We do not want on our register and in our census, the untouchables classified as a separate class. Sikhs may remain Sikhs in perpetuity, so may Mohammadans, so may Europeans. Will Untouchables remain Untouchables in perpetuity? I would far rather that Hinduism die than untouchability lived. It will create a division in Hinduism which I possibly cannot look forward to with any satisfaction whatever... if I was the only person to resist it with my life. (Proceedings of Federal Structure and Minorities Committee, Indian Round Table Conference, [Second Session] 7th September 1931-1st December 1931, Vol, III : 1346).

Ambedkar and Rao Bahadur R. Srinivasan submitted another memorandum in support of the claims of the DCs. The lack of compromise between the leaders of Indian groups made the British Prime Minister to adjourn the Committee meeting *sine die* with a suggestion to put a signed requisition, authorising the Prime Minister to arbitrate and give decision on the communal issue. This was signed by Gandhi but Ambedkar refused to do so (Moon 1991:74). The memorandom asserted that the demand of the untouchables were so reasonable that no arbitration was necessary in this regard (*Ibid*).

On August 4, 1932, the British Prime Minister announced the Communal Award, also known as the Macdonald Award. Accordingly, apart from many others, the DCs were also recognised as a minority. Reacting to it, Gandhi commenced his fast unto death. Finally, there was compromise between the caste-Hindus, represented by Madan Mohan Malviya, and the DCs represented by Ambedkar. Now joint electorates were provided for DCs, and 148 seats were reserved for them.[2] It had a unique feature whereby the DCs were asked to elect four representatives separately in the primary elections, who in turn would be the candidates to be elected by the general electorate in the constituency. Apart from this, in the Central legislature there was a provision for 18 per cent reservation for the DCs in British India. The system of primary election to a panel of candidates to the Central and

---

2 It was raised to 151 according to Government of India Act 1935, making adjustments for Bihar and Orissa as a whole (Chatterjee 1996:24-242).

Provincial legislatures was to come to an end after the first ten years, unless earlier terminated by mutual agreement between the concerned communities. The Depressed Class were not to be discriminated against for being member of such community, while being considered for appointments to public services. Every province was to earmark adequate educational grants for providing educational facilities to the members of the Depressed Classes (Moon 1991:85-88).

The freedom movement against British rule was gradually becoming aggressive. On the other hand, the Second World War had started and the Congress led governments in the Provinces resigned. There arose a constitutional crisis that led to the Cripps Mission negotiating with the leaders of Indian political parties on the issue. The proposals laid down by Cripps were not acceptable to Ambedkar and M. C. Rajah and they categorically wrote:

> The depressed classes would regard it a breach of faith if a constitution was forced upon them by His Majesty's Government which had not received their free and voluntary consent and did not contain within itself the provisions necessary for safeguarding their interests (Quoted in Chatterjee 1996:253).

Apprehensive of the consequences of a Constituent Assembly without proper representation to the DCs, Ambedkar felt that in the present circumstances they will be a hopeless minority. Caste-Hindus would have the right to nominate their representatives to the Constituent Assembly and these representatives of DCs would be the tools in the hands of caste-Hindus. This will lead to wiping out the safeguards granted to the Depressed Classes in the existing constitution (Moon 1990:336-43).

On October 29, 1942, Ambedkar as a member of Executive Council submitted a memorandum to the Governor-General. It contained the grievances of the SCs and suggested remedies for their removal. It demanded a fixed amount and number of representatives in different government institutions, like the appointment of Scheduled Caste Officer to protect their services rights; representatives on the Federal Public Service Commission; appointment of two representatives of SCs in Central Board of Education; apprenticeship in government printing press and government railway workshop; providing adequate publicity of social and political grievances of SCs and providing a footing in the Government Contracts system in the Public Works Department for the SCs (Chatterjee 1996:256-258).

In response to the memorandum, seats in the Council of State, an additional seat in the Central Assembly, reservation in Indian Civil Services, technical training at railway workshops and school of mines, and annual provision of three lakh rupees as scholarship for technical education were provided by the government. It also extended the benefit of 81/2 per cent of vacancies in Central and Subordinate Services, including Railways to be reserved for them. The age limit was raised by three years and examination fees reduced to ¼ for them (*Ibid*: 258).

In another effort to solve the Constituent Assembly tussle, the Cabinet Mission arrived in India on March 23, 1946. Ambedkar stated to this delegation thus:

> We do not want a Constituent Assembly at all. It would be dominated by the caste-Hindus and the Scheduled Caste members would be nothing more than a small minority which would always be outvoted if a three-quarters or two-thirds majority were required for the Assembly's decisions…moreover there would be an immense amount of corruption in the Assembly; members would be bought over to vote against the interests of their communities… separate electorates were fundamental since without them the Scheduled Castes would never have their own representatives (Mansergh 1970:144-147).

The Cabinet Mission did not entertain the issues raised by Ambedkar. Subsequently , the elections were held for the Constituent Assembly and the process completed by the end of July 1946. The Congress won 206 seats, Muslim League 74, Independent 8, Unionist Party 3, Akali Partiy 3, Communist 1, and the Scheduled Caste Federation (SCF) also got one seat (Chatterjee 1996:262).

The SCF met on June 4, 1946 and demanded that:

(a) The SCs should have the right to be represented in the legislatures through separate electorates,

(b) The constitution should contain a provision, making it obligatory on the government to undertake formation of separate settlements for the SCs, and

(c) An SC member who tops the last primary elections should be made a member of the Advisory Committee and allowed to elect five other representatives of the SCs in the Committee. It was also conveyed that if the demands were not accepted, it would resort to direct action (Mansergh 1970:808-12).

Ambedkar resisted the proposals of the Cabinet Mission and produced the analysis of the Constituent Assembly elections. Addressing a letter to the British Prime Minister, he requested the following:

(a) to state openly that His Majesty's Government hold that the SCs were a minority within the meaning of paragraph 20 of the Cabinet Mission's Statement'.

(b) before singing the treaty of cessation of sovereignty, satisfactory safeguards would be provided to SCs to live free from the fear of the majority.

(c) the Interim Government should have at least two SC representation to SCs (Moon 1991:509-10).

In support of his claim for SCF to be the genuine representative of SCs, Ambedkar produced the figures from the December 1945 primary elections. According to it where only SCs voted, the Federation received more votes than the Congress in Madras, Bombay and the Central Provinces (*Ibid* 1991:366-75).

Policies for Tribals

Due to their inaccessibility, the tribal areas were the last to come under the British rule. The tribals resented the curtailment of their accessibility to forest wealth, and violently opposed it. Consequently, the British adopted a policy of pacification through indirect rule with respect to tribal areas and treated them differently from the rest of the country. In this regard the Scheduled Districts Act of 1874 was enacted, to keep large tracts of tribal areas outside the jurisdiction of normal administration. The administration policy was prudently based on non-interference in their affairs. In accordance with this policy, the Government of the Madras Province, formulated the Agency Rules in 1924, whereby the local chiefs of the tribal areas were recognised by the British government for administrative purposes. Later on, an Act called 'Excluded and Partially Excluded Area Act 1935' provided for non-applicability of any legislation of the Provincial governments to tribal areas except on the power to pass special regulations for tribals, with prior permission of the Governor-General.

Sri Thakkar Bapa Committee, which was appointed to study the position of Excluded and Partially Excluded Areas Policy of Britishers, made many recommendations of which the most relevant had been that the State should bear the responsibility of the tribal people and protect the tribal lands and prevent their exploitation by the money-lenders.

With reference to the north-east, the British Government by and large following the policy of non-intervention in customary and economic life of the people. The first Inner Line Regulation was introduced in 1873 for all the districts of the eastern frontiers of Bengal. Land was allowed to be governed by tribal laws, and outsiders were prohibited to acquire land in these areas (Pathy 1997:152).

Reservations in jobs for tribals was also advocated and subsequently instructions were issued in December 1947, asking the appointing authorities to keep in view the recruitment of tribal people. In 1949, orders were issued to provide fee and age concessions at par with the SCs (PCWSCT 1953-54:2).

Safeguards for Dalits Enshrined in the Constitution of India

The British Government formulated some policies aimed at the upliftment of the Dalits. Later on the Constituent Assembly discussed Dalit issues in detail and continued some of the previous measures, while adding some other provisions in this regard.

These provisions can be divided into four major groups:

Policy against Adverse Discrimination

Abolition of untouchability under article 17 and enforcement of any disability arising out of untouchablility was made a punishable offence in accordance with law (CAD 29 November 1948:669).

The Constitution did not offer any definition of "Untouchability". But there was a discussion on the subject wherein a member proposed amendment to the clause 11 of the Draft Constitution, saying that the article sought to prohibit untouchability on the ground of religion or caste (CAD 29 November 1948:665) and not on other matters. However, the proposed amendment was nullified and left for the interpretation of the courts.

The Constitution did not merely abolish untouchability and its practice but its enforcement was also considered to be an offence as per the law. Subsequently, Untouchability Offences Act 1995 was also enacted which provided for more provisions to punish certain kinds of historically prevalent obnoxious patterns of behaviour, which the society at large considered a right to exercise.

Policy for Compensatory Discrimination

To bring Dalits in the mainstream of the country, the founding fathers of the Constitution made some provisions which could empower them and compensate against the discriminations inflicted upon them. These are as below:

Political Reservations

The major breakthrough for political reservations for SCs was attained by the Communal Award of 1932 and the subsequent compromise between the caste-Hindus and the Depressed Classes by the Poona Pact. The Award provided for special constituencies for SCs, where they alone could contest. The question was further discussed by the Constituent Assembly and the demand for 'separate electorates' was again raised by Dr. Ambedkar (Shiva Rao 1967:67).However the Constituent Assembly rejected this demand, in favour of joint electorates with reserved seats, as agreed under the Poona Pact. Thus the Constitution provided for reservation of seats in legislatures for SC/STs.[3]

The provision for reservations was adopted as a protective measure without which it was feared that the SCs and STs would be unable to secure adequate representation in elected bodies; having neither the resources nor the experience for entering into an open competition in the political process and decision-making. Thus these provisions were included, not merely because they were 'minorities', but more so on the ground that they had been suffering from social handicaps for centuries altogether.

The provision for reservation of seats was initially intended to be purely temporary. Dr. Ambedkar even moved an amendment in the Constituent Assembly, according to which it was to cease after ten years and it was accepted and adopted (CAD August 1949:674). However, this period has been extending every time upon its expiry and recently it was extended till 2010.

Article 332 provides Reservation of seats for Scheduled Castes and the Scheduled Tribes in the legislative assemblies of the States. It has to be in proportion to the population of these groups in the respective states (except for the Scheduled Tribes in the autonomous Districts of Assam). One major difference with regard to Assam's autonomous districts is that any one who is not an ST of the autonomous district shall be ineligible for election in the Legislative Assembly.

3 The Article 330 of the Constitution lays down that the seats shall be reserved in the House of the people for the SCs and STs in accordance with their population except the STs in the autonomous districts of Assam.

According to Article 334, political reservations will cease after fifty years from the commencement of the Constitution, provided that nothing in this Article shall effect any representation in the House of the People or in the Legislative Assembly a State until the dissolution of the then existing House or Assembly, as the case may be.

Job Reservations

Material benefits are vital for the interests of any marginalised community struggling for the social upliftment. The objective of socio-economic equality was intended to be fulfilled by Article 16 (4). It states: "nothing…shall prevent the State from making any provision in the reservation of appointments or posts in the services under the State in favour of "backward classes citizens". This is an exception to the Article 16 (1), which ensures to provide equality of opportunity to all citizens in matters relating to employment or appointment to any office under the State. *Prima-facie* it seems to non-counter the previous Article.

Article 335 that specifically provides reservations for SCs and STs in the jobs states:

> the claims of the members of the Scheduled Castes and Scheduled Tribes shall be taken into consideration in consistence with the maintenance of efficiency and administration in the making of appointments to services and posts in connection with the affairs of the Union or of a State.

A time limit was demanded on this issue by a member, H. N. Kunjru in the Constituent Assembly, but it was rejected by (CAD 30 November 1948). So no time limit was imposed on reservations in the service sector for Dalits.

Education Development

Ambedkar's three commandments, viz., educate, agitate, and organise, is a well known political dictum among his fellow community. The 1931 Census records point out that the literacy rate among Depressed Classes was merely 1.9 per cent. Taking stock of the grim conditions of their literacy rate, the framers of the Constitution under Article 29 of the Constitution provided: "no citizen shall be denied admission into any educational institution maintained by the State, or receiving aid out of the State funds, on grounds of religion, race, caste, language, or any of them". In addition the provision under Article 29 (2) specifically mentions that special care will be taken for the educational and economic interests of the weaker sections.

Monitoring System

The framers of the Constitution were well aware of the fact that the special provision in favour of SC/STs cannot be implemented properly till there is an authority to monitor the whole issue of their welfare. In this regard Article 338 provided that:

(a) there shall be a Special Officer for the Scheduled Castes and Scheduled Tribes to be appointed by the President.

(b) it shall be the duty of the Special Officer to investigate all matters relating to the safeguards provided for the Scheduled Castes and Scheduled Tribes and report to the President upon the working of those safeguards at such intervals as the President may direct. Further, the President shall cause all such reports to be laid before each House of the Parliament.

Article 339 provides for the Union to exercise control over the administration of Scheduled Areas and for the Welfare of STs. It also lays down, that the President shall appoint a Commission to report on the administration of the Scheduled Areas and the Welfare of Scheduled Tribes in the states, at the expiry of ten years from the commencement of the constitution.

Inclusion or Exclusion of SCs and STs in/from the List

Under Article 341 and 342, the President by an order or the Parliament by a law can include or exclude communities into or from the SC/ST list.

Summary of the Reports of CSCT and NCSCT

Initially, the status of the CSCT was that of a Secretary in the Government of India, but the Committee on the welfare of SC/STs in its first report reviewed the working of the office in 1969. Consequently the 46th Constitution Amendment Bill tried to amend the Article 338 whereby the Special Officer was to be replaced by a multi-member SC/ST Commission (James and Reddy 1979:1100-03). Later on, to strengthen the Commission, an amendment was introduced which is known as the Constitution (65th Amendment) Act 1990.

We reiterate that the president study is concerned with the role of Parliament in shaping the policies on Dalits between 1985-95, thus we shall analyse not only the NCSCT Reports but also the reports on the CSCT that existed prior to 1992.

The NCSCT was bestowed upon wide ranging powers after the conferment of constitutional status.

Under clause 5 of the amended Article 338, the functions of the Commission can be broadly divided into 4 areas:

(a) Investigation;
(b) Monitoring;
(c) Evaluation; and
(d) Participation in the Planning Process and Policy Matters.

Prior to the 65th Constitutional Amendment, the CSCT and the Commission for SC/STs had some powers to investigate and monitor the functioning of welfare measures for Dalits. But due to the lack of an evaluative system and the lack of well-defined powers they were incapable of suggesting construction measures to safeguard the interests of Dalits.

The NCSCT not only can investigate and evaluate the provisions but also can participate and advice in the planning process for socio-economic development of the Dalits. It was to associate itself with the Planning Commission and various other Ministries while in formulating development programmes for Dalits.

It has been made obligatory for the Central and the State Governments to keep in touch with the NCSCT on major policy matters which affect the Dalit community. With these wide-ranging functions and powers, the NCSCT has the potential to play an important role in the development of the deprived sections of the society. Recommendations contained in its reports submitted to the President of India have been widely appreciated, but the lack of their implementation has been lamented by the Commission (Mathur 2000).

The following discussion provides a summary and analysis of the Reports of NCSCT and the CSCT.

Recommendations of the Reports of the CSCT and NCSCT

In its report for the year 1985, the Commission made 43 recommendations. These emphasised implementation of the existing provisions with minor modifications to sharpen the relevant portions of constitutional safeguards. Most significant of these recommendations were to ensure proper representation in group 'A' and 'B' jobs for Dalits, exchange of SC/STs against each other in case of non-availability of candidates, low cost housing, building an opinion against untouchability, providing promotions and other incentives for those government officials who help in registering the complaints of SC/STs, implementation of existing economic programmes, assessment of the working of Scheduled Caste Development Corporation's programmes, growth of various centres in Tribal areas and SC *bastis*, simplification of bank loan procedures, appraisals of anti-poverty programmes, etc. Apart from attempts at the strict implementation of existing measures, the Commission's recommendations also addressed some policy issues. It suggested formulation of certain policies for the effective implementation of the continuing welfare schemes. These are as follows:

(a) to provide constitutional status to the Commission and to vest it with the power of Commission of Enquiry Act 1952,
(b) there should be a 'Special recruitment drive' for vacant posts in the groups 'A' and 'B' services,
(c) the outley for the welfare programmes for Dalits (such as Special Component Plan (SCP) and Tribal Sub-Plan (TSP) should be in accordance with the population of these sections,
(d) to prosecute officials found responsible for the abatement of offences against SC/STs,
(e) to establish special courts to deal with untouchability related cases in order to avoid denial of justice for a longer period,
(f) for the days of attendance in courts or other government institutions the wages should be paid not only to the victims but also to the witnesses, and
(g) to transform the process and mindset of the people, it was also recommended that there is need for change in the curriculum and it asked the mass-media to be sympathetic towards the issues of Dalits and provide sufficient coverage to the issues concerning them.

Recommendations of the Commissioner for SC/STs : 1986-91

The Commissioner in its reports for 1986-91 undertook a comprehensive analysis of the welfare measures being carried by the Government of India and various State Governments. The Report for 1986-87 contains 34 recommendations aimed at uplifting Dalits. On analysing these recommendations category-wise it is found that of these 34 recommendations, 21 recommendations concern the SC/STs jointly. But the STs remain a major concern of the report, where 13 recommendations exclusively deal with them. Whereas, no recommendation was made for SCs specifically.

Concern for Economic Development of SC/STs

Dalit problem is multi-dimensional. Thus its solution does not lie in one mechanism but in various measures such as social, political, and economic. Economic development is considered to be the base for any sort of change. For the economic development of SC/STs, the Commissioner suggested following safeguards:

1. Check the Land Alienation

1. The Central Government should prepare a model regulation or law to prevent alienation of land belonging to the SC/STs, and restore illegally or irregularly transferred lands to them. This law should be stringent.
2. There should be no transfer of SC/STs land to individuals belonging to other communities.
3. The prohibition should also apply in case of realisation of dues from SC/STs by the individuals.
4. There should be provisions for compulsory restoration of land after the decision of a court in favour of SC/STs.
5. If anybody tries to occupy the land within 3 years of the date of retroaction, the person should be convicted.

2. Mechanisms of Land Distribution:

1. Land should be allotted to the tiller. Being the prime resource for Dalits, lands should not be disturbed;
2. Share cropping should formally be recognised under the law and Tiller should be entitled to not less than 2/3 of gross produce;
3. Wherever land is held by a Trust or co-operative society, where all members are not actual tillers, land should be taken over by the State and distributed to the landless people, and the State should assume the responsibility of a Trust.
4. There should be drastic reduction in the ceiling limit of land based on the quality of land, productivity, and the possibility of the extent of development;
5. If corporate bodies have excess area, it should be taken over by the State and distributed to the landless; and
6. The State should create a fund for Dalits to purchase land and it should be interest-free and recoverable in not less than 10 year's time.

3. Improvement in Wages and Working Conditions

The Union Government was asked to take urgent measures to improve the working conditions of labour in the unorganised sector, wherein the percentage of Dalit population is high. Some of the specific measures recommended were:

(a) special attention should be paid to economic activities traditionally associated with Dalits.
(b) minimum wages should be fixed.
(c) in the case of scavenging, strong measures should be taken, to ensure that children below 14 years do not undertake it. Wherever parents are engaged in scavenging, their children should get free education in residential institutions upto the age of 14.
(d) there should be established leather co-operatives to remove the contractors. And effort should be made to upgrade the skills and establish strong marketing network for the benefit of leather-workers.

4. *Job Reservations*

The Government should formulate a comprehensive policy of reservation for SC/STs in Government and Public Sector Undertakings (PSUs). This should include:

(a) a comprehensive law on reservations,
(b) a policy which is sensitive to local situation,
(c) the Commissioner's advice with reference to dereservation of vacancies in Government should be binding, and
(d) *safai* work should be organised on co-operative lines.

There was no reference to reservation in private enterprises.

5. *Welfare Measures*

Since reservations in employment have a limited scope, welfare schemes in the shape of direct financial help or comprehensive plans for the development of Dalits, have also been recommended by the Commissioner.

They are as follows:

(a) provisions of separate budget for SC/STs, and formulation of programmes to target the people and not their location in a particular area or State,
(b) the items in the Tribal Sub-Plan should comprise primarily those items which concern the development of the tribals,
(c) a separate budget for power and irrigation projects,
(d) the Special Central Assistance remaining unutilised at the end of 5 years should be converted into Special Education Fund

which can be spent on the elementary education of Dalit children.

6. The Government of India has been asked to prepare a 'comprehensive policy paper' for Dalits to ensure equality in all spheres of national life. For this purpose:
   (a) there is need for comprehensive employment generation programme,
   (b) the economic activities like animal husbandry, poultry etc., that constitute subsidiary occupation to the marignalised sections should be decentralised, according to the needs of local conditions,
   (c) small worker-entrepreneur model be adopted and needful financial, technical and organisational support be provided to ensure economic development of Dalits.
7. The Union Government in consultation with the State Governments should prepare a comprehensive plan for Dalits to extend advantages of opportunities being created in the proposed growth centres and the existing townships. For the same purpose, the government may create a special fund.
8. There is a need for the extension of positive discrimination policy to the non-Government enterprises in organised sectors getting benefits of institutional finance, apart from various Ministries/Departments/Public Sector Units. The newly emerging assets such as residential houses and commercial complexes being created in private sector in urban centres with the State assistance should have due reservation for Dalits.
9. Suitable measures should be taken to ensure that the Eighth Five Year Plan contains a clear perspective and explicit objective that members of SC/STs under SCP and TSP are able to reach the general level of development within two Five Year Plans.
10. The National Development Council shall look into the consequences of growing 'economic inequality' and 'unrestrained consumerism' and its implications on the socio-economic conditions of Dalits.

Concern for Social Development of Dalits

Social development of Dalits primarily imply abolishing of the existing discriminatory practices such as untouchability and the safeguarding of civil rights that have been denied to Dalits. Forcing bonded labour and child labour on Dalits, etc., also come within the purview of social developmental concerns. Apart from statutory measures against adverse discrimination, there are some developmental measures like education, health, housing, etc., which may help Dalits to overcome the structural discriminations.

1. In its first recommendation itself, the Commissioner suggested to make Protection of Civil Rights Act 1976 more stringent. The Government was urged to support those officials working for equality in the society. Usually, civil servants working for Dalit cause were transferred for political reasons. Thus a need was felt to avoid shifting of those officials standing by the poor. The prominent public figures favouring untouchability have been asked to be dealt with firmly and promptly, and their property counteracted through strong legal action.
2. Regarding atrocities, a system of regular review by the District Magistrate on a monthly basis and a similar review by the Chief Secretary at the State level, has been suggested and a report was to be prepared, to be forwarded to the Commissioner. Thus a three-tier review has been provided for against atrocities and discriminations of similar kind.
3. It was also recommended that force should not be used in civil matters related to Dalits. If an officer wants to use 'force' against them then a detailed report should be prepared with full facts of the case and reasons given for the use of force. Also the reaction of people has to be sent to the officer designated by the Commissioner for SC/STs seven days in advance. Any officer violating these norms shall be liable for penal action.
4. If violations of safeguards for Dalits occur due to wilful neglect by the authorities then appropriate action should be taken. And these cases should get attention of the Central and State Cabinets. Further, a convention should be established or a law could also be promulgated to make reference of such cases to the Supreme Court where the authorities knowingly function in a way whereby the Dalits are denied the constitutional safeguards.
5. There is a need to establish forums at Blocks, District, States, and National levels, which may continue a dialogue with the social activists or voluntary organisations working for the mobilisation of Dalits. And these forums can be used to resolve the conflict situations which may arise from time to time.

6. In the social development of a person, education plays an important role and so the report has duly asked to give highest priority to the education of Dalits. There are four major aspects of this recommendations:
   (a) necessary outlays should be earmarked for education in the general outlay for the development of Dalits.
   (b) there is a need for special programmes in those areas where the literacy rate of Dalits is very low.
   (c) various scholarships should be reviewed from time to time according to the 'Cost of Education Index'.
   (d) presently, the scholarship is received by the students at the end of the month. But it should reach him/her before the month.

Concern for Overall Development of Dalits

Some of the recommendations of the Commissioner touch upon both the issues of economic development and social upliftment, and few other aspects which need the attention of the government. These are:

1. The Ministry of Welfare should function as a 'nodal agency' with the responsibilities of reviewing the poverty alleviation programmes and should look into all matters which have implications for the welfare of Dalits before the matter goes for the consideration of the Cabinet where a final decision is taken. This nodal agency has to be under the charge of the Prime Minister at the Centre or Chief Minister at the State level respectively.
2. A Status paper on the social and economic conditions of Dalits should be prepared by the Government of India. It should contain the differential positions of Dalits vis-à-vis non-Dalits. For this purpose, following measures have been suggested:
   (a) each Ministry has to prepare a status paper concerning its responsibilities towards Dalits.
   (b) there is need to look whether a change is necessary in the normal flow of information concerning Dalits.
   (c) The responsibility for various surveys can be bestowed upon the National Sample Survey Organisation, as it has necessary mechanism for the purpose.
3. The Government may consider to organise student volunteer corporations, especially those belonging to the Dalit community, who may function for mobilising people for participation in the economic activities.

4. The National Development Council has been directed to constitute a Standing Committee to consider all the matters having implications for Dalits. This standing Committee has to find out the possible acts of commission, aberrations, and distortions impinging upon the development of Dalits.
5. There is a need to formulate proper procedures for the certification of Dalits in the List. All the claims should be thoroughly examined by a team of experts. For inclusion of various groups in the category, the geographical, historical, ethnic, and linguistic dimensions should be examined. The Dalit students should be issued permanent community certificates along with computer numbers to be maintained by the School boards.
6. As indicated in *Table 2.1*, apart from the common concern for the SC/STs, the report of the Commissioner has dealt with specific measures for STs. These recommendations are also divided into three parts, viz., economic, social, and overall development.

Table 2.1: Section-wise Recommendations 1987-87

Area	*Joint*	*ST*	*SC*	*Total*
Economic Development	8	6	0	14
Social Upliftment	8	2	0	10
Overall/particular	5	5	0	10
Total	21	13	0	34

Source: Reports of the Commission for SC/STs 1986.

Economic Concern for Tribals

1. A dialogue should be started by the Central Government engaging the State Governments, regarding alleged unauthorised occupation of forestland. And effort should be made to associate tribal people as partners in the management of forests.
2. The Special Central Assistance outlay for the welfare of tribal people should be raised. And a separate sub-plan should be formulated for dispersed tribal people.
3. The Tribe Sub-Plan should be prepared in a way that there is constant advancement and amelioration of tribal people. Education, health, and mobilisation of tribals for developing their inner strength and enhancing their sense of social position should be the priority. In the Eighth Five-Year Plan, the Integrated Tribal

Development Projects (ITDP) should implement the programme of the plan from below. Those tribal areas or population facing special problems should be identified for microplans with ITDP.

4. Reasonable share should be ensured in the new assets being created and new enterprises being established:
   (a) In tribal areas 50 per cent of assets and enterprises should be earmarked for tribal people.
   (b) If tribal land is taken by an outsider, the tribals should be associated with the enterprise as share-holders
   (c) All corporate enterprises in tribal areas should have a partnership in the share-holding of tribal people
   (d) There should be no tax on the ancestral property of tribals.
   (e) The Finance Commission should give special attention in Scheduled areas and the Central Government should give directions to State Governments to provide systematic care for Scheduled areas.
   (f) There is a need for an annual review of the admission of Scheduled areas by a Cabinet Committee in the Central Government.

Concern for Social Development of Tribals

1. The Central Government should issue directives to State Government to ensure effective implementation of the schemes of excise, forest credit, and marketing. Time-bound measures should be taken to avoid further exploitation of the tribal people. They should participate in the management and development of social forestry.
2. The development of primitive tribal communities should be streamlined so that the left out population of tribals are also included in the development programmes. An expert group may be constituted for the same purpose. The All India Institute of Medical Sciences and the National Institute of Nutrition may also be asked to provide help for the biological survival of the primitive tribes.

Concern for Overall or General Development of Tribals

1. All the on-going projects for the tribals and also the pending ones should be reviewed and it should be ensured that all safeguards provided for them in the constitution are honoured in the real spirit. And they should not remain unrepresented simply because they do not have the necessary equipment to articulate their cause. A

national consensus and policy frame need to be developed regarding their access to and command over resources and their displacement for 'development' purposes.

2. To extend ordinary laws to Scheduled Area, a suitable procedure should be adopted so that a regular review can be done. And the adaptation of these laws may be considered by the Supreme Court in case of non-action by the Executive.
3. In the Scheduled Areas, comprehensive regulations for the maintenance of peace and ensuring good administration such as single line of administrative authority, a special code for conduct governing the public servants, suitable institutions at village level which are answerable to the people in accordance with local customs, etc., should be put in place. They should work as protection against backlash of development.
4. The Finance Commission accepted the compensatory measures for officials working in adverse conditions of tribal areas in principle. Accordingly, it directed that the government should work in preparing a graded comprehensive scheme of incentives, taking into account the inaccessibility of the places of posting and the kind of the social services available in such areas for the officials.
5. *Panchayati Raj* Institutions should be established in consonance with the traditions of tribal people. The *panchayat* institutions should shoulder wider responsibilities covering every day life and the management of local resources, particularly land and the forest.

Recommendations of the Reports of the Commissioner for the SC/STs 1987-1991

Since the Commissioner for the period 1986-91 was the same person, the recommendations for 1986-87 cast a major shadow on the following years as well.

The 1987-89 report can be termed to be general in comparison to 1986-87 report, that touched upon even the minute elements that needed the attention of the Government. In this report, the emerging scenario at the all India level has been analysed. Here it was observed that a dualistic system was rapidly gaining ground, and which hampered the interests of under-privileged sections of the society.

During this period there was a tremendous growth of social consciousness among the deprived sections. The emergent contestation for power and resources at the social level resulted in an intractable problem of laws created by the State. In this context, the Commissioner's opinion that some laws created by the State, particularly where the State was encroaching into the rights of tribal people's lands and forests, were not in accordance with the spirit of the constitution. Further, he assested that there is no use of specific recommendations, when the foundation of the system itself is faulty.

Even as the above observations were being made, the Commissioner came up with the following recommendations in his Report for 1987-89:

(a) there is need to restructure the legal-framework in a way that the life of the common man occupies a central theme in it. And all the unconstitutional elements, particularly those concerned with the command over resources, ownership of means of productions, and entitlement of labour should be identified and replaced.

(b) A profession providing livelihood to the common man should be recognised as his/her right and the State should protect that right.

(c) A system of self-government needs to be established in the tribal areas for the management of day-to-day affairs.

(d) The State should refrain from using force against the peaceful struggles of the people. And the people's resolve to create and perpetuate the systems based on their basic values should be honoured.

(e) The developmental paradigm needs to be redefined so that those are in harmony with the prevailing conditions.

(f) The substance of all policies should be in consonance with the solution of the common man's day-to-day problems.

The Report expected a serious discussion at the national level on the fundamental questions regarding human rights, democratic values, and constitutional schemes. It also expressed hope that decisions will be taken in a manner that the dreams of the Constitution's founding fathers can be realised.

The 1989-91 report has been basically a correspondence of the Commission with the Prime Minister, Lok Sabha Speaker and the President of India. The issues raised in 1986-87 and 1987-89 Reports are repeated once again. The Report regrets the lack of prompt response from the government's side in the implementation of these recommendations.

The appointment of the Commissioner under the Article 338 also takes prominence in the Report. It has been suggested in this Report that the Commissioner's office should be kept away from political rivalries and the incumbents should not have any party affiliations. This was felt necessary in order to maintain sanctity of the office and discharge the duties without the fear of changing political colours of successive governments.

Recommendations of the Reports of the National Commission for SC/STs 1992-95

After the 65th Amendment Bill, the NCSCT was established. It submitted its first report for the year 1992-93 on 15 August to the President of India. Later on it submitted reports for 1993-94 and 1994-95. The following is the summary of recommendations by the NCSCT:

Education

In its First Report the National Commission asked for:

(a) Special coaching for Dalits.
(b) Collecting exact figures about their education.
(c) Checking drop-outs in education.
(d) Enhancing scholarship according to the price-index.
(e) Motivating Dalit children for education, whose parents are engaged in 'unclean' occupations.

In the Second Report, the central themes of concern were:

(a) Higher education of Dalits. Universities and the HRD Ministry should find out the causes of poor representation of Dalits in colleges and universities.
(b) Revision of merit list by the Ministry of Health and Family Welfare.
(c) Prior permission from the National Commission for changing any policy for the Dalits.

The 1994-95 Report asks:

(a) To develop a perspective plan for ensuring equal standards of education for Dalits in comparison with general category.
(b) Use of such a language which would facilitate Dalit children's acquisition of knowledge from the vast expanses of print and visual media.
(c) To evolve a National Education Policy wherein primary schools should be opened in tribal areas on priority basis.

(d) Developing communicative skills among tribals.

(e) Establishing residential schools for Dalits and developing a support system for them in education. In higher education, the government aided institutions which do not provide admission to Dalits should be directed to do so and the Government should earmark remedial courses and scholarships for higher education.

Apart from the above measures HRD Ministry was asked:

(a) To monitor the comparison between Dalits and non-Dalits.

(b) To provide monetary and non-monetary incentives to Dalit students.

(c) To encourage NGOs to establish schools in Dalit dominated areas.

Adverse Discrimination or Atrocities

In its First report, the National Commission has also suggested the measures to be taken for the effective implementation of the Prevention of Atrocities Act (PAA). They were:

(a) The Postmaster can be assigned the duty of telegraphically sending the complaints of the victims.

(b) The Act (PAA) be made part of examinations, regulations and orientation courses.

(c) Publishing it through mass-media and NGOs.

(d) Identifying the atrocity-prone areas.

(e) Making local administration more vigilant.

(f) Setting up special courts to dispose of the criminal cases quickly.

(g) Providing a relief of one lakh to the victim of atrocities.

It was also suggested as a matter of policy that the subject of atrocities should be transferred to the Ministry of Home Affairs (MHA) from the Welfare Ministry, which is the case at present.

The Second Report asked for a series of studies to be carried out on the working of special courts, atrocity-prone areas, relief distribution to the affected persons, disposal of cases by the police and courts vis-à-vis problems faced by the victims. It recommended that SHOs should be trained to implement the PAA properly.

The 1994-95 Report also recommend for the speedy implementation of PAA in its true spirit.

Economic Development

The Report for 1992-93 recommends to fix up higher proportion for TSP and SCP in the plan outlay, than population of Dalits. It also proposes that PAA can be used to settle the land-related disputes. It also suggests that the employment generation programmes need to be given priority for some more years till the Dalits get economically stablised. It also asks for speeding up the pace of implementation of development programmes for Dalits.

The suggestions of the Report on the implementation of reservations in case of recruitment are significant. These are as below:

(a) Dalits falling into the merit list should not be considered against the reserved quota.
(b) Ending the practice of direct recruitment where Dalit candidates are not available for promotion.
(c) Reviewing the procedure of writing the CRs of Dalit officers.

The Report for 1993-94 required the government: (i) to direct the thrust of planning towards Dalit sections in rural India and ask the central ministries to give an account of programmes/schemes undertaken, and (ii) to identify the poorest of the poor and direct the benefits of Employment Generation Programmes to them.

On the land question, it suggested:

(a) To bring down the land ceiling in states as far as possible.
(b) To set up land tribunals to expedite the cases of disputes.
(c) Financial assistance to the allottees.
(d) The Ministry of Rural Development should urge the State to report the progress with respect to the alienation, restoration and possession of land given to tribals.
(e) To check the illegal transfer of tribal land to the non-tribals. It also suggested that if there is a provision to transfer land with permission from competent authorities, such provision should be deleted from the legislations.

With respect to safeguards in recruitment in the public sector the Report recommended:

(a) Proper implementation of reservations in universities and colleges and suggested amending the UGC and University Act, if need be.
(b) In the absence of Dalit candidates the non-Dalit should have ad-hoc appointment, not permanent.

(c) Asked to fulfill the backlog and clearly mention the number of reserved seats.
(d) In case of litigation regarding the appointment of Dalits candidates, if a case is decided in favour of the candidate then the management should be prohibited to go in for appeal.
(e) Seventy five per cent sweeper posts to be reserved for those engaged traditionally in the occupation.
(f) Those engaged in scavenging can be diversified to group 'D' services.
(g) PSU Executives/ Directors should invite Dalit Unions to address their grievances.

The verification of the caste certificates of Dalits was also paid attention to. It was suggested that (i) Dalit women's identity be decided on the basis of her father's identity and not on the basis of the husband and, (ii) completion of verification of certificates should be done within three months to avoid harassment to Dalit candidates.

The 1994-95 Report, while deliberating upon economic issues, repeated its previous recommendations apart from the need:

(a) To review the functioning of Scheduled Caste Development Corporations and Tribal Development.
(b) To provide education and accommodation facilities to the employees working in tribal areas.
(c) To monitor the NGOs working in tribal areas.
(d) To have a radical departure with regard to the Tribal Sub-Plan
(e) To convert Integrated Tribal Development Projects in to ITD Agencies and their registration as societies so that they could be subject to an internal evaluation system.
(f) To address the water problem in north-east.
(g) To upgrade skills and technology to control drought conditions in the predominantly tribal districts of Kalahandi and Nuapada of Orissa.

On reservations in Public Service, it directed:

(a) To have a special recruitment drive for group 'A' and 'B' services.
(b) To ask the liaison officers to inspect the maintenance of the Roster System and suggested that they should be made responsible for its maintenance.
(c) To provide a respectable status to SC/ST employees.

(d) To embody the main principles of reservations in the Act of Parliament to avoid its violations.

This report discussed the problem of the flow of 'fake' certificates being used by non-Dalits at length and suggested that steps be taken to alter the methods of issuing the same. The non-Dalits have been using fake certificates to get jobs in the government sector, and for admissions in the educational institutions as well.

The 1994-95 Report of the National Commission also recommended some significant suggestions for Dalits through 'Research and Evaluation Studies'.

The analysis of the above recommendations show distinctions between the reports prepared in the pre-constitutional and post-constitutional status of the National Commission for SC/STs. The CSCT reports have raised some major policy issues whereas in the NCSCT Reports emphasis lies on the implementation part.

The PCR Act 1976 has been recommended to be made more stringent so that it could put a check on the multiplication of atrocities. The formation of regular review Committees, not only at the Central but also at the State, District and Block levels forms the major part of the recommendation on violation of civil rights of Dalits. Willful negligence on the part of the concerned officers with respect to atrocities on Dalits is suggested to be dealt with strictly. In its post-constitutional status, the National Commission recommends to implement the Prevention of Atrocities Act 1989 effectively. It has been suggested that as Dalits are scared to approach the police in case of atrocities, the Postmaster of the area could be asked to receive the complaint of the victim and he/she in turn should send it to the competent authority. Setting up of special courts and training the officials to implement the act has also been emphasised for the success of the policy.

In the previous reports, the need to formulate a comprehensive policy on reservations in jobs has been emphatically recommended so that the Non-Government Organisations also provide proper representation to Dalits and the Government's institutions, and ministries are asked to fill up the back log. But in the latter reports, there is a shift towards proper implementation of the reservation policy in PSUs, colleges and universities, Special Recruitment drives, and appointing liaison officers have been recommended.

On the educational front, the earmarking of necessary outlays for the educational development of Dalits and complementing the cost of

Education Index and the Scholarship was emphasised by CSCT reports whereas in the latter reports, provision for special coaching, checking drop-outs, and motivating the children of parents engaged in the 'unclean' occupation has been recommended. A major policy issue finds place in the latter reports where the Government was entrusted with task of formulating a policy for the admission from the National Commission, while changing any policy on education that concerns Dalits.

The Commissioner in its 1986-87 report gave special attention to the upliftment of the tribals and recommended that the Finance Commission should pay special attention to the Scheduled Areas/ participation of tribals in the management and development, and above all, make 'single line administration' and special code of conduct compulsory for government personnel to work in the tribal areas. But the latter reports do not recommend any policy changes, but merely seek proper implementation of the existing ones.

Few of the other significant policy concerns of pre-constitutional National Commission include:

(a) A status paper on the socio-economic conditions of Dalits
(b) Asking National Development Council to constitute a Standing Committee on Dalit issues
(c) Making the Welfare Ministry a nodal agency for poverty alleviation programmes. And finally, it has been recommended that the substance of the polices must be in consonance with solution of the common man's everyday problems.

After being granted constitutional status, the National Commission for SC/STs touched the areas generally discussed in the previous reports, such as establishing land tribunals, monitoring of NGO's functioning for the development of Dalits, and reviewing the functioning of SC/ST Development Corporations.

Thus policy areas find more discussion in the pre-constitutional National Commission with minor modifications and changes in the latter phase.

Summing Up

The reports once tabled on the floor of the House are discussed by the legislators. These can be then utilised by both the MPs and the government as inputs for policy formulation. On the basis of above analysis, a framework of policy inputs emerges that broadly includes the following issues:

(a) To provide constitutional status to the Commission for SC/STs.

(b) Special recruitment drive to fulfill the backlog.

(c) To rationalise land distribution mechanisms and setting up of land tribunals for checking land alienation.

(d) Making Protection of Civil Rights Act more stringent to check atrocities. It could include:
- — action against erring authorities,
- — review panel comprising District Magistrates and Chief Secretaries,
- — setting up special courts,
- — identification of atrocity-prone areas.

(e) Special educational programmes.

(f) Ministry of Welfare to become nodal agency for the Welfare of SC/STs.

(g) Policy of positive discrimination in government funded NGOs and other government aided private institutions.

(h) Special policies for tribals. These should aim at the following:
- — not to acquire their land without consensus,
- — constitution of a commission of Scheduled Areas and welfare of STs.
- — to provide share in newly created assets and enterprises in tribal areas,
- — no use of force against their struggles.
- — to review all the ongoing projects in tribal area.

(i) Comprehensive changes in overall system.
- — status paper on Dalit development,
- — prior permission of NCSCT to change present policies,
- — National Development Council to constitute Standing Committee on Dalit aspects,
- — Research and analysis studies to examine impact of welfare programmes,

(j) Scavengers to be promoted to group 'D' jobs.

(k) To legislate new Act to embody main principles of reservations.

These issues need to be examined while looking into the legislative deliberations because they are indicative of contemporary policy needs of Dalits.

3

Discrimination, Reservation and Globalisation: Reports and Response

The policy of protective discrimination primarily functions as an instrument of social justice and secondarily as one of social transformation. Social transformation is not a natural phenomenon but the result of the rise of political consciousness among the people that eventually leads to various interventionist measures. These pave the way for the improvement of their social condition. Such changes are not necessarily radical and may occur through an evolutionary process. No social system changes completely and even the most radical changes like revolutions seldom bring change in all features of a social structure. Hence all social changes remain uneven and partial (Cohen 1979:3). When we talk of the policy of protective discrimination it encompasses the idea of planning not merely from the standpoint of social consciousness but also enforcement by the State, in the form of social legislations. The State institutions like administrative apparatus, political executive, courts, and above all legislatures are major instruments of social legislations.

In this study, an attempt has been made to scrutinise the role of Legislature *i.e.*, the Lok Sabha in the formulation of legislations for the SC/STs.

As stated earlier, the Lok Sabha provides ample opportunities to its Members to participate in governmental affairs through: (i) oral or written questions posed by MPs, and (ii) participation by members in debates on Bills, Resolutions, and Statements made by the government on the floor of the House. These two occasions can also be understood in terms of the direct and indirect influence on the decisions of the government. The Questions are instruments of indirect influence building measure used by the parliamentarians, and indicate a preparatory phase of influencing the decision-making process (Narayana 1980:433). Direct influence is exercised during the debate and discussion on various proposals of the government, *viz.*, Bills,

Resolutions, etc. Although the reports of the CSCT and the Commission fall in the latter category, here too the Members do not exercise a direct influence on the decisions of the government. The reply of the concerned Minister is indicative more of the policies in existence than about the formulation of new policies. In majority of the cases the government assures the House of formulation of new proposals in the near future. Thus it is basically during the discussion on the Bills that the MPs influence the decision-making process directly. However, we are concerned only with the reports of the CSCT and the Commission. Under Article 338 (3), it has been clearly mentioned that the Commission would investigate all the matters relating to the safeguards of the SC/STs under the Constitution. There is no other comparable authority which has been bestowed upon with this sort of power and asked to prepare a report on the functioning of the welfare measures for this section. Also, its review of the conditions prevailing at various levels gains importance in the context of developing/modifying or changing the policies in favour of the SC/STs.

In 1985, the 3rd and the 4th reports of the Commission for the years 1980-81 and 1981-82 were discussed. Likewise, the 28th and 29th reports of the erstwhile CSCT for 1986-87 and 1987-88, and the 5th, 6th, 7th and 8th reports of the same body for 1982-86, were debated in 1994. The newly constituted NCSCT's reports from 1992 onwards were not deliberated upon by the Lok Sabha till 1995.

Several studies on the leadership in Parliament have observed that it being elite in nature remains alienated from the large mass of citizens and therefore is unable to represent the interests of citizens. Guttsman's study (1964) on British parliamentary elite over a period of hundred years revealed that occupationally and educationally the MPs come from socially privileged classes. This makes them more anxious towards maintaining the social structure. They support their own privileges through the system and thus control the economic resources of the community through political influence. The study observes that they show little interest in framing policies for the under-privileged sections. Studies on Indian legislators by Mathur, *et. al.*, (1993), also observe a lack of concern among them for the development of a large mass of people. Their constitutional concerns do not reflect upon long-term perspectives. As a case in point, there is a poor representation of demands and needs of the drought affected people before the Government on the floor of the House by the legislators. In the final analysis it says that :

> Legislative interventions on drought reveals the MP as substantially committed neither to his constituents nor to the national interest, much less to the lofty abstractions such as reason and conscience... Parliament as a whole has a fairly limited influence on policy-making, which remains the exclusive preserve of the Government..... (p 116).

These studies show the ineffectiveness of Parliament to hold the Executive responsible for providing developmental direction to the policies formulated by the regime in power. It is equally true that policy issues being complex and technical in nature cannot be easily comprehended by the ordinary MPs.[1]

There could be arguments in favour of a lack of concern among the MPs on electronics, or science and technology policies, as they need technical and scientific understanding. But negligence of simple issues such as poverty alleviation, atrocities, etc., that need relatively simple and ordinary understanding on the part of the legislators, cannot be defended on the same ground. The consequences of poverty, untouchability, atrocities, etc., have a long term effect on Dalits and we expect that the concern of the MPs, particularly of Dalit MPs, should find proper articulation.

Democratic representation expects accountability from representatives and it becomes quite obvious when special interests are distinctly represented in it, as is the case of Dalits in India. Emancipatory politics requires genuine concern of the representatives, not merely for the power and prestige in serving constituencies but to ensure adequate representation and protection of Dalit interests. It also includes competing for political power within the party as well as in the Legislature (Duskin 1972:208, 210-211). Only vocal and well-informed MP can force the Treasury benches to be responsive and accountable towards the plight of the Dalits and make his/her presence felt. An entry into the Legislature is no assurance to become a ruling force. It is equally necessary to capture economic, ideological, and cultural power to demolish the dominance of the ruling class maintained at such power centres (Guru 1993:45).

It has been rightly pointed out that the law-making process for the welfare of Dalits has been bugged by both tardiness and apathy, though the major problems confronted by them have been identified for long

---

1 The studies on electronics and science and technology policies undertaken in 1985 by R.B. Jain and Rahman and Haritash respectively, also point towards this.

(Narayana 1980:440). Here the emphasis is on the perspective being adopted and developed in the Lok Sabha with regard to the Reports of the Commission and the CSCT by the Members in the House. The reports of the CSCT and Commission for SC/STs provide framework for the legislators to emphatically argue in favour of formulating policies of a specific nature for them.

The recommendations of the Commission(s) function as guidelines and inputs for the legislators to make policy decisions and for the legislature to function as a "demand input processor", to use Wahlke's (1978) phrase. Also the policy inputs contained in the reports of the NCSCT help legislators to develop their perspectives for policy demands. The relationship between the reports of NCSCT and the perspectives adopted by legislators on the floor of the house would help us to examine their responses *vis-à-vis* the feedback provided and would subsequently ascertain our knowledge of the gaps, therein. The average citizen, both as spectator and as voter does not know much about the issues to mount the policy demands that could be raised by the institutional apparatus like NCSCT. Apart from citizens or constituents, political parties, pressure groups, cabinet colleagues, etc., can also put demands to the government that can become policy input mechanism for the Legislature. But these are extra-legislative and extra-constitutional, whereas the NCSCT Report being constitutional in nature remains a prime policy input mechanism for the legislators. These reports may be utilised during the legislative deliberations and we shall examine how far the reports are used to develop policy perspectives. Floor debates have been considered the most important form of deliberation (Gerald Solomon and Donald Wolfenrbergos 1994). Being confronted with the shortage of time and resources on the one hand and the need to take too many decisions on the other, legislators are not in a position to deliberate upon each and every issue. Thus, they need to be specific. The NCSCT reports make it easier for them to obtain information relevant to their needs during deliberations.

There are two perspectives to assess the responsiveness of the legislators. One which satisfy the immediate demands of the people. The other which creates new demands according to the circumstances and needs in the long-term perspective. Thus representation can be divided into two categories: 1) *Phenomenal Representation*, and 2) *Enduring Representation*. The former has short-term objectives, where with regard to Dalits, increasing funds for welfare activities, vacancies for recruitment, scholarships for education, etc. became the concerns of the representative. Here the representative may ask to implement the present schemes and programmes without suggesting changes in their implementation mechanism. The latter is concerned with long-term objectives where an attempt is made not only to strengthen existing institutional mechanisms but also to create new ones to implement policies. It also terms the present Dalit policy paradigm as inadequate, demanding additional attention, and offering alternatives policies.

Nevertheless, the effectiveness of the legislator to influence Dalit policy substantially depends on the perspectives adopted, even though legislative deliberations may not be conscious articulations with one or the other of these perspectives. The NCSCT reports also deal with both short-term and long-term objectives. The legislative deliberations also explicitly or implicitly refer to one of these perspectives only.

While participating in a debate on the reports, a stage can be set by the legislators to take the Government to task on the conditions of Dalits. Being equipped with statistics and recommendations of the NCSCT, Dalit legislators in particular are expected to be more serious to use the occasion for the improvement of the Dalit lot.

An examination of the discussion on the two Motions that took place in the Lok Sabha in 1985 and 1994 on the Commission and the CSCT's reports shows prevalence of both 'phenomenal' and 'enduring' representation among the legislators. These reports are based not only on the facts and figures of the Dalit Policy paradigm but also recommend the Government to take steps both in terms of proper policy implementation and policy shifts.

Most of the time legislators during the discussions were involved in policy issues as they also raised minor issues which reflected on phenomenal representation. Out of the seventy-three legislators who spoke on the two Motions, seventeen MPs apart from raising policy issues deliberated on: (i) inadequate and untimely scholarships to the Dalit students, (ii) fulfilling or increasing vacancies in various central government departments, and (iii) demanding more funds for welfare activities. Eleven of these MPs belonged to reserved constituencies. Some of the instances are cited below:

Anadi Charan Das [Jajpur]

> The stipend you are giving under educational facilities is totally inadequate. It is not sufficient to continue the studies. Therefore, the amount of stipend should be increased so that our children are benefited by these stipends. Similarly, under the women education programme also very little amount has

been made available. More funds should be allocated for this purpose also (LSD 26 November 1985:313).

R.P. Suman [Akbarpur]

Even after 38 years of independence, the representation which should have been upto 22.5 per cent has reached only 5.68 per cent. With this speed it would possibly take hundred, two hundred or four hundred years. Similarly, in 1982-83 in civil services, 963 candidates were selected. Of these, only 26 candidates belong to the backward classes. This is the state of affairs at present. We regret that we are not marching forward with the speed we had anticipated in starting these welfare programmes (LSD 28 November 1985:278).

Manikrao Hodlya Gavit [Nandurbar]

There is a huge backlog in services under Central Government, State Governments and Public Sector Undertakings in every state, there is backlog in appointments of scheduled castes and scheduled tribes in Primary and Middle Schools and Colleges. The institutions working there even do not inform the concerned authorities regarding this backlog. The Welfare Ministry should look into the matter and brought to the notice of Chief Minister and Chief Secretary of the State (LSD 7 December 1994:248).

R. Annanambi [Pollachi]

More funds should be allocated for these schemes. A sum of Rs. 6000 is not enough for constructing a house. A minimum of Rs. 10,000 should be given for a house. Similarly, instead of limiting 25 houses for a Block, at least 100 houses should be constructed in a Block. Naturally more funds should be allocated by the Centre for achieving this objective (LSD 28 November 1985:295).

The only major difference pertaining to the discussion on the issue of phenomenal representation that took place in the years 1985 and 1994 is that in the former the demand was to increase scholarships, vacancies in jobs, and funds. But in the latter year it was meant for providing the scholarship in time, fulfilling the existing or increased reserved quota in jobs. Quite interestingly during the 1994 discussion there was no demand to provide more funds for welfare activities. Apart from the above aspects of phenomenal representation there emerges a more concrete thing, which relates to the simple demand for the implementation of existing policies without asking for changes or strengthening the mechanisms responsible for their implementation.

A conscious and assertive electorate can force the representative to be articulative, accountable and responsive. Having got elected through joint electorates, the Dalit representative has to maintain a balance between the constituency needs and the needs of his/her Dalit constituents (Guru: 1986). Thus he/she functions at two levels – general and particular. Here, we are concerned with the SC/ST representatives, who are expected to respond to the needs of the Dalit masses. For effective representation, participation is the primary condition for the representative. But participation requires sufficient articulation which can be achieved through proper understanding of the problem. For this, the representative needs to be already well-informed about the conditions and expectations of the constituents. However, the examination of the question of political articulation involves two issues– one signifies the character of representation, whereas the other, the content of representation. In this chapter, we shall deal with the latter aspect of representation.

Perspectives on Implementation of Policies and Programmes

The hostility regarding the non-implementation of legislative measures and the common rules and regulations for Dalits was faced by Ambedkar during his encounters with the officialdom. Observing the attitude of personnels in implementation process he stated:

> The official is anti-untouchables (read Dalit) and pro-Hindu. Whenever he has any authority or discretion it is always exercised to the prejudice of the untouchables.... The police and Magistrate are sometimes corrupt. If they were only corrupt, things would not perhaps be so bad because an official would not perhaps be so bad because an official who is corrupt is open to purchase of either party. But the additional misfortune is that the police and Magistrate are often more partial than corrupt. It is this partiality to the Hindus and the antipathy to the untouchables which results in the denial of protection and justice to the untouchables. There is no cure to this partiality to the one and the antipathy to the other. It is founded in the social and religious repugnance which is inborn in every Hindu. The police and Magistrate by reason of their motives, interest and their breeding do not sympathise with the living forces operating

> among the untouchables. They are not charged with the wants, the pains, the cravings and the desires which actuate the untouchables. Consequently, they are openly hostile and inimical to their aspirations, do not help them to advance, disfavour their cause and snap at everything that smacks of pride and self-respect. On the other hand they share the feelings of the Hindus sympathise with them in the attempt to maintain their power, authority, prestige and their disunity over the untouchables. In any conflict between the two, they act as the agents of the Hindus in suppressing the revolt of the untouchables and participate quite openly and without shame in the nefarious attempt of all Hindus to do everything possible by all means, fair or foul, to "teach the untouchables a lesson" and hold down in their own place (Moon 1989:269-70).

It is significant to note that of the 36 Members who participated in debate in 1985, only six of them found no major fault in the policies of the government, and pointed to but only flaws in the administrative apparatus. It needs to be noted that they belonged to the Congress party; four were SC/STs (two each), the other two were from general constituencies. All of them were equivocally concerned with misappropriation, under-utilisation of funds and non-implementation of the existing policies of the government. Some of their observations are as below:

Ram Payare Panika [Robertsganj]

> So far as the question of their (Dalits) economic, educational and social development is concerned, all the hon. Members have dealt at length on it. I would like to point out that all the policies of the Central Government are all right but the fault lies in their implementation at different levels. Due to lack of time-bound programme the desired results are not being achieved and the policies and guidelines are not being implemented properly (LSD 28 November 1985:353).

Satyanarayan Jatiya [Ujjain]

> We are considering protection of the rights which were made to strengthen the concept of equality. We aimed for such an objective but are we being able to achieve this objective? That is why, several programmes, tribal sub-plans, schemes for ensuring a special share of Scheduled Castes can definitely prove to be important towards development but it is not being implemented and even if is being implemented at some places,

it is not satisfactory. If their pace and functioning is made satisfactory, their outcome can also be satisfactory (LSD 8 December 1994:268).

Though the Members in the 10th Lok Sabha were also concerned with the non-implementation of the policies but none of them uttered sweeping statements as was done in the 8th Lok Sabha. The policies were being correctly formulated but a lot was left to be desired when it came to implementation. The non-implementation of polices—an aspect that kept rearing its head during the discussions not only retards the development of this section materially but also makes the realisation of the objectives of liberty, equality, justice and fraternity a Herculean task.

The demands for implementation have no meaning without asking for strengthening of the implementing agencies. It indicates a phenomenal representation but its nature differed during 1985 and 1994 because in the former, emphasis was on simple implementation of the existing policies, whereas in the latter, implementation was termed unsatisfactory and need was felt to alter the mechanisms of implementation.

Moreover, terming the implementation process as unsatisfactory is not sufficient to force the Government to make its enforcing agencies more capable. The nature of the Dalit problem is distinct and so it needs specific treatment in a long term perspective. It needs situation-sensitive strategies which have both a combative as well as a preventive orientation. The deliberations in the Lok Sabha are not necessarily conscious articulations with short-term or long-term perspectives. Having shown the prevalence of 'phenomenal' representations in the above discussion, we now turn to 'enduring' representation, where MPs not only aired dissatisfaction with the implementation process but also referred to the inadequacy of a few existing policies, inefficiency in some others and, argued for modifications and changes in those with regard to the empowerment of Dalits. We examine enduring representation first in terms of strengthening implementing agencies and then in terms of policy shifts.

Constitutional development during the last fifty years has helped in finding ways not only with regard to alternative policies but also alternative mechanisms of implementing these polices. The recent debate on the President K.R. Narayan's remarks to judge "whether it is the Constitution that has failed or we have failed the constitution", highlights the need to examine the implementation process and those who implement the policies. Arguing for changes, it has been stated that "if some changes in the Constitution can help reform those who implement it, then it should certainly be looked into"(Nayyar 2000:3742). These observations emphatically raise the need to look into the perspectives adopted by the legislators to strengthen the mechanisms of implementation of Dalit policies.

Perspectives on Monitoring Agencies-CSCT and Commission for SC/STs

Most of the participants in the debate referred to the weak status of the Commission for SC/STs and its inability to get the information from various ministries and departments, leaving aside the question of inquiry into the malpractices prevalent at different levels. Almost all the Members (apart from six mentioned earlier) consistently pursued and argued for the need to give more teeth to the Commission and strengthen it to function effectively in monitoring the development of these sections. Mere allocation of resources is not sufficient condition for development but it needs to be seen whether the allocated resources reach the people or not. To make possible for the allocated safeguards to reach the masses was one of the most frequently emphasised demands put by the legislators.

K. Jeevarathinam [Arakkonam]

> Unfortunately this Commission does not have the powers to enquire into the petitions submitted by the Scheduled Caste workers about their not getting minimum wages under the Act. This commission should be given powers under the Commission of Inquiry Act. Then only the Commission can look into the genuine grievances of these people and penalise those who deny them the minimum wages. I suggest that the Hon. Minister of Social Welfare should do the needful in this matter, and ensure that the Scheduled Caste agricultural labourers get the minimum wages.
>
> The issues relating to land ceilings and the updating of land records have been included in the new 20-Point Programme. Unless the State Governments pay serious attention to these two issues, the Scheduled Caste landless agricultural workers will not make any progress in their life. This Commission has to remain a silent spectator if the State Governments do not implement the recommendations made by it in these two matters. And when this Commission is given the constitutional status and mandatory powers, then alone it

> can function effectively. I request that the Hon. Minister should expeditiously forward the constitutional Amendment Bill for empowering the Commission with mandatory powers (LSD 28 November 1985:290).

Thus during the debate on the Commission's report in 1985 it was demanded that the Commission should be given the constitutional status. Subsequently an Act was passed in 1990 by the Parliament to provide constitutional status to the Commission for SC/STs. It was clubbed with the CSCT and was named 'National Commission for SC/STs.'

It was believed that the NCSCT would be able to monitor the functioning of the policies for SC/STs in an efficient manner. However, the Members during the debate on the Reports of the CSCT in 1994 were apprehensive about the role played by it during the last three years of its existence. One of the participants went up to the extent of calling it a 'toothless tiger', though the Members by and large were more bothered about improving the functioning of the National Commission than suggesting major policy shift in its institutional apparatus. For instance:

Manjay Lal [Samastipur]

> This Commission has been given wide powers. Out of these, 3 or 4 powers are very effective. The Commission has the powers to check atrocities on downtrodden, provide immediate relief to the sufferers and rehabilitate them. It is the duty of the Commission to see that the people belonging to Scheduled Castes get promotion in government services and they are not subjected to any mental torture. This Commission has also been empowered to oversee the works undertaken by the State Governments as well as the Union Government under different schemes meant for the Scheduled Castes and Scheduled Tribes. This enjoins the powers to call for any document from any court and order an inquiry after examining the documents. Though this Commission enjoys such wide powers, yet it does not have its own budget and the staff to oversee its functioning. In this way, the Commission depends on the Ministry of Welfare (LSD 24 August 1994:617).

Welfare Ministry as a Nodal Agency

One significant aspect of the discussion was to constitute a separate Ministry for the welfare of SC/STs or at least to have a special minister for them. It was also observed that with this change the National Commission would also get strengthened and its reports could be implemented in a proper way. The special Minister and the National Commission could have co-ordination with the governments at the State and the UT level. In this regard Dwarka Nath Das [Karimganj] argued:

> Sir, in my opinion, there should be a Minister of State entirely for Scheduled Castes and Scheduled Tribes under the Welfare Ministry because welfare is a very broad term to cover all aspects of the people of India. That is why there should be a particular Minister under the Ministry of Welfare. There should be a network of State and UT level Commissions under the supervision of the National Commission to look into the problems and to implement the national policies relating to Scheduled Castes and Scheduled Tribes. I will suggest that after every five years there should be a detailed survey of SC and ST people to assess about their stages of development educationally, socially and economically (LSD 7 December 1994:237).

In January 1982, the Ministry of Welfare was declared a nodal agency for the overall policy, planning, and co-ordination for the development of SC/STs. Not only was it made a nodal agency but was also given the responsibility of co-ordination with the Central Ministries, State Governments, and Union Territories. In spite of the amendment in the procedures, the Members aired their dissatisfaction and demanded the constitution of a separate ministry or if that was not possible, then at least a department for the same. This was voiced by a concerned Member on the following terms:

> Let there be a separate Department to deal with the SC/ST people of the country. But it is an unfortunate thing for us that a few days ago the Cabinet was reshuffled and a new Department has been created Department of Welfare for the Scheduled Castes and Scheduled Tribes though it was not mentioned. May I know who will deal with the atrocities part of it? Would you be able to deal with that job? Certainly not, It is with the Home Ministry itself. So, the problem of the SC and STs has been divided in many parts. Some parts will be dealt with by the Home Ministry, some by the Welfare Ministry and some by some other Ministry. In this way are you going to solve their problem (Amar Roy Pradhan [Coochbehar] LSD 26 November 1985:319-20).

Though a separate department was created as the watchdog for the welfare of SC/STs, it remains to be analysed what role did the separate department play in monitoring the implementation of policies and programmes of the Central Government. A department without committed bureaucrats proves to be the cutting edge in case of transfer of sincere incumbents. It happened to the Department of Rural Development in 1990's. It became handicapped in the absence of committed administrators who were transferred to the Department of Finance that became the power-house of economic liberalisation (Mendelsohn and Vicziany 1998:166).

Perspectives on Atrocities

Atrocities on Dalits is the consistent feature of the Indian society in the context of the problem of untouchability. Most of the atrocities are committed in the rural areas. The prime reason for such atrocities relates to the land question in one form or the other. The Reports of the NCSCT have repeatedly attracted the attention of the government in this regard. Although the abolition of untouchability was given comprehensive treatment in the Untouchability Offences Act (UOA) and later on in the protection of Civil Rights Act (PCRA), the number of atrocities has not registered any slump. The Reports of NCSCT reveal that atrocities which are physical in nature are committed more in the rural than in urban areas and in most cases the reason is the landlessness of Dalits.

During the debate on the 1985 Report, thirteen out of twenty Members of the atrocity prone areas (Andhra Pradesh, Madhya Pradesh, Bihar, and Uttar Pradesh, etc.) touched upon the subject in one way or the other. They were not happy with the implementation of PCRA, and wanted more stringent laws to punish the guilty.

The following excerpt substantiates the perspective on atrocities in the Lok Sabha in this context:

R. P. Suman [Akbarpur]

> So far as atrocities on the Scheduled Castes and the Scheduled Tribes are concerned, you will see that the number of such incidents have doubled during 1981-82. It has been stated in the report that the number of cases of atrocities increased by 112 per cent during 1982-83. Despite that, it is said that the number of such incidents is decreasing. I request the Government to take this matter seriously, otherwise their number will continue to increase. In order to prevent such

> incidents, action should be taken on the basis of the recommendations made in this report (LSD 28 November 1985:279).

The continuation of this practice has also been confirmed by the United Nations Committee on the Elimination of Racial Discrimination. In its review under the auspices of the convention on the Elimination of All forms of Racial Discrimination in 1996, the Committee states:

Although constitutional provisions and legal texts exist to abolish untouchability and to protect the members of Scheduled Castes and Scheduled Tribes... widespread discrimination against those people, and the relative impunity of those who abuse them, points to the limited effects of these measures...(Human Rights Watch 1999:26).

To constitute special courts to deal with the atrocities has been a long standing demand. Even a cursory look into the cases of conviction, shows quite a disturbing emerging scenario. In 1962 the conviction rate had declined to 23 per cent as compared to 1951 and this has further compounded with the lowering of conviction rate to 12 per cent in 1982 (Mendelsohn and Vicziany 1998:128). Thus the politico-legal system dealing with atrocities allows leeway to offenders, with a mechanism of self-defence, through which they get out of the administrative apparatus easily. In this connection K.S. Rao [Machilipatam] stated:

> When we hear that some offences are committed against them, this should not be left to the normal courts; there must be special courts exclusively meant for dealing with these offences committed on them; and the government must see that a time limit should be fixed for giving judgement in those offences (LSD 25 November 1985:371).

Perspectives on Land Reforms

Landlessness is the major handicap of Dalit population, particularly the SCs, among whom nearly 50 per cent of the households cultivate less than 0.01 hectare land each. Nearly two-third of them in the rural areas are agricultural labourers and are totally dependent upon wage employment. (Mungekar 2001:9) Land to the tiller, has been the slogan of various regimes but the land ceiling has not been properly implemented according to the legislators. Though during a discussion in 1985 on the CSCTs reports, the land distribution question was raised by nine out of thirty-six MPs, the deliberations reflected more dissatisfaction with implementation than asking for policy shift. But in 1994 it was the other way round, where the Members wanted change in the policy and even argued for incorporating land reforms in the 9th

Schedule so that big landlords are not able to question the executive decisions in the courts. Following excerpt clearly suggests this.

Dattarau Bandaru [Secundrabad]

> Some time ago the Hon. Prime Minister had called the Chief Minister's conference and he said that within the next two years we must verify the fact as to how much land should be distributed State-wise. But till now, no figures are available. I demanded that the government should bring a Bill in Parliament to include land reforms in the Ninth Schedule of the Constitution. I know that during the Janata Dal Government all the parties including the BJP and the CPI (M), has all agreed to include this in the Ninth Schedule. I personally request the Home Minister to take suitable action. The caste system and the feudal system are dependent on land. If land is bifurcated and given to small beneficiaries, I feel that definitely the caste system will be eliminated (LSD 23 August 1994:624).

The persistent problem of landlessness has been considered as the most potent cause of atrocities. The Reports of the CSCT and the Commission also maintain that most victims of abuse are landless agricultural labourers. Lack of access to land make Dalits economically vulnerable and their dependency is exploited by the upper and middle caste landlords, who abuse the Dalits and go unpunished (Human Rights Watch 1999:28). In the past landlessness gave rise to Naxalite movements in different parts of the country, namely the *Telangana* uprisings in Andhra Pradesh and the *Tebhaga* movement in West Bengal. There also has been an upsurge of naxalism in Bihar in the last few years.

Together with these, the disenchantment with the functioning of the Ministry of Welfare in terms of Dalit policies is also amply reflected in the observations of the Members during the debates. The inability of the Ministry to take legal action against the violators of law forms the basis for this. One of the members, K.D. Sultanpuri went to the extent of suggesting that the department should be put under the Prime Minister's Office, so that there is constant vigilance and monitoring of the prevailing conditions (LSD December 7, 1994:227). The demand to shift the subject of atrocities on Dalits from Welfare Ministry to Ministry of Home Affairs has been consistent and many other MPs also reiterated the proposition.

Perspective on Job Reservations

The issue of job reservation has been dealt in Phenomenal representation where short-term and stereotype issues were discussed. It was meant simply for either increasing or filling the vacancies. But legislators also wanted special attention in this regard and came out with concrete suggestions. Hence we differentiate between Phenomenal and enduring representation in job reservation, as in latter alternative policy mechanisms are suggested with long-term objectives. Compensatory discrimination in government jobs has been the most controversial aspect of the policy. And it has been continuously considered the most effective measure to counter poverty and discrimination prevalent in village life. But the critics of reservation hold the policy responsible for the dilution of standards without taking cognisance of the changes in the economy and polity in recent times (Natraj 1999:2384). It is also equally true that the class which benefits by these reservations is the socially mobile group among Dalits. During the discussion on the Commission's reports in 1985, the Members were apprehensive about the enactments of the provisions and regretted the non-implementation, as it was a meagre number that benefited due to this policy. However, the 1994 discussion shows that the legislators not only raised the issue of non-implementation but also suggested measures like going for special recruitment drive. The Members raised the issue of the punishment to those government officials found guilty of not implementing the policy. For this they demanded special attention.

The anti-reservation movement in some parts of the country developed antagonism between Dalits and their counterparts. The persons authorised to fulfill the reserved quota did not want to appoint SC/ST candidates. A wide gap has been shown in various reports of the Welfare Ministry between the posts available and those filled up with these candidates. The issue was raised during the discussion in 1994, by U.H. Patel [Bulsar] who stated:

> Mere talks or formulation of guidelines will not deliver the goods. The powers given by the Constitution to the Central government will have to be used. For this necessary orders will have to be issued. Why are the State governments or other institutions not issuing orders for filling up the reserved posts? I request the Central Government to prepare a time-bound programme for filling up the reserved posts and take up this work on war-footing (LSD 26 November 1985:315).

Similarly Simon Tigga [Khunti] opined

> In the end I would like to say one thing more. So far as the question of reservation for them is concerned, persons at the lower level indulge in bungling. I do not say that Government does not want to ensure reservation. Many laws have been enacted to provide reservation to them and Government desires that they get due representation in services, but government servants not implementing machinery should be held responsible and the persons found guilty should be awarded punishment. They are unable to get their reserved quota as these officers do not observe the rules. On the other hand influential persons organise agitation for abolishing the reservation system. The result is that a situation of class war is developing in our country. Government should pay special attention towards it. With these words, I thank you for giving me an opportunity to express my views in this regard (LSD 26 November 1994:289).

Perspective on Promotions in Services

The Mandal Commission verdict withdrew reservations in promotions for SC/STs with prospective effect. The issue of reservations in promotions has been raised many times in the Parliament. Although statements were issued by the Minister to clear the cloud prevalent at that time, the fact remains that various departments did not implement it on one pretext or the other. The issue was again raised by many Members during the debate on the Reports in 1994, and the Government was asked to come out with a comprehensive Bill to take care of the interests of Dalits in services.

Thus, Jagpal Singh [Haridwar] spoke

> The Mandal Commission case is lying pending with the Supreme Court. The Scheduled Castes and Scheduled Tribes are not a party to it but the Apex Court gave the decision that there will be restriction on the promotions of the Scheduled Castes and Scheduled Tribes. They were not given reservation in their promotion. This question has been raised at least 10 times here. The Hon. Minister has assured that they have not implemented this decision and reservation will be given at the time of promotion also. I may submit here that order of the Supreme Court is treated as a law unless the Parliament changes it. If the Parliament does not change the relevant rule or law, the order of the Supreme Court remains in force.

> Today all the departments have stopped reservation in promotion. You may keep on giving orders after orders, nothing will happen. Those orders are of the Department of Personnel and not yours. Those orders have not been executed any where till date. The reservation in promotion in each department has been stopped; everything is in backlog. These vacancies are not being filled. Then why the Government is keeping silence on such an order? (LSD 23 August 1994:499).

To counter the biased behaviour of the judiciary, one of the legislators, G.M.C. Balayogi [Amalapuram] went up to the extent of putting the reservation policy under the 9th Schedule of the Constitution (LSD 24 August 1994:503-4).

In the light of the non-fulfilment of reserved quota and the non-percolation of benefits to the poor, some of the Members raised the issue of reviewing the 'Policy of Reservation'. They desired to know the exact position of those who got elevated due to the policy. Further they wanted to develop a comprehensive strategy for their development. Rasa Singh Rawat [Ajmer] than stated:

> What is their condition today? How much reservation and other facilities have been provided to them? Only some handful forward classes are getting benefit of it and other people are still leading their lives on pavements. They are still reeling under the same conditions. Similarly, how many Harijans have reached the high posts? There are some handful people who are getting most of these facilities and rests are still facing the situation of negligence. Is the time not ripe even after 47 years of independence to review the reservation policy of the Government? Had it been reviewed, it would have become clear as to how many persons have got employment, how many posts are lying vacant and what are the reasons for not filling up these vacancies. It would have also become clear as to what extent this policy has brought about uniformity and goodwill in the society (LSD 8 December 1994:294).

Similarly, Bhagwan Shankar Rawat [Agra] stated

> I also would like to say one more thing that it should also be reviewed whether the benefits of reservation have reached these classes or not. Except some particular groups among 1-2 castes, no other Scheduled Castes people could get benefits of this reservation policy. We have to think over the existing bottlenecks while formulating new policy so that all people

belonging to Scheduled Castes could be benefited. Hence it should be reviewed at once, and a comprehensive strategy should be formulated for their development (LSD 8 December 1994:298).

Perspectives on Privatisation, Liberalisation and Globalisation

The privatisation and liberalisation process started by the Rajiv Gandhi Government in 1985 is considered to have had a deleterious effect on the Dalit masses as the opportunities for jobs were reduced in the government departments and the public sector undertakings.

The debate among economists and social philosophers has highlighted the limitations of the market to provide social justice. It is difficult to arrive at a generally acceptable consensus and evaluate the available alternatives (Vaidyanathan 2001:1810). When market forces occupy the centre-stage of growth and development, the State's power to intervene is reduced. The market excludes those without income as consumers or buyers due to their lack of purchasing power. The exclusion deprives them of "entitlements" (Sen 1981). Thus the weaker sections will fall short of entitlements with the setting in motion of the liberalisation process and the most obvious victims among the weaker sections ate the SC/STs in particular. Compensatory discrimination policy has become stereotyped around public sector reservations and the Dalits particularly saw it to be "a haven for employment" (Omvedt 2001).

Though the V.P. Singh regime did not expedite the liberalisation process after Rajiv Gandhi government, but the P.V. Narsimha Rao regime (1991-96) accelerated the process. In such circumstances, the issue of reservations in private sector to safeguard the interests of deprived sections was addressed by the parliamentarians, to sustain the development of SC/STs. Even the PCWSCT presented two reports on the subject, but the Members showed dissatisfaction during the discussions on the inaction of the Government in this regard. Even till today there is no assurance on the subject by the State. The following excerpts substantiate MPs perspectives on the liberalisation process *vis-à-vis* Dalits.

G.M.C. Balayogi [Amalapuram]

As a part of the liberalisation programme, the Government is going in for privatising the public sector units and even nationalised banks. This privatisation is inflicting a death blow to the Scheduled Castes, Scheduled Tribes and

> minority sections of the society. With privatisation all the reservations available to these sections in Government Undertakings will be taken away at once. The Private companies and Undertakings are averse to the policy of reservations. Hence, the legislation to guarantee reservation in Private Sector. Thus, the Government can save SCs/STs and other minority sections from being deprived of the Reservation facility duly guaranteed by the Constitution. Hope, the Government would come forward with the necessary Bill before this House soon (LSD 24 August 1994:563).

Realising the implications of lack of reservations in private sector, the Prime Minister gave a statement to assure the house to look into the matter of safeguarding the interests of SC/STs. The following excerpt of his statement highlights only assurances, not any positive course of actions:

> We will certainly examine this – Measures for welfare of Scheduled Castes and Scheduled Tribes, especially with regard to the reservations in private and public and multinational corporations. In view of the new economic policy this is again an extremely important point. But right now, as the law stands, as the Constitution stands, it is not possible for me to give any commitment. All I can say, we can put our heads together and find a way as to how we can cope with this new situation in the new context (LSD 24 August 1994:541-2).

Whatever statements the Government may come out with, it goes without saying that the liberalisation process thwarts the survival of the weak. The Welfare State is shedding its responsibility of providing socio-economic security to the poor, particularly to the Dalits. Liberalisation of economy in general and globalisation in particular is increasing the interdependence and interconnectedness of the world within a logic of an advancing modernity which signifies a risk, and an uncertainty that leads to vulnerability (Harriss 2001:2034).

We must say that, the Dalit Question requires long–term strategies, which would involve long-term prescriptions for its solution. Though the Members did not categorically mention about how to shape a strategy, they pointed out the failures of the existing mechanism to uplift Dalit masses and suggested various measures in this regard. A long list of measures can be compiled from the suggestions made by them with both long-term, and short-term perspectives. In brief, the following suggestions broadly indicate the perspectives adopted.

Suggestions by the MPs During Discussion on the Reports 1985 and 1994

Atrocities

- Exclusive courts to tackle Dalit cases
- Special police force to combat the atrocities
- Allotment of land with mutual consent to avoid atrocities
- Punish encroachment in tribal areas
- Implement minimum wage law strictly to stop atrocities

Service Sector

- Representation of Dalits in Interview Boards
- Filling up of reserved vacancies in Ministries/Departments and Pubic Sector Undertakings
- Efforts to be made at the Central and the State level to fill up the vacancies
- To appoint eligible Class IV employees in Class III to fulfill the quota
- Recruiting Dalits in the Army
- Special training for promotions
- Punishment to those, not fulfilling the reserved quota
- Pre-training to absorb the eligible candidates in case of non-suitability
- Tackle the adverse remarks in CRs

Education

- More stipends to the Dalit students
- Dalit students in merit list not to be included in the reserved category list
- Food for education programme to attract children
- Construction of hostels at District and Block levels
- Ensuring that scholarship reaches to the students in time
- To tackle separately Dalit education question in the New Education Policy
- Hostels for tribal girls
- Education for awareness
- More *Ashram* schools in tribal areas
- Making education not only free but also compulsory

- Increasing the number of scholarships with revision
- Special programmes to increase the literacy rate of Dalits
- Mid-day meal and mother-tongue education to tribal children
- Mental development in terms of confidence building.

Land Reforms

- Amending the law on land
- Updating the land-records
- Allotment of land with mutual consensus
- Expedite the land reforms
- Check the slipping of Dalit land to non-Dalits
- Land reform to check atrocities
- Land reforms implementation with police protection
- Not only allotting land but also giving possession.
- To remove impediments to make Dalits real land-owners
- Tackling the middle-man concept in tribal areas
- Avoid double entry of land in tribal areas – both in Revenue record and in forest land
- First rehabilitation of tribals, then acquisition of land
- Distribution of land in Government's possession

Housing

- Abolish the concept of separate houses away from village community
- Provide good material for Dalit Housing schemes
- *Pucca* houses for slum clearance
- Habitation of Dalits only at District and *Taluqa* levels

Miscellaneous

- Flush system for scavengers
- Rehabilitation of scavengers
- Special arrangements for water and electricity
- Making SC/ST Development Corporations more efficient
- Judiciary not to intervene in the fixing up of quota
- Legal cells at different levels
- Recruiting sincere and dedicated officers in Tribal areas and concerned departments
- Streamline the administration for proper implementation of Schemes

1994 Discussion

Atrocities

- Exploitations of tribals shifted from money-lender to the government officials
- Appointment of Dalit judges in special courts
- Residential schools for SC/STs
- Rehabilitation of tribals before starting a project
- To start mobile special courts
- Implementation of land ceiling act
- Violation of human rights by not allowing conversion should be stopped
- Commission not to depend on SP/DMs for reports
- Constituting *Bhumi Sena* to give possession of land
- Legal action against public servants who violate laws on Dalits
- No repetition of Nagpur stampede kind of incidents
- Stop illegal possession of land
- Officers to be made responsible for atrocities

Education

- Residential schools in SC/ST areas
- Mid-day meal scheme
- Scholarship to be sufficient and in time
- Hostel for SC/ST students, specially tribal girls
- Developing mechanism against drop-out of Dalit students
- No diversion of funds for SC/ST education
- More *Ashram* schools
- Provide adequate staff in schools in SC/ST areas
- Scholarships according to price index
- More educational institutions
- Encouragement among SC/ST students for higher education
- Training Institution for Dalits
- Opening of SC/ST hostels in every district
- Quality education to eradicate untouchability

Service Sector

- Special recruitment centres in tribal areas
- SC/STs members in interview boards
- Special coaching for students to get into service
- Punishing the guilty officers

- Filling up backlog
- Providing jobs to educated youth
- Reservation to be put under the 9th Schedule
- District-wise reservation to tribals in TSP areas

Miscellaneous

- Co-operatives in tribal areas
- Five-times enhancement of the budget on Dalits
- Sanction of loan to be made simple
- Development of industrial infrastructure for unemployed youth
- Small scale industries and sheds to Dalits
- Providing feedback to handloom sector
- Monitoring of loans under SCDFC and banks
- Commission should not depend on SP/DMs
- New commission to bring in Castes/Tribes in the list
- Commission to consult the States
- Discussion on parliamentary committee to be made compulsory
- Proportional representation to Dalits in industries
- More powers to the Ministry of Welfare
- Time-bound programme to implement the recommendation contained in the reports of the CSCT
- Master–plan for mobilisation of irrigation resources
- Need to abolish casteism
- Electrification of Ambedkar grams
- Provide assistance for proper house construction

Summing Up

Deliberations by the legislators reveal that there was both Phenomenal as well as Enduring representations. Their articulations for increasing: (i) the funds for welfare activities, (ii) vacancies in various departments and fulfilling them, (iii) scholarships for students, etc., were relatively low because only seventeen out of the seventy-three legislators intervened in these aspects. Interestingly, a majority of them belonged to reserved constituencies. Another significant aspect of the deliberations was that in 1985 if the concern was for raising scholarships, funds and reserved vacancies, in 1994 it was against the delay in scholarship[2] and non-fulfilment of existing reserved vacancies.

---

2 There was a revision in scholarships in 1989 by the Central Government.

It is surprising to note that constituency concerns even with regard to short-term objectives were ambiguously absent. Neither did the legislators bother about the lack of funds for developmental activities concerning Dalits in their constituencies, nor did they raise the issue of atrocities in their areas.[3]

Legislative deliberations appear to be more concerned with the Enduring representation. Though some of the members' articulations exhibited Phenomenal representation but most of them gave equal treatment to long-term policy objectives as well. Before the conferment of constitutional status to the Commission they kept raising this issue throughout the 1985 discussion. However, the constitutional status of 1990 failed to altogether satisfy them, as they wanted the wide ranging powers bestowed upon the Commission to be strengthened with adequate budget and staff to oversee its functioning. Another aspect for the proper implementation of safeguards was related to the constitution of a separate ministry for SC/STs or to bring Dalit subject under the MHA. With regard to containing atrocities against Dalits, the legislators were not happy with the PCRA. They wanted:

(a) a more stringent act to punish the guilty,
(b) establishment of more special courts, and
(c) appointment of Dalit personnels in atrocity-prone areas etc. Another concern of the MPs was to amend the laws on land reforms for a proper distribution of land to the landless Dalits.

With regard to the compensatory discrimination, they argued for a Special Recruitment Drive to fulfill the backlog. In 1992, the Mandal Commission judgement on the withdrawal of SC/ST reservations in promotions attracted the attention of the parliamentarians and they took up the matter during the 1994 discussion on the Reports. The MPs seem to have been aware of adverse impact of the liberalisation process and asked the Government to come out with the necessary Bill to safeguard the Dalit interests.

One major policy question on the constitution of a commission to report on the administration of the Schedule Areas and the welfare of STs under Article 339, was missing during the debates both in 1985 and 1994. Though some questions on education (particularly for Scholarships) were asked, the issue of providing the SC/STs with better

---

3 Participants were from atrocity-prone areas like Andhra Pradesh, Bihar, Rajasthan, Uttar Pradesh etc., and the reports provided sufficient data and evidences.

educational facilities and making them self-reliant was not addressed adequately during the debates.

While replying to both the Motions, the Government seems to have been able to satisfy the Members, that it was in following a coherent policy towards the Dalit problem. In the 1985 reply to a Motion, the Minister of Welfare, Rajendra Kumari Bajpai convinced the Members with regard to the existence of Review Committees at the State, District and *Taluqa* levels for the welfare of these groups. She mentioned that now the family, instead of the area was being taken as a unit in the Tribal Sub-Plan. The lack of prosecution of offenders due to absence of evidence (even though the PCRA was stringent enough to punish the guilty) was accepted by her. She admitted that "everything is not fine and everything is not right at every level but the responsibility lies on the State Governments, as the policies are basically implemented by them." She however, "assured to see to in that the guidelines of the Central Government are followed" (LSD 28 November 1985:261-269). It is rightly pointed out that public accountability remains a serious problem for ensuring proper choice of beneficiaries and proper use of funds. In spite of availability of information there are no proper and efficient institutional mechanisms for lodging complaints or seeking redressal of grievances (Vaidyanathan 2001:1819). The Minister of State for Welfare, Giridhar Gomango told the Members that the Ministry of Welfare was already working as a nodal agency so that polices are implemented. He mentioned that the allocation of Business Rules 1961 have been amended in 1982 and accordingly:

> The Ministry of Welfare will be nodal ministry of overall policy, planning and co-ordination for programmes of development for SC/STs with regard to sectoral programmes and schemes of development for these communities. Policy-making, planning, monitoring evaluation etc. also will be the responsibility of this Ministry and co-ordinate with not only concerned central Ministries, but also with State Governments and Union Territories (LSD 28 November 1985: 334-336).

None of the two Ministers replied satisfactorily to the question of constitutional status to the NCSCT. It was merely reiterated that the matter would be looked into. On the special recruitment drive it was said that it was the responsibility of the Department of Personnel and Training.

The Members alleged that the Ministry of Welfare does not have any power to look into the law and order problem, handicapped as it is, in taking action against the errant person(s). This issue was ignored by the Ministers. Hence the question had to be shifted to the MHA. But the Government ignored the issue of shifting the SC/ST question from the Ministry of Welfare to the Ministry of Home Affairs.

One issue raised by a majority of the MPs was related to the question of hardening punishment to the officers responsible for non-implementation of policies. The Ministers neither stated what is being done nor promised to come out with measures or policies to check the conduct of the officials *vis-à-vis* Dalits. The responsibility was put on the state governments as "the task of implementation of policies was theirs and not of the Central Government". It was stated by the Minister that at the most, the Central Government could send orders to the State Governments, if specific cases of policy violations came to light.

Replying to the Motion on the reports in 1994, the Minister of State for Welfare, K.V. Thangabalu, basically provided the facts and figures in the form of the funds allocated in various sectors, for the upliftment of SC/STs. For instance, the allocation of Rs. 6 crores for implementing PAA to the states. The Union Territories were provided with Rs. 2600 crores for SCP and Rs. 2629 for TSP and Rs. 492.07 crores were sanctioned to the National SC/ST Finance Development Corporations, etc. Apart from this, he mentioned about the programmes and schemes being implemented to commemorate the Ambedkar Centenary such as Ambedkar Chairs in Universities, the Ambedkar Award, allocation of Rs. four crores for a film on Ambedkar to be made by the National Film Development Corporation, the translation of writings and speeches in various languages, etc. (LSD 9 December 1994:226-42). But he was unable to provide figures for those erring officials who were responsible for the non-fulfilment of backlogs. The Minister was also unable to convince the Members on the lowering of funds to the National Commission for *Safai Karamcharis* from 5000 crores to 500 crores.

Regarding the atrocities on Dalits, he came out with figures which showed the scale declining from 3500 to 3000. He claimed to have identified forty-eight atrocity-prone areas. However, he made no mention of such regions or even the states where the magnitude is higher. Time and again the issue of law and order being the State subject emerged and the Minister shifted the responsibility on to the states for non-implementation of programmes. Mention was also made for having written to Chief Minister and to the latter's response in terms of the instructions given to the District Magistrates and Superintendents of Police for checking atrocities.

The Minister shared the concern on the scholarship revision and allocation of more grants for this, reservation in promotions, and assured to look into these matters. These were narrow concerns and only implementational aspects of the reservation policy attracted the attention of the Minister. However, major policy issues like the need for legislation to ensure promotions, policy of representation in private sectors, promotions of scavengers to group 'D' services, providing share to tribals in newly created assets, reviewing the ongoing projects in tribal areas, constitution of a commission to report on the administration of Scheduled Areas, and welfare of STs in the States, escaped the attention of the Minister. Even though some Members reminded him of these issues, he chose to ignore these, as he reeled out statistics and ignored the policy aspects.

The Government in 1985 was unable to satisfy the MPs and a member, R.P. Suman, who raised the issue of punishment to erring officers (who failed to implement the policies meant for upliftment of SC/STs), wanted some assurance, as no state government was paying heed to orders and guidelines issued by the Central Government. He went on to blame that it was happening only with regard to Dalits.

In 1994, Ramvilas Paswan, Bhogendra Jha, Ram Nihori Rao, and Nitish Kumar intervened during the proceedings regarding the various issues of punishment to officials, land not being in possession of Dalits, funds being misused, and use of welfare hostels for non-official purposes, respectively. Coming to the rescue of the Minister, the Deputy Speaker remarked that he has understood the question and that the Members should rely on the assurances given by him. The House was finally adjourned till the next working day.

The discussion on the Reports shows that Dalit policies were indeed deliberated upon by the Lok Sabha. And the legislators' emphasis was more on policy aspects, *i.e.* on the Enduring representation. The Enduring representation was more towards strengthening the mechanism of policy implementation than pursuing representation of Dalits in 'untouched areas' such as private sectors, Supreme Court, and High Courts, etc. Simultaneously stray demands were made for such provisions but not pursued in the reply of the Ministers.

The Government's overall response remained wanting with regard to the demands of the Dalits. Data was provided on various aspects of present Dalit policies and demands on 'untouched areas' were usually ignored. Even if assurance was given, no time-bound programmes to materialise the assurances was announced. As far as reservations in central services was concerned, other ministries were roped in to say that it did not come within the purview of the Ministry of Welfare. When the legislators reminded them of its role of co-ordination regarding safeguarding the Dalit interests, the ministers casually responded with statements like, "orders in specific matters can be issued' or ' the matter will be looked into."

In 1994, interventions on the reply of the Minister were greater as compared to 1985. It shows that the Dalit issue had become quite provocative in the post-Mandal period. Though, the MPs may not have been able to change the policy perceptions of the Government during the debates on the Reports, several policy issues, whether to alter the implementation strategies or to demand new policies or at least to make the Government realise the need for policy change with regard to Dalits, was put forward by the MPs.

4

Output Policy: The Parliamentary Deliberations

A policy can be the product of already existing, systemic modifications, or a product of completely fresh proposals of demands put to the political system by various individuals, groups or institutions. Legislations become source of various policies and are often result of proposals of the government and deliberations by the legislators in a political system. Policy outcomes of the existing legislations create conditions either for the continuation or alteration of such arrangements. In the previous chapter, an analysis was made to ascertain the perspectives of the MPs in response to the reports of the Commissioner and the Commission. It was found that there are gaps between the reports presented and perspectives adopted by the MPs. Again there were differences between the MPs perspectives and the Ministers responses relating to the policies towards Dalits. Where MPs emphasised on the need for policy adoptions, the Ministers chose not to heed the demands. And even if sometimes promises were made, no time bound assurance was given to fulfill them. The perspectives adopted in the Lok Sabha on Dalit policies in the last chapter show a prevalence of disenchantment among the Members over the existing safeguards for these sections. Whether with regard to the functioning of the Commission or PCRA or about the economic policies, the Members have not only shown their dis-satisfaction regarding the implementation of those policies but also felt the need for alteration in their safeguards.

The impact of the perspectives adopted by the Members and the subsequent policy formulation by the Government is examined here. The issue of policy outputs of the perspectives taken during policy-making is the major concern here. Policy outputs indicate the actual decisions taken by the Government, as distinct from what is regarded as given assurances. Policy outputs constitute a body of specific inducements for the members of a political system to support it (Easton 1957). The government may come out with an alternative legislation that may not be entirely a voluntary initiative but may be the result of outside pressure, *i.e.*, of interest groups, of concerned individuals, or of representatives in legislatures etc. We examined the impact of perspectives adopted by the MPs, as Policy output is influenced by the policy responsiveness of the representatives that relates to their decision-making conduct in a given field of policy (Eulau and Wahlke 1978:63). Not only can policy initiative be influenced by the representatives in legislatures, the policy content may also be altered through the addition or deletion of some clauses on the floor of the House.

Conceptualisation of Legislative Deliberations and Policy Output

Here, the representation *vis-à-vis* policy output of the legislative interventions is examined. The policy responsiveness also indicates the attitude of the representatives towards their constituents. Mere representation is not a guarantee for participation, and similarly participation is not an insurance of effective representation. It requires the proper judgement of policies, as it is on the basis of this that the question of supporting or rejecting the policy initiatives as taken by the Treasury benches can be properly understood. Thus in this case, policy output is about how far the legislations brought by the Government on the floor of the House would have an impact on the Parliament's involvement. Parliament's involvement in selected areas could furnish with ample material to discuss the role played by it in formulating and controlling policies (Jain 1983: 560).

Here we make an attempt to develop linkages between the NCSCT reports of the Commissioner, and the Commission, and the perspectives adopted by the MPs and the Government's proposals to formulate policies for Dalits on the floor of the House. The focus is not only on the deliberations by the MPs but also on the examination of the role of the MPs to modify, amend, or alter the policy or legislations proposed by the Government on the one hand and Government's responses to the propositions of the MPs on the other. Thus, the concern is about the Enduring representation of the MPs in policy formulation in the Lok Sabha and examination of the role of Parliament as an institution to function for the welfare and development of Dalit masses. The policy responsiveness of the legislators in the House towards their Dalit constituents apparently is the subject-matter of the present chapter.[1] It is

1 Special representation of Blacks in American Congress had been primarily based on the premise that Black constituents have distinct needs and interests that differ from the White constituents (Swain 1993:7-10), and they are disproportionately affected by problems such as crime, drugs, poverty discrimination and poor health.

examined whether Dalit legislators in the Lok Sabha differ in their responses in comparison with their counterparts while they address the issue of the legislations meant for Dalits.

How legislators participate in discussion with response to policy proposals in terms of Legislations and Statements by the Government? How legislators respond to government proposals and finally become instrumental in formulating policies for Dalits needs examination.

Below is an attempt to exert the policy output of parliamentary interventions. For the purpose of exerting the role of legislators, this process can be divided into three stages:

1. Analogy between Legislative Perspectives and Policy Proposals of the Government

   The purpose here is to probe the resemblances and gaps between broader legislative perspectives adopted during discussion on the reports of the Commissioner and the Commission for SC/STs and the nomenclatures of legislations proposed by the Government.

2. Contextualisation of Legislative Responses to Policy Proposals

   Bills, Resolutions, and Statements by the Minister/Government constitute policy proposals of the regime in power for consideration of the legislature. At various points of time, the legislators respond to such proposals which may contain major policy themes. We need to contextualise legislative responses to the policy proposals and develop a relationship between the two as the demands are put before the Government during deliberations. The nature of this representation can be divided into two parts:

   (a) *Enduring Representation of Customary Character*, where opinions are expressed and suggestions are made to include or exclude some themes of a Bill, a Statement, etc, and

   (b) *Enduring Representation of Specific Character,* where demands are pursued before passing a Bill in the form of amendments regarding specific themes.[2]

   The reports of PCWSCT have also been examined in this perspective.

Moreover, politicians representing districts with higher African-American population differ in their response to the needs and interests of these constituents (Canon 1999: 353).

2 In the later discussion we have used representation of Customary character instead of Enduring representation of customary character and representation of specific character instead of enduring representation of customary character.

3. Impact of Legislative Interventions on Policy Proposals

   The amendments or changes proposed by the legislators may or may not be accommodated by the Government. Proposals may be passed without incorporating the suggestions made by the Legislature, thus reducing it to insignificance. These in turn would reflect upon the consequences of the legislative interventions on the policy outputs which finally go to become policies.

Legislative deliberations during the discussion on the NCSCT reports appear to be concerned both with the short-term objectives, *i.e.* Phenomenal representation and also long-term objectives *i.e.* enduring representation. Here the focus is only on the Enduring representation, as the study focuses upon long-term objectives or policy aspects.

There has been a consistent rise in the scale of atrocities during 1985-95 and the legislators were not satisfied with the results produced by PCRA (1976) so they demanded a more stringent legislation to deal with the atrocities. The Government came with a legislation called the Scheduled Castes and Scheduled Tribes (Prevention of Atrocities) Bill 1989.

To strengthen the existing institutional mechanism, they argued for strengthening the Commission for SC/STs by providing it with a constitutional status so that it can function as a premier monitoring agency *vis-à-vis* Dalit policies. It was also argued that the Dalit issues should be transferred from the Ministry of Welfare to the Ministry of Home Affairs. Though Government introduced the Sixty-fifth Constitutional Amendment Bill to strengthen and bestow constitutional status to the Commission, it did not propose transfer of Dalit issues from MW to MHA.

The legislators were also concerned to improve the conditions of the *Safai Karamcharis*. Thus, a National Commission for *Safai Karamcharis* (NCSCK) was constituted that was to function as a monitoring and advisory body for the abolition of scavenging, that is mainly carried out by those belonging to Dalit communities.

Another important concern of the MPs during the discussion on Reports of the Commissioner in 1994 was to safeguard the interests of SC/St employees regarding promotions in reservations withdrawn by the Supreme Court in the Mandal Commission verdict. In this regard 77th Constitutional Amendment Bill was passed in 1995.

Though four more legislations were introduced by the Government, these were primarily for inclusion of more communities under the SC/ST category rather than to alter the Dalit policy paradigm. However, we shall discuss the Constitution (Scheduled Castes) Orders (Amendment) Bill because Dalits who converted to Buddhism were reinducted in the SC list. If observed carefully, the legislations by the Government reveal how during this period the emphasis was on the extension of safeguards to a few more communities rather than, the development of policies to safeguard the Dalit interests.

There were legislative perspectives adopted on land distribution, reservation in government jobs, special recruitment drive to fulfil backlog, special policies for tribals, representation in private sector due to privatisation, liberalisation and globalisation, etc. But sadly enough, no legislation was introduced by the regimes in power on these crucial matters.

There were twelve Statements made by Ministers in the House which can be divided into two parts: (a) *Instantaneous Statements*, and (b) *Policy Statements*: (i) Statements for continuation of policies, and (ii) Statements of policy shifts or changes. The former has short-term connotations, whereas the latter long-term. Out of the twelve Statements, seven were Instantaneous Statements[3] and five were Policy Statements.

Among policy Statements, two were Statements for continuation of policy *viz.*:

1. Continuation of the scheme for the supply of wheat/rice at specially subsidised rates in Integrated Tribal Development Areas and Tribal majority States for one more year from 1st April 1990 (LSD 18 April 1990), and
2. Enhanced subsidy for SCs under IRDP (LSD 26 April 1990); and, three were Statements of policy shifts, *viz.*:

---

[3](i) Anti-reservation agitation and Communal incidents in Gujrat (LSD 29 July 1985).
(ii) The incidence of violence/arson in the House of Sh. Ramvilas Paswan, M.P., on 22nd May 1991 (LSD 19 August 1991).
(iii) The incident relating to atrocities on members of Scheduled Castes in West Numar Khargon District of Madhya Pradesh. (LSD 9 September 1991).
(iv) Alleged rape of tribal women in Tripura (LSD 24 April 1992).
(v) The incident of roiting and arson on the issue of installing the statue of Dr. B. R.. Ambedkar in a plot in Parwana Road in Khureji under Police Station Krishna Nagar, Delhi (LSD 8 May 1995).
(vi) The reported incident of intimidation of Kr. Mayawati and others in the State Guest House of Lucknow, Uttar Pradesh on June 1, 1995 (LSD 3 June 1995).

(a) liberalisation of orders with a view to improving the representation of SC/STs in central posts/ services (LSD 19 April 1990),

(b) reservations in promotions for SC/STs in the wake of the judgement by the Supreme Court (LSD 23 December 1992), and

(c) the previous Statement regarding reservation in promotions was repeated (LSD 15 August 1993).

The Statements by the Government show their concern more for short-term objectives because seven out of the twelve Statements were Instantaneous. And among the five Policy Statements one was repeated by the Minister next year. This shows lack of policy proposals in response to the legislative perspectives adopted and a repetition of the existing measures in one form or the other. Thus there seems to be a little similarity in the legislative perspectives and policy proposals of the Government. In this regard, some of the areas left out by the legislations have been taken care of by the Policy Statements.

It reflects that there is some affinity between the broader legislative perspectives and policy proposals of the Government, whether in terms of nomenclatures of legislations proposed or Policy Statements issued by the Government on the floor of Lok Sabha.

At the same time, the most crucial legislative perspectives in the emerging eco-socio-political scenario, whether it is reservation in the private sector due to the policy of liberalisation and privatisation where role of the State is shrinking, or the matter of land redistribution among Dalits, none have been taken care of by the Government.

The analogy between legislative perspectives and policy proposals of the Government indicate gaps in terms of Bills introduced and Statements issued by the Government in the Lok Sabha. It needs to be probed, what the legislators deliberated upon while participating in the debate on various Bills and Statements of the Government. First, we shall find how they approve of the themes contained in the Bills and the Statements, or how they advance modifications or reject them. Secondly, how far these modifications are pursued in terms of amendments, while passing the Bills. The PCWSCT's role in policy formulation has also been examined. We shall see whether it is able to raise the issues left unadddressed on the floor of the House by the Government and bridge the gaps in terms of policy formulation.

A Test Case of Policy Proposals: Reservation in Jobs for Dalits

The job reservations have been an important aspect of compensatory discrimination for Dalits. It has become an instrument to secure employment and occupational mobility and gaining freedom from the age-old vices of poverty and subordination.

Initially the reservations were made applicable on an all-India basis but later on it was felt that in majority of the cases, Group 'A' & 'B' services attract candidates from all over India, whereas for Group 'C' & 'D', only those residing in the nearby localities or areas are attracted. In accordance an order was issued in 1985 by the DOPT, wherein it was stated that the recruitment for Group 'C' & 'D' would be carried on the basis of the population percentage of SC/STs in a particular region as per the 1981 census. This order came into effect from June 1, 1985.

Though the backlash against reservation has been continuing since the adoption of the Constitution, its opposition has become more evident during the last twenty years. Innumerable limitations of job reservations could be found in various studies conducted in the recent past. The latest among these by Mandelsohn and Vicziany (1998) underline four major problems which are linked to its structural and functional flaws. They are:

(a) only a small proportion could be benefited even with the cent-per cent reservations
(b) habitual lack of bureaucratic performance due to traditional discrimination practiced against these communities
(c) backlash and violent protests by the caste-Hindus
(d) doubts about the value desired from maintaining the policy of Compensatory Discrimination.

On 19 April 1989, the Minister for Personnel, Public Grievances and Pensions gave a Statement on the floor of the House to liberalise the orders for improving the representation of SC/STs in the Central Government. Two decisions were taken in this regard. These are: a) there will be ban on dereservation in all cases of direct recruitment in Group A, B, C & D vacancies, and it will be permitted only in group 'A' in exceptional cases and with prior permission of the Ministry of Personnel, and b) the restriction with regard to promotional reservations was revised to 75 per cent instead of existing 66.75 per cent in case of direct recruitment.

The Statement attracted the attention of the House and forced the Government to have a discussion on the subject. Subsequently a debate was held for three days (4 and 11 May 1989)[4] in which 36 Members participated on the Motion moved by E. Ayyapa Reddy (Kurnool), who argued that if there is no dearth of candidates as per Union Public Service Commission's reports then why the quota is not being fulfilled in the central services (LSD 4 May 1969: 410). Members were critical of the non-implementation of policies meant for Dalit upliftment. The liberalisation of orders was pointed out to be the consequence of apathy and lack of political will of the government to achieve the set targets. Apprehensions were expressed over the non-implementation and it was maintained that reservation will have to be continued till the society keeps discriminating on the basis of caste.

The biased principles, prejudiced notions and the changing names of discrimination, *viz.*, the pretext of non-availability of SC/ST candidates, their non-suitability, and finally the incapability of SC/ST candidates, were concerns which were also raised by the Members. Anadi Charan Das [Jajpur] categorically pointed out that in the garb of non-suitability, the authorities appoint non-Dalits against the reserved vacancies (LSD 11 May 1989:150). The unsuitability argument attracted the attention of majority of the Members who wanted stringent action to be taken against the officials found guilty of bypassing the reservation policy and ignoring the interests of the weaker sections of the society. Ram Ratan Ram [Hajipur] urged the government to pass a central act to provide legal safeguards against the dereservation of vacancies. Without legal security, it was argued, the violation of reservation policy may continue for longer period (LSD 12 May 1989: 30) Similar views for the constitutional amendment were expressed by Thampan Thomas [Mavelikara]. Demand for a Special Tribunal to accomplish the cases related with the compensatory discrimination in services for SC/STs was enunciated by some other Members. As per the information of the NCSCT as many as 8, 858 petitions were attended and action taken wherever the allegations or grievances warranted intervention by the Commission (NCSCT 1992:62) The gravity of the problem could be visualised with these figures and the Members were concerned to devise the institutional safeguards for these sections by instituting a special tribunal to speed up the cases related to service sector. Merely instituting a Special tribunal could not solve the deep-rooted problems. Therefore, a demand to facilitate the

---

4 Calling Attention Motion was converted in to Rule 193.

process was also put in terms of having a time-bound programme for the fulfilment of quota (LSD 4 May 1985: 430, 450, 11 May 1989: 138, and 12 May 1989: 47). It was impressed upon by various Members that the institutions run with any kind of assistance from the Government should also be asked to follow the reservation policy as prevalent in the government institutions and departments. Some desperate and idiosyncratic opinions were also aired, such as having cent-percent reservations till the required quota is not fulfilled (Keyur Bhushan [Raipur], (LSD 11 May 1989:139), reservations until arrangements to provide modern education and training is achieved to all the SC/STs (LSD 4 May 1989: 425), etc. These opinions however, did not have many receivers.

Some doubts were also raised on the percolation of benefits to the people at the lowest levels who are not able to send their children to the schools and colleges. The opinion that a section within the SC/STs is taking away all the benefits of compensatory discrimination, was also placed by Syed Shahabuddin [Kishangunj] (LSD 12 May 1989: 149). However, there were no takers of such opinions.

Replying to the debate, the Minister of State for Personal, Public Grievances and Pensions, and Home Affairs thanked the Members for participating in the debate and pointed out how the number of reserved seats have been on the rise since 1968 and that how non-fulfillment had led to acute backlog (LSD 12 May 1989: 72-83). Ayyapa Reddy [Kurnool] asserted that it means backlog can be attributed to official negligence and the Minister admitted the inbuilt bias in the system against SC/ST recruitment. A Special Recruitment Drive was to be started from 1st June 1989 to fulfill the backlog in various Central Government departments. He also told the House that a policy for SC/ST candidates who come on merit basis not to be adjusted against reserved vacancies has also been adopted by the government.

On non-implementation of derservation in promotions, the Minister stated that due to the 'zone of consideration', no one can pretend that SC/ST candidates are not available and the power of dereservation had been delegated to ministries and departments. If things happened adversely then the Government may have to consider centralising this power in one ministry, he asserted.

In the course of Minister's reply Ayyapa Reddy and Thampan Thomas intervened but those interventions were not specifically related to the Statement, which showed a sense of satisfaction among the Members on the Minister's reply.

Thus the discussion in response to the Statement on 'Liberalisation of Order for Improving Representation of SC/STs in Central Government Posts/Services' is indicative more of representation of a customary character, where MPs raised policy matters in relation to Dalits but the Government did not alter its stand except for the objectives of the Statement. The non-pursuance of issues raised during discussion by the MPs itself shows absence of representation of a specific character.

Therefore, except the Statement's implications on the Dalit policy output, the Members' deliberations during the discussion had no impact on the Government. There were merely assurances in the form of the centralisation of power of dereservation in one ministry, acceptance of in-built bias against Dalit recruitment among the officials, etc. However, the Minister's Statement and its implications could be ascertained with the considerable fulfillment of backlog with three SRDs undertaken between 1989 to 1993.[5]

Scheduled Castes and Scheduled Tribes (Prevention of Atrocities) Bill 1989.

At the time of the Constitution making, it was not merely the form of government that was undergoing transformation but various cultural, regional, and linguistic realities at the social level were also being redefined. There was an attempt to change the basic Indian social realities like gender inequality, caste prejudices, and inflicted cultural inferiority in the form of untouchability etc. Article 17 of the Constitution specifically deals with untouchability. While going through the Constituent Assembly Debates, one cannot ignore a general attitude of sympathy and generosity among the Members on the issue (Kanananaikel 1982:17). Untouchability was evident in various forms in the society but it was primarily concerned with the protection of the individuals and not the group because social boycott based on conduct was not covered by the Article 17. (Devrajiah vs. Padmanna, AIR 1961 Madras:35-39). While explaining the tyranny of socio-economic boycott of the Scheduled Castes, Ambedkar stated:

> This boycott is often planned on such an extensive scale as to include the prevention of the Depressed Classes from using the commonly used path and the stoppage of sale of the

---

5 The SRDs were undertaken in 1989, 1990 and 1991 to fill up the backlog of reservation for SC/STs.

> necessities of life by the village *Bania*. According to evidence, sometimes small causes suffice for the proclamation of a social boycott against the Depressed classes (Moon 1979: 46-47)

Untouchability is not merely a social stigma which is aimed at avoiding proximity with a group of people, but also an ideology of social violence aimed at these groups. It is a kind of conflict between two unequals where the relatively weak wishes to be socially equal with the relatively strong, and the weak resists and tries to oppose the injustice and exploitation by the other (Ram 1995: 270). If we look at Dalits from this perspective, we come closer to understanding the social and physical violence perpetrated by the caste Hindus against them.

In 1974, the MHA termed the crimes against Dalits as 'atrocity' and classified it into four categories, *viz*., murder, grievous hurt, arson, and rape (Commissioner 1988).

Atrocities of one type or the other have been inflicted upon Dalits through the ages due to their subjugation at socio-economic, religious, and political levels. On the account of the dominance of caste-Hindus, Dalits rarely dared to openly defy their dictates and so there was hardly a question of protest on their behalf. Even though there were cases of few individual resentment, it usually had violent repercussions, and hence, collective protests were non-existent.

In the post-independence period and more particularly in the last two decades, the cases of physical violence on the Dalits have increased due to the rise in their collective consciousness and strong reactions to the injustices heaped on them. This is clearly borne out by the Government reports. Thus, the more the united protests of the collective consciousness of Dalits, the more the chances increased for physical violence on them by their counterparts.

Apart from the growing socio-political consciousness, there are two other major causes which fan the rising atrocities. One is the dispute over possession of surplus land allotted by the State. The other is the non-payment or underpayment of minimum agricultural wages by the land-owning communities.

Statistics reveal that the post-independence period has witnessed a steep increase in the atrocities against Dalits. There has been an increase of 86.3 per cent in the cases of atrocities committed during 1951-61 in the entire country. But during the 1961-71 and 1971-81 periods, the percentage increase remained 69.4 per cent and 63.9 respectively. Yet again, 1977 saw the manifestation of a 75.5 per cent increase in the atrocities on Dalits as compared to the year 1976 (NCSCT 1992:95).

Article 17 for abolition of untouchability was not adequate enough to deal with various related offences. Subsequently the Untouchability Offences Act (UOA) 1955 was enacted to give effect to the abolition of untouchability. But even this Act could not check untouchability cases which were increasingly growing day-by-day. In the light of the emerging conditions, the UOA was renamed 'as Protection of Civil Rights Act (PCRA) 1976 which made untouchability as a non-compoundable offence. Separate provisions were made with regard to enforcing religious disabilities, social disabilities refusing to admit persons to hospitals, denying them sale of goods or services, etc. Similarly, a collective fine was imposed on the residents of any area who were involved directly or latently in such an offence or its abatement. In situations where the concerned persons failed to render assistance or failed to apprehend the offenders, or anyone suppressing material evidences regarding the commission of such offences, was also made punishable.

The PCRA also provided assistance to the aggrieved persons. Under the Section 15(a) of the Act, responsibility was legally fixed on the State Governments to take measures necessary for ensuring that the rights originating from the abolition of untouchability were made available to the victim in the form of legal aid, appointing officers for the supervision of prosecution under the Act, and setting up Special Courts or Committees at various levels to assist the State governments in implementation of the measures prescribed in the Act.

However, even the PCRA could not put a check on the continued violence on Dalits, all over the country. The cases of atrocities, exploitation and discrimination on account of caste untouchability registered an increase every year. To cease atrocities and its changing nature, the government introduced another Bill named the Scheduled Castes and Scheduled Tribes (Prevention of Atrocities) Bill 1989. While introducing the Bill, the Minister of Welfare Rajendra Kumari Bajpai stated:

> During 1988, there were a little over 15,000 offences against Scheduled Castes and 3380 cases in respect of Scheduled Castes and 783 in respect of Scheduled Tribes. Of these heinous offences such as murder, arson, rape and grievous hurt were about 3300 cases accounted for Scheduled Castes and 783 in case of Scheduled Tribes. There were other

minor offences also. This shows the attitude and tendency of the other caste people. They did not want the SC/STs to be respected in the society. The nature of these offences in many Stales indicated that these were not isolated instances but represented a trend in the country (LSD 14 August, 1989: 59).

Further she enumerated a number of reasons behind the introduction of the Bill. These included suppression of voices of equality, dishonour to a person, particularly to a Dalit woman, to question the manhood of male-members, land relations, dumping carcass in the vicinity of Dalit house, etc. There appears to be a new phenomenon of atrocities arising from no specific cause but Dalit assertion for self-respect (Krishanan 1993:423) Nowadays, there is a collective outrage against them, if they disown the traditional caste calling, a collective violence is perpetuated on Dalits if they ask for wage raise, land disputes, etc., that leads to physical torture, burning alive, dismantling of their dwellings, molestation, and rape of their womenfolk (Ram 1977: 111-121).

Some of the major themes included in the Bill or Prevention of Atrocities Act 1989 (PAA) can be divided into three parts:

(a) Punitive Actions
(b) Preventive Actions
(c) Miscellaneous Aspects

Punitive action relates to the punishment for offences of atrocities and those for the neglect of duties on the part of executive officers. It explains thoroughly about 15 types of offences and a minimum of six months punishment for the offender that could be extended upto five years with fine. Even an indirect involvement in an offence is punishable. The willful neglect of duty by a public servant except those belonging to SC/STs has also been brought under punishable offence. Subsequent offences grants enhanced punishment of minimum one year. Even forfeiture of property could take place with the order of the Special Court. To prevent the offence, removal of a person likely to commit atrocity may take place and if he does not leave the area on his / her own, he / she can be arrested as a preventive measure. State Governments can impose collective fine as well on the area of the people, who do not raise voice to restrain a person or a group to commit atrocity. Executive officers can also take preventive action in the atrocity prone area.

Under the miscellaneous aspects a special court for each district has been prescribed with a special public prosecutor for the purpose of conducting cases.

The State Governments have been asked to take measures for effective implementation of the Act and provide infrastructural facilities to the victim and the witness, for not only meeting the travelling and maintenance expenses but also for the economic and social rehabilitation of the victim. A periodic review of the implementation and identification of atrocity-prone areas also occupy a major part of the Act.

A comparison between the PCRA and the PAA points to negligible difference between the two, so far as objectives are concerned. The difference is in terms of details of the atrocities and their nature on the one hand and provisions for strict punishments and implementation on the other. The PCRA described atrocities under various heads like enforcement of religious and social disabilities and denying excess to public places. Whereas the PAA talks more of social disabilities in terms of committing atrocity or intending to commit atrocity. Another major difference with regard to the PAA relates to the provisions of Special Courts, Special Public Prosecutor, forfeiture of property of certain persons, and externment of prospective offender that was absent in the PCRA. Earlier the minimum punishment was one month but under the PAA it is six months. The PAA explains untouchability in terms of atrocities, whereas the PCRA portrayed untouchability in terms of disabilities. The most significant proposition of the PAA is the protection of STs which was explicitly absent under the PCRA.

Overall thirty five Members participated in a two-day (14 and 16 August 1989) debate on the Bill. On both the days, the issue of low presence was raised by the Members. On 14 August, 1989 it was alleged that no opposition Member were present (the opposition alleged the political reasons for bringing out the legislation on the eve of elections). It is interesting to note that out of thirty-five Members, eight did not speak much about the Bill and only made indirect and usual suggestions, *viz*., to punish those not implementing the laws and misutilising the funds (LSD 14 August 1989: 103 & 16 August 1989: 25,52).

The denial to lodge an FIR by the police occupied center-stage. During the discussion the Members wanted to know what action the Government contemplates which would deal with the officials who indulge in the negligence of duty. On the question of FIR and negligence of duty by the concerned personnel, the Minister responded that such offences have been dealt in clause 4 of the Bill which says:

> whoever being a public servant but not being Scheduled caste or Scheduled Tribe willfully neglects his duties required to be performed by him under the Act shall be punishable with imprisonment—for a term which shall not be less than six months, which may be extended to one year.

Digvijay Singh [Rajgarh], Lacchi Ram [Jallaur] and Janak Raj Gupta [Jammu] questioned the exemption of SC/ST officials in this regard (LSD 14 August 1989:97 and 16 August 1989: 20,74). They wanted to bring these officials also in the net, for the negligence of duty. Syed Shahabuddin [Kishanganj] moved an amendment in this regard but it was squashed by the House. The rationale behind exemption of the SC/ST officials as pointed out by the Minister was that the focus of the Bill was about atrocities committed by one section of the people on the other and the purpose of bill was to check such ideals prevailing in the society. It was further added that even if the SC/ST officials indulge in negligence of duty, they can be dealt with through the ordinary law of the land in this regard (LSD 16 August 1989: 100).

The discharge of quantum for rehabilitation and compensation in favour of the victims of atrocities was another significant theme of the Bill. A few suggestions like fixing up the amount for the purpose by the Central Government, constructing houses under the National Housing Policy for the victims, etc., were made by the Members. Vir Sen [Khurja] raised the issue of providing compensation to an unmarried girl who has been a victim of rape, providing her rehabilitation. In this regard an amendment was moved by Syed Shahabuddin to "compensate them fully for the loss of damage to the movable and immovable property, and for loss of life and physical injury in accordance with the prescribed scale." Responding to the amendment, the Minister pointed out that the Bill incorporates broader outlines, and minute aspects shall be taken care of while framing the rules. On the assurance by the Minister, the Member withdrew the amendment.

A few other important themes of the debate were externment of the offender from the area; appointment of SC/ST officials in sensitive areas, punitive fine for the people in the area of atrocities, establishing monitoring cells at the district level, and, involving MPs and MLAs at various stages in the administrative machinery to arrest violence against SC/STs.

Ram Ratan Ram [Hajipur] alleged that the choice to extern the area remains with the prospective offender (LSD 14 August 1989: 68). Some others suggested that instead of asking a prospective offender to leave the area, the person must be arrested (LSD 16 August 1989:62). Reacting to the sentiments expressed by the Members, the Minister reminded that being an order of the Special Court, the offender has to comply with it under section 10 and 11 of the Bill which states "anyone who does not comply with the externment order shall be arrested and put into police custody."

The demand for appointing SC/ST officials in the areas where Dalits are likely to be subjected to atrocities surfaced time and again in the Lok Sabha and the Members repeatedly demanded for it (LSD 14 August, 1989: 70,90 and 16 August; 1989: 54).

The prime reason for this demand was pointed out to be the biased sympathy towards people of their own social background among the caste-Hindu officials, and their obvious insensitivity towards the Dalit sections. Syed Shahabuddin moved yet another amendment to substantiate the feeling of the House which sought to provide "due representation of the Scheduled Castes and Scheduled Tribes in the administrative machinery so as to give the local administration a composite character." The Minister evaded the concern by asking for the fulfillment of the backlog, instead of seeking due representation in all branches of law and order machinery, to the SC/STs (LSD 16 August 1989: 96).

Regarding punitive fine, members wanted the *Panchayat* or the Revenue Block to be taken as unit to impose collective fine on those who do not react to an atrocity being committed. Most of the atrocities are committed in the rural areas and the dominant sections are insensitive to the offences against Dalits.

There was no new provision in the Bill to empower the State government to impose collective fine if the inhabitants of an area were found guilty of abetting the commission of offence or harbouring the offender in direct or indirect way by either suppressing the material evidence or failing to discover or apprehend the offenders. What was proposed was just a repetition of section 10A of PCRA. But through this the citizen was made accountable, who was supposed to be vigilant as well as instrumental in avoiding a crime.[6]

---

6 For constituting Monitoring cells care has been taken in the framing of rules, wherein both at the State and District level vigilance and Monitoring Committees are supposed to be established. At the State level Chief Minister/ Governor (in case

Ram Ratan Ram [Hajipur], Syed Shahabuddin [Kishanganj] and Janak Raj Gupta [Jammu] in particular raised the question of summary trial for quick disposal and to prosecute the offenders. K. Kunjabu [Adoor] and Rambhagat Paswan [Rosera] wanted appointment of Dalits as Special Court judges, and justice to the victims at the doorsteps, respectively to avoid the witnesses turning hostile (LSD 16 August 1989: 54, 77).

In the case of speeding up the trial of the accused, the State Governments need to be in touch with the Chief Justice of the High Courts, to specify for each district a court of session to be termed as special court to try the offences under the Act. Regarding these two main demands, the Bill proposed not only the constitution of a Special Court but also to appoint a Special Public Prosecutor having an experience of not less than seven years.

The legislators raised several pertinent questions during the debate on the Bill which were not part of it, *e.g.*, exemption of Dalit officials, rehabilitation and compensation to the victim of atrocity, appointment of SC/ST officials in atrocity-prone areas, taking *Panchayat* or Revenue Block as unit to impose collective fine etc. It indicates that legislators took enough interest in Dalit policy paradigm, thereby showing prevalence of Enduring representation of a customary character. But there are some grim areas untouched by the MPs which include how Centre should deal with the States which do not implement the provisions of PAA in the right spirit as well as the way in which to make people aware of the existence of such an Act.

At the same time, the legislators who raised questions, not addressed in the Bill did not pursue these, while passing it, because none except Syed Shahabuddin moved amendments to the Bill. Even the eight amendments moved by Syed Shahabuddin were withdrawn on the assurance by the Minister, to look into those while framing the rules. No Dalit MP supported these amendments.

The debate on the Bill shows that both Dalit and non-Dalit MPs not only participate but also raise issues on the proposed legislation. Apart from discussing issues like lodging of FIRs, strict action against culprits, special courts, etc., the MPs also raised those issues which were not part of the Bill *e.g.* rehabilitation of the victims of atrocity, appointment of SC/ST officials in atrocity-prone areas, to fix collective

---

of President's rule) and at the District level, the District Magistrate occupy the position of chairman at their respective levels. The MLA & MPs find place in the Monitoring committee at the District level.

fine on the *Panchayat* or Block prone to atrocities, etc. At the same time, some crucial aspects of implementation and spreading awareness among the people regarding the provisions of the Act have been ignored by both Dalit and non-Dalit MPs. The maintenance of law and order is a subject of the State. How to deal with the States defying the provisions by not implementing them was largely neglected by the MPs. The non-implementation of programmes and schemes being the major aspect of Dalit policies, should have been put forward more emphatically, rather than being ignored. Secondly, sensitisation of the people, and informing the society about the prevalence of such legislation was completely ignored by the MPs. The MPs could have asked to use the Government and the private media to spread awareness about such an important legislation.

The pursuance of issues raised during the debate while passing the Bill was completely absent among the Dalit MPs, whereas a non-Dalit MP of Janta Party moved eight amendments. It shows that the non-Dalits from the Opposition were more active in legislature as compared to Dalit MPs either from the ruling party or from the Opposition. Most of the issues uncovered in the Bill have been taken care of while framing the Rules. It is a different matter that these rules were framed under the Janata Dal and not the Congress government.

Debate on Atrocities apart from Discussion on the Bill and NCSCT Reports

Although the PAA was passed in 1989, but its constituent were framed in 1990 and it came into force from 1992 onwards. Significantly, during this period many atrocities were committed in which large number of Dalits were killed, and the Lok Sabha discussed them under various legislative rules.

Thus apart from the discussion during the NCSCT Reports, atrocities on Dalits were debated in the Lok Sabha three times under the Rule 193, and once each under the Adjournment Motion and the Private Member's Resolution. Before adoption of PAA (1989), atrocities were discussed in 1988 under Rule 193, where the emphasis of the discussion was not much different from the discussion during the Commission's Reports or during passing of the 1989 Bill. The only difference was in terms of strengthening the safeguards under Compensatory Discrimination for providing representation in the Army, private sector, public schools, etc. A few major demands that came up during the discussion in August 1988 catered to liquidation of various caste armies prevalent in Bihar, providing arms to Dalits, and declaring central Bihar a disturbed area (LSD 12 August 1988: 355, 370, 373, 433, 350, 449).

However, PAA (1989) was unable to contain atrocities on Dalits. The atrocities kept multiplying every year, as the NCSCT Reports (1992-95) suggest. After enforcement of the new Act, major massacres particularly in the states of Uttar Pradesh and Bihar took place, and this led to debate in the House.

The discussion after passing of the PAA shows a major shift in the opinions of the legislators regarding atrocities on Dalits. Apart from the non-implementation of the Act, and the acquittal of the perpetrators of atrocities due to lack of evidence, etc., the emphasis now was to transform the caste-based Indian society and bring about a change in the mind set that either commits or supports the atrocities on Dalits due to the social sanction of untouchability and the caste-system. The following excerpts from the Lok Sabha debates by the MPs indicate prevalence of such opinions.

R. Mallu [Nagarkurnool], a Member stated

> I would like to suggest certain things for the permanent solution of this problem. Unless you attack the caste-system, you are not going to succeed in solving the problem. The incidents that took place in Tsundur in Andhra Pradesh or in Uttar Pradesh or in Bihar are only sporadic incidents. Actually such incidents are taking place in all over India, in all the villages.... It is not the individual but caste that comes in the way (LSD 19 August 1991: 267-8).

Another discussion under the Adjournment Motion on the reported incidents of atrocities on Dalits in various parts of the country with particular reference to Uttar Pradesh and Bihar, show the amount of dissatisfaction on the legal safeguards among the legislators. Here Santosh Kumar Gangwar [Bareilly] spoke thus:

> Sir, the subject being discussed today has been discussed unlimited times since independence but what has been the outcome? Whatever be the deliberations, the end-result is always the same ... The social equality is not possible until we stop mental exploitation and mental torture (LSD 25 February 1991: 538-9).

Similarly Dinesh Singh [Pratapgrah] stated

> Several of the Hon. Members said that the psyche of the society will have to be changed. As long as the psyche of the society is not changed, these types of incidents will continue to take place (LSD 25 February 1991: 598).

Suggesting solutions, Members argued for a need for social transformation and particularly to opt for mass movement. After three years of the above discussion, a Private Member's Resolution was adopted in 1994, which reflect upon the arguments for social movements, as legal system was found unhelpful for the Dalits at large. In this vein Hanan Mollah [Uleberia] stated:

> You are aware Sir, that Scheduled Castes and Scheduled Tribes, as we understand by the very word are the victims of casteism. Casteism is the worst kind of crime against humanity in the world. Though we, the Indians, feel pride in saying that we are one of the oldest civilised countries in the world, at the same time, we also feel ashamed that we are carrying on this oldest crime of casteism in our society… we have to participate in the social movements and fight for the right of the SC/STs. Then only the real emancipation of the SC & ST can take place (LSD 30 May 1995: 279-82).

The above affirmations display that there is a major shift in the opinion of the MPs. The emphasis shifted from the question of different governance, on to the initiatives of the civil society and to transform the basic Indian social reality, *i.e.*, the caste system.

The Constitution (Sixty-Fifth Amendment) Bill 1990 or National Commission for SC/STs

To equip the Commission for SCs and STs with constitutional powers has been a long-standing demand of the Lok Sabha. Even before setting up of the Commission in 1978, the Members had been pleading to strengthen the office of the Commissioner and also deplored the lack of co-operation from state governments in providing the required information. (Narayana 1980: 453).

Instead of strengthening the Commissioner's position, the Janata Party Government appointed a Commission and made the Commissioner a member of the Commission *vide* Ministry of Home Affairs Resolution dated 21 July 1978. Apart from the Commissioner, there were four other members including a Chairperson. Though it was stated that the functioning of the Commission would not lesson the authority of the Commissioner but its function broadly corresponded with him. This disenchanted the Commissioner who in its 27th Report categorically maintained that there are two alternatives to strengthen the monitoring system under the Article 338. One was either to replace the Commission with a multi-member Commission and the second was to retain both the offices with clearly demarcated functions and status. In case the latter option is accepted then, "it would be desirable to appropriately revise the functions assigned to the Commission so that these do not overlap with the functions assigned to the Commissioner under the Constitution..." (27th Report of the Commissioner for SC/STs, 1979-81: 49-50). These observations had no impact on the Government and the *status quo* was maintained till 1990. Thereby, the Commission and the Commissioner existed simultaneously and both presented their reports. But during 1981-90, on many occasions, none of the two had the required composition. From 1981 to 1986, the post of Commissioner was lying vacant, whereas the Commission did not either have the full-members or there was no Chairperson to head the meetings and prepare requisite reports during the said period.

The legislative perspectives have shown that one of the major demands during 1985-95 related to the conferment of constitutional status to the Commission and to provide it more powers to investigate, monitor, participate and advise in the matters of Dalits. The major themes of the Bill introduced in 1990 can be divided into three parts:

Composition of the Commission

(a) Duties of the Commission
(b) Powers of the Commission

The Bill proposed five member Commission, which included one Chairperson and a Vice-Chairperson with three other members to be appointed by the President of India.

So far as duties were concerned, it was to perform the following:

(a) To investigate and monitor all matters relating to Dalit interests.
(b) To examine specific complaints of deprivation of rights to these sections.
(c) To present annual reports to the President, and in response the Government was to table the reports in Parliament with Action Taken Report and also mention the reason for not taking action.

(d) To advise on effective implementation of measures for protection, welfare, and socio-economic development.

(e) To send a copy of the report or part thereof to the concerned State Governments, and the Government was to table the Action Taken Report before the State Legislative Assembly.

The only power the Commission had was to regulate its own procedures.

The debate on the 3rd and 4th Reports of the Commission for 1980-81 did put up a strong demand for providing constitutional status to it. It has been clearly mentioned in the previous chapter that the discussion on reports of the Commission and Commissioner provide a contextual framework on the functioning of the policies and programmes for SC/STs, and most of the Members strongly pleaded for strengthening of the Commission not through some vague orders or guidelines but with a constitutional amendment Bill. However, during the time, the Minister of Welfare smartly ignored the issue by stating that "the Government will certainly look into how effectively the Commission can work" (LSD 29 November 1985: 262).

During the discussion on the Bill, nineteen Members participated in the debate in the House. One of the eldest Members of the House N.G. Ranga [Guntur] stated that there was no need to be very optimistic about the capacity of the Bill to provide the services and protection to the concerned people, but he did not object to passing of the Bill (LSD 28 May, 1990: 124). Yet another Member called the exercise another "small step" to boost the downtrodden (*Ibid*: 129). However, the MPs brought in other issues related to Dalits, like economic measures to make the Commission successful. It was suggested that misutilisation of funds should be looked into by the Commission (LSD 28 May 1990: 132), and the Central Government should be made accountable for the implementation of the Special Component Plan and Tribal Sub-Plan, which are premier programmes to uplift Dalits. The fact that land reforms implementation needs special legislation to ensure effective intervention of the Commission was argued by Matilal Handra [Jhargram] (LSD 28May 1990: 140). Arvind Netam [Kankar] wanted a separate Tribunal for SC/ST employees on the lines of Central Administrative Tribunal (LSD 23 May 1990: 138). All said and done, a majority of the Dalit Members were apprehensive about the success of the Commission and reiterated their demand to look after the implementation of the rules and regulations formulated under the Bill (K.D. Sultanpuri, Kusuma. Krishna Murthi, Arvind Netam, Kumari Mayawati, Ramlal Rahi, etc., LSD 29 May 1990).

Another area of suspicion among the Members was the dependence of the Commission on the State governments which have hardly been co-operative in providing the required information to the Commission. To avoid the gaps in formulation and implementation Piyarelal Handoo [Anantnag] asked the Government to confer not only the powers of monitoring and enforcement but also to implement the welfare programmes for Dalits to the Commission, so that the objectives set in the Constitution could be realised (*Ibid*: 143).

One of the most frequent observations during the debate was to bring the Commission under MHA. Although there was no consensus on the issue, but most of the Members suggested the Commission to be either under MHA or to be an independent body like UPSC or CAG, but not under the jurisdiction of MW. It was only Mayawati of Bahujan Samaj Party, who argued for the Commission to be under the direct jurisdiction of MW (LSD 29 May 1990: 140) K.S Chavada [Patan]. She went on to even suggest that a new Ministry should be created for the Welfare of SC/STs under which the commission should also function or the welfare functions should be brought under the MHA (*Ibid* : 124)

It is interesting to note that the three amendments suggested by Ramdhan, the then Chairperson of the Commission and Member of Lok Sabha from Lalganj, were introduced and incorporated in the Bill. The Government Amendments included:

1. the appointment of some more Members in the Commission, apart from the Chairperson and Vice-Chairperson
2. the substitution of 'examine' with "inquire into" regarding the complaints against the government functionaries *vis-à-vis* the programmes for the positive discrimination for SC/STs
3. to participate and advise in the planning process of socio-economic development of SC/STs and to evaluate the progress of their development under the union and any State.

Ramdhan wanted the number of members to be six instead of three. He was also not in favour of a Vice-Chairperson in the Commission. It was on the plea of the non-existence of such a post in case of Backward Class Commission or Minorities Commission.

P.R. Kumarmangalam [Salem] moved two amendments: (i) to increase the number of Commission Members to ten, and ii) to elect the Members of the Commission from amongst the Members of the Lok Sabha. But the Government did not accept any of the two suggestions. Whereas K.D. Sultanpuri [Simla] moved seven amendments. Three related to the omission of the post of Vice-Chairperson, the fourth related to the Chairperson who belonged to SC/ST communities, while the fifth was for appointing the commission for a period of five years. The sixth amendment was to ensure the fulfillment of the SC/ST quota in lower courts, public sector undertakings, State and Central Government offices, and the last one being to direct the State governments to remove all the impediments coming in the way of economic welfare of SC/STs. Also included was the question of taking action against those States which would show non-compliance with regard to these concerns. Eventually, K.D. Sultanpuri withdrew all the amendments on the assurances of the Minister of Welfare for inclusion of the relevant amendments, while formulating rules and regulations concerning the Bill.[7] Jose Fenandez [Nominated], Anandi Charan Das [Jajpur] and K.V. Thomas [Ernakulam] also gave notices to introduce amendments but they did not move them.

As per the status of the Commission as a nodal agency to safeguard the interests of the SC/STs, it has been given powers to investigate, monitor, and inquire into specific complaints with regard to the usurpation of rights and welfare provisions for them. It can ask any office or department under the State or Central Government to send requisite information and investigate into the complaints received by it. It also monitors the implementation of the existing policy decisions with regard to these sections. As a monitoring agency, it has to present annual or special reports to the President and can make recommendations that should be adopted by the Union or the States in safeguarding the measures for the protection, welfare, and socio-economic development of the concerned groups. Also the President can ask at times to discharge some other functions in this regard as per the laws passed by the Parliament.

The most important function that was absent in the provisions of the erstwhile Commissioner and the Commission was related to the powers of the Commission to function as a Civil Court. Now it got the following powers:

(a) summoning and enforcing the attendance of any person from any part of the country,
(b) requiring the discovery and production of any document,
(c) receiving evidences on affidavits,

---

7 To appoint the Chairperson only from amongst the SC/ST communities was incorporated under the rules.

(d) requisitioning any public record or its copy from any court or office,
(e) asking for examination of witnesses and document,
(f) any other matter that may be determined by the President.

These provisions were not part of the original Bill but were introduced while passing. These are indicative of the legislators' impact on the policy output because they demanded to confer it the status of the Commission of Inquiry, 1962. It was due to the Commissioner's role in the policy process and planning that a controversy erupted in the 1970s, wherein the CSCT's role was questioned regarding his involvement in it. But to avoid this controversy, the 65th Amendment Bill categorically carved out its role in the planning process as a participant as well as an advisor to evaluate the progress of SC/ST's under the Central and the State Governments. The powers of the NCSCT have not only been confined to the participation in the planning process but it has also been made obligatory on the part of the State and Central Governments to consult the NCSCT on all major policy matters that have direct or indirect impact on the concerned collectives of the Indian society.

The Members' articulations show presence of both, the representation of customary, as well as the specific character, where demands are raised to encompass a few more themes in the Bill, and then pursue these while passing it through. The real impact of the demands does not occur during the deliberations on the floor of the House, but before the Bill comes to the House as is evident from the amendments to the original Bill by Ramdhan which were incorporated as the Government's amendments. The amendments by K. D. Sultanpuri regarding the Chairperson of the Commission to be only from SC/ST communities and P.R. Kumarmangalam regarding electing the Members of the Commission from amongst the MPs of the Lok Sabha were not included by the Minister. Though initially they insisted upon for their inclusion but after the Ministers' response on the debate, they withdrew their amendments. Ramdhan's insistence to increase the numbers from five to six members was also left out and even the voting on it could not help it to get incorporated in the Bill.

The discussion on the 65th Amendment Bill reflects the prevalence of both Enduring representation of customary and specific character, where not only suggestions are made but also amendments moved to incorporate those in the original Bill. The major issues raised during the debate had been to bring the Commission under MHA or to create a special Ministry, to look into the implementation of the rules and regulations of the Bill, misutilisation of funds, etc., which were directly concerned with the Bill. Some of the Members raised issues which were indirectly related such as special tribunal for SC/STs on the lines of Central Administrative Tribunal, attention towards land reforms, asking the Commission to implement welfare programmes as well as monitoring them, etc.

If we look at the amendments introduced by the Members we find that the focus was on increasing the number of members in the Commission or on the indirect issues such as fulfilment of quota, directing State governments to remove all the impediments hindering welfare of SC/STs, etc. Many members who gave notice for more amendments, did not do so, while passing the Bill. Thus we see that the focus of the discussion, remained on indirectly concerned aspects, and not on strengthening the Commission by providing it with more powers and functions which would help Dalits. The overall impression of the Legislature's involvement remains unsatisfactory with a few successes like acceptance of three amendments proposed by the MP from Lalganj constituency.

Thus so for as demands for amendments are concerned, those raised by the Members indicate the representation of the specific character prevalent among the Members but the impact of such demands on the policy output is seen to be negligible. On the other hand, the perspectives of the Members adopted during deliberations show some impact because the Government included a number of themes in the original Bill.

After enforcement of NCSCT, a debate on the erstwhile Commissioner and the Commission's reports was held in 1994 in which 41 Members participated in the discussion. Among them only nine Members referred to the functioning and status of the present Commission. One of the major observations was to present and discuss the annual reports of the Commission in time on the floor of the House. Some Members raised the issue of flaws in the functioning of the Commission as it could not direct the State Governments to take necessary steps where excesses on Dalits were committed (K.D. Sultanpuri [Shimla] 7 December 1994). They also raised the issue of the reports being confined to the redtapism prevalent in the bureaucracy, and the establishment of a network between the Union Commission and the State Commissions to function in a proper and efficient way (Dwarkanath Das [Karimganj] *Ibid*: 236, 237). The vast majority of the Members were satisfied with the power conferred on the

Commission but the non-Dalit MPs, Ramashray Prasad Singh and Rasa Singh Rawat were not satisfied with its powers and functions. They maintained that even the Constitutional status has not helped the Dalit masses and there is a need to make it more competent. Arguing on these lines Rasa Singh Rawat [Ajmer] stated:

Sir, one thing I would like to say through you that this Commission should be made competent, strong and effective. At present it is like a toothless tiger. This Commission cannot take any action. Whenever any incident of atrocity occurs and news are read in the newspapers, the Chairman of the Commission, or Minister goes there to get information. But the inhuman act that has been committed cannot be undone and later on matter is hushed up and no action is taken. The exploitation and oppression which is being done of these classes should be checked. That is why I would say that the Commission for Scheduled Castes and Scheduled Tribes should be strengthened and it should be empowered to accomplish the task with which it has been entrusted (LSD 8 December 1994:295).

The Commission's inability to check atrocities has always been raised and rightly so because it does not work or has not been entrusted with the powers of taking preventive action and even if it suggests so, then the implementation has to be done by the State not by the Central Government. Thus on the one hand the Commission lacks the power to exercise preventive measures and on the other hand, its jurisdiction does not provide it to function as a criminal court and that is why on most occasions, its criticism lies not in its functioning but in its structure itself which fails in taking punitive action against the culprits in case of violation of laws regarding SC/STs.

The Commission's capacity against the adverse discrimination is marginal as compared to the compensatory discrimination. Its power to function as a Civil Court with regard to the socio-economic development of Dalits and its constant monitoring and reviewing the implementation of programmes, policies, rules, and regulations against adverse discrimination has been marginal.

Constitution (SCs) Orders (Amendment) Bill 1990

The Constitution has been amended several times to include new communities in the SC/ST list. Though the Constitution does not allow any kind of discrimination on the basis of religion, but the SCs, other than 'Hindus', have not been allowed to get the benefits of reservations. Among such groups, have been the neo-Buddhists who converted from amongst the SCs to Buddhism. Though the Government of Maharashtra had provided them the facilities long back but it was denied by the Central Government till 1990.[8]

On 24 May 1990, the Minister of Labour and Welfare, Ramvilas Paswan introduced a Bill in the Lok Sabha to provide the facilities available to those SCs who adopted Buddhism. The Bill was already passed by the Rajya Sabha. Twenty-eight MPs participated during the discussion on 28 and 29 May 1990 on the Bill. Twenty seven MPs supported the Bill and only one MP, Eduardo Faleiro (Mormugaon) opposed the Bill but abstained from voting, and it was passed with a consensus. There were three categories under which majority of the MPs spoke:

(a) those, supporting the Bill without mentioning support for other religious converts to be given facilities under Dalit policy Paradigm
(b) those arguing in favour of other converts
(c) those who explicitly opposed the move to provide facilities to all categories other than Buddhists.

The emphasis of the debate was whether SCs converted to Christianity or Islam should also be given the same facilities as available to their counterparts. Fifteen Members argued in its favour. The very basis of secularism of the Indian Constitution was questioned by most of them. If there is a discrimination on the basis of religion in providing facilities to other religious converts then the secular credentials of the Indian State need to be questioned. This was opined by the legislators among whom K. S. Rao [Machilipatanam] was the most vocal (LSD 28 May 1990:55). Another significant argument was that the educational and economic status of a person cannot change overnight due to conversion. Though other religions may not recognise caste or untouchability, yet those who practice untouchability continue to do so and the life of such converts remains miserable, hence the need for amendment was argued by G. M. Banatwala [Ponnani] (LSD 28 May 1990: 78). Interestingly, majority of the MPs who stood in favour of extension of such facilities to other religious converts were from southern states, as conversion whether to Christianity, Islam or Buddhism has been a basic feature of the society in these States. They emphatically pointed out that the demand to provide the facilities to other religious converts is quite legitimate and these converts are none

8 Constitution (Scheduled Castes) orders (Amendment) Bill 1956 denied the facilities to other than Hindus but later on Sikhs also availed it.

but the same SCs with the same social and economic disabilities. The inhuman treatment of caste-Hindus was held to be the prime reason for conversion that has neither changed their economic nor social status. Another major argument was based on the religious freedom provided to the citizens by the Indian Constitution which proclaims that no citizen shall be discriminated against on the basis of religion. Thus it was opined that in absence of these facilities to the Christians and Muslim converts, the right to freely profess and practice any religion was hardly meaningful.

Supporting the Government's move to provide facilities to Buddhists, converted from Scheduled Castes, Mayawati (Bijnor) opined against some Members who held that Buddhism was part of Hinduism, and also criticised the Government for taking a long time to confer the facilities (LSD 28 May 1990: 73). Five MPs supported the Government's move to pass this legislation, but these MPs did not mention about providing reservations to other religious converts. Implicitly we can say, they were neither against nor in favour of other religious converts on the issue. Among them, four belonged to the reserved constituencies and one to the unreserved. Among the twenty-eight Members, five vehemently opposed the demand for the inclusion of Muslim and Christian SCs in the list. They argued that the case for Buddhist converts, and Muslim and Christian converts was entirely different. Those converting to Buddhism adopted this measure against the evil of untouchability and it was not for material benefits. It was a kind of protest, whereas, people converting to Christianity in particular do so for financial benefits or under threat was their allegation. The following observation substantiates their opinion in which Ram Ganesh Kapse [Thane] stated:

> ...the people who adopted Islam or Christianity felt that conversion has taken place either under pressure or for pecuniary benefits (LSD 28 May 1990: 57).

Replying to the debate, the Minister of Welfare Ramvilas Paswan said that the Government did not have a negative attitude towards other converts but it needed a general consensus in the House as is present for Buddhist converts. He also remarked that if it would not have required a general consensus then the 8th Lok Sabha in which Congress had 3/4 majority could have passed a Bill in the regard (LSD 29 May 1990:88-107).

Due to these remarks of the Minister, MPs like G. M. Banatwala, S. Benjamin Shikiho Sema, and N. Danis, who had proposed amendments to include Christian and Muslim SCs, did not pursue them and hoped that in future, the Government will include them to benefit all the converts and preserve the secular character of the Indian Constitution.

The MPs showed both representation of customary and specific character. They may have argued in favour of inclusion of the other communities in the SC list but they did not pursue increasing the proportion of reservations due to addition of Buddhists. Replying to the debate, the Minister himself gave assurance on various issues, *viz.*, increasing the percentage of reservation, inclusion of land reforms in the 9th Schedule, a policy for proper rehabilitation of the persons involved in manual scavenging, and continuation of special recruitment drives (SRDs).

One explanation for legislators not asking for larger questions could be passing of the Constitution (Sixty-eighth) Amendment Bill during the same period, where the policy issues were being discussed on a larger scale.

National Commission for *Safai Karamcharis* Bill

Safai Karamcharis, who are mostly Dalits, are considered to be at the lowest rung of the social order. "The process of liberation of scavengers involves not only value conflict, rehabilitation and change in the means of livelihood, it is also closely related to the change in social status and patterns of social relationship" (Pathak 1996:14). Thus a national scheme for the elimination of scavenging and disposal of 'night soil' by human beings was initiated by the Central Government in March 1991. It had two integral components, *viz.*, a) to restructure the mechanism of caring human excreta by introducing water borne latrines, and b) to rehabilitate the scavengers in other occupations by training them. This scheme involved the Ministry of Urban Development (MUD), the Ministry of Welfare (MW), and the State governments. The onus of conversion of dry latrines into water borne ones rested with MUD, rehabilitation was to be taken care of by MW, and the outlay on margin money was to be shared by State and Central Governments in the ratio of 49:51.

Ramesh Chandra (1999) enumerated a number of flaws in implementation of the scheme. He mentions these as:

(a) the Government cannot bear the expenses of providing water born latrines to all the people country-wide
(b) the rate of stipend, which is Rs. 150 per month has been very low for each trainee

(c) Banks have shown reluctance to sanction loans to those scavengers who were found defaulters in other schemes

(d) training gets weakened by poor enrolment of people due to lack of initiatives, and poor co-ordination and inadequate facilities, etc.

The All India *Safai Mazdoor Congress* has been demanding the constitution of a National Commission for *Safai Karamcharis* since 1990 (session held in 7th and 8th July 1990). On the eve of the 102nd birth anniversary of Dr. Ambedkar, the Prime Minister Narsimharao pointed out that a Bill was to be introduced in this regard so that the menace of scavenging could be abolished completely (*Nav Bharat Times* (Hindi) Jaipur: 15 April 1993).

It was on 12th August 1993 that the National Commission for *Safai Karamcharis* Bill was introduced in the Lok Sabha. The main function of the Commission was to recommend specific programmes of action towards elimination of inequalities in status, facilities and opportunities for *Safai Karamcharis*, and, a time-bound action plan. Pointing out the major functions of the Commission while introducing the Bill, the Minister of State for Welfare said that it will be primarily dealing with the manual scavengers of urban areas. It would look into the conversion of dry latrines into water borne latrines, and liberation and rehabilitation of those engaged in this occupation. Scavenging was to be ended by March 1997 as per the provisions of the Bill. The Commission was to recommend the policies and programmes to improve the living conditions of s*afai karamacharis*; and, the Commission's reports was to be presented before the Parliament and State Legislatures. He further stated that the 'Government has drawn a comprehensive scheme for rehabilitation of all the seven lakh scavengers and their dependants (LSD 12 August 1993).

Twenty-five Members of Parliament participated in the debate on the Bill. Most of the members emphasised on providing alternative employment to the scavengers (LSD 13 August 1993: 279, 289 and 16 August 1993: 296, 306, 311, 315, 326; 331) The Members suggested that due to lack of alternative arrangements for scavengers' employment, there would be no change in the basic status of their reality. Without alternative employment, they will have no means to get their bread and butter. In spite of the filthiness of the occupation, their survival depends on it. Thus it was pointed out that success of the removal of scavenging depends on the alternative mechanism of employment for their survival.

The second important aspect addressed by the Members was that the State should provide free education to the children of the scavengers (LSD 16 August 1993: 286, 290, 303, 314, 316, 320, 323). It was argued during the discussion that even if the present scavengers are able to get alternative means of livelihood, it may not ensure the abolition of the system in the absence of proper and free education to their children. The need was felt not only for education but also for uniform education so that the hierarchical system of education could not become a hindrance in getting employment opportunities to their children who would only be admitted in government run schools.

A demand was raised that arrangements like the *Sulabh Sauchalyas* could help in abolishing the system of carrying human excreta on head. (LSD 16 August, 1993, 290, 322, 323, 332) One of the members raised the issue of non-recruitment of scavengers by the *Sulabh International* - considered to be the pioneer organisation in the field of alternative arrangement of scavenging.

The other much debated issue concerned the relationship between NCSK and State Governments (LSD 16 August 1993: 297, 298, 326, etc.). The implementation of the schemes depended on the State Governments so the Members argued that without proper co-ordination between the Commission and these governments, the objective of the Bill stands defeated. They wanted establishment of committees at the levels of Central and State governments.

The other issues raised by the members included special training to the scavengers, representation of Dalits in judiciary, regular salaries to the *Safai Karamcharis*, abolition of contract system, and last but not the least, changing the attitude of society towards this section of the society.

The Members were basically concerned with the implementation part of the Bill and suggested some broad guidelines for action but none of them commented on the functions given to the Commission or the administrative apparatus essential for the proper functioning of the Commission. Opposition members expressed dismay over the amount earmarked for the eradication of scavenging being too inadequate. Sayed Shahabuddin also criticised the Government for not being clear in its mind about the objectives of the Commission. The Minister responding to the debate stated that for the identification and rehabilitation of scavengers Rs. 111.23 crores have been released to the State Governments. The SCSTFDC would be directly incharge of the programme in collaboration with MUD. Out of Rs. 905 crores 105 crores had been earmarked for training, and the rest for rehabilitation.

The NCSK is to monitor the implementation of the programme and advise the Government for proper functioning of the scheme for ending the practice of carrying night-soil on the head by human beings and to rehabilitate them in alternative occupations.

A careful observation of the legislative responses to the NCSK Bill point out that the MPs were more concerned with the implementation part of the functions of the Commission and not for strengthening the Commission itself. They did not even ask obvious questions on how the Commission will deal with the State Governments or the individuals found guilty of manual scavenging. They could have argued for the status of a Civil Court to the Commission to handle the cases of violation of the law on manual scavenging, for which precedence existed under the NCSCT that functions as a Civil Court.

As the legislative interventions were not specifically for the Commission, the amendments were not moved by the Members on the Bill and the Bill was passed in its original form.[9] The legislators behaviour of not moving amendments to the Bill, again reveals the MPs satisfaction with whatever the Government proposes.

Constitution (Eighty-Sixth) Amendment Bill[10]

The demand for reservation in promotion was raised several times during the Question Hour and debates on Dalit policy aspects. These demands were the product of the Supreme Court judgement in the *Indira Sahni Vs Union of India* case, popularly known as Mandal Commission verdict, wherein the Court decided against the promotional reservation for Backward Classes prospectively. This was to be applicable only after five years beginning from 16 November 1992. For the continuation of the provision of reservation in promotions for Dalits, a constitutional amendment Bill was introduced by the Government on 2 June, 1995. A total of twenty-two legislators participated during the discussion on the Bill.

Apart form other concerns, the MPs raised four major demands: (i) inclusion of Other Backward Class under the ambit of the Bill, (ii) punishment to officials indulging in non-fulfillment of quota, (iii) anyone could approach the court regarding the discrimination

---

9 The legislators having moved no amendment, again reveal the MPs satisfaction with whatever the Government proposes.

10 After passing the Bill, it became the Constitution (Seventy-Seventh) Amendment Act.

between SC/STs and OBCs pertaining to promotions, and (iv) to deal with the question of writing Confidential Reports (CRs).

Majority of the legislators argued for the inclusion of OBCs in the Bill because reservations were provided to them also in the services under the State, after the Mandal Commission verdict. Members argued that as per the provision of the Constitution, Backward Classes include SCs, STs and OBCs. So there was no need to create confusion among the people by separating them, which shows a discriminating attitude and slackness on the part of the Government. Reflecting towards the mood of the House in this regard, Mumtaz Ansari [Kodarma] asserted that "section of the House is raising no objection to the inclusion of OBCs also" (LSD 2 June 1995: 332). Nitish Kumar [Barh] observed that as the Supreme Court covered various issues while giving its judgement in the case, similarly the Government also needs to "cover all the issues and bring a comprehensive Bill in which a ceiling of 50 per cent should also go " (LSD 2 June 1995: 324).

The legislators were also apprehensive of someone going to the court of law against the Bill, as it was discriminatory in nature against the OBCs and the court could term the Bill to be unconstitutional in the present form.

The following excerpt would indicate prevalence of this opinion:

Anandi Charan Das (Jaipur):

> Article 16(4) deals with backward classes and all the people are covered in it. The provision of reservation has been made in section 335. It should also be included otherwise Supreme Court might be approached (LSD 2 June 1995; 359).

Another important feature of the debate was related to the punishment of officials indulging in any sort of recklessness with regard to non-fulfillment of reservations. They suggested various measures in this regard, *viz.*, fixing up the penalty against the officials, sending them to jail, making a criminal case against them, suspending or terminating them, etc. Reflecting upon the opinion of the House in this regard, Ratilal Varma [Dhanduka] pointed out that "the laws are quite good but the people who have to enforce these are prejudiced, their intentions are malafide" (LSD 2 June 1995: 339).

The related concern of the discussion had been about writing of adverse remarks against SC/ST personnels in their CRs. Some of them observed that the non-Dalits may not like Dalits to be their bosses and spoil their CRs. The following statement of the MP, Manikrao Hodlya Gavit [Nandarbar] needs to be mentioned:

> "Now reservations in promotions will be given but when CR would be examined, and bad remarks given by officers will be seen in the confidential reports of SC&ST employees, then their promotion may be stopped. Therefore, Government should see how to check this tendency (LSD 2 June 1995: 348).

On the other hand, GMC Balayogi, K.D. Sultanpuri raised the issues of representation of SC/STs in High Courts and Supreme Courts. Rupchand Murmu questioned the intentions of the Government on land reforms that was needed for the overall development of the SC/STs and its non-implementation in the absence of sincerity and honest will. Kalka Das wanted steps to be taken for reservation in private sector. Geeta Mukherjee raised the question for providing in-house training to SC/ST officials so that the hindrance in their promotion could be stopped.

Responding to the debate, the Minister of Welfare, Sitaram Kesari said that it was a long pending demand to provide promotional reservations to the SC/STs in view of the Mandal verdict and so far as the question of similar provision for OBCs was concerned, he assured the House that he will bring the Bill after a consensus is built on it.

When the motion was put for voting, four Members[11] introduced their amendments while a few others supported them. But, on assurances from the Minister, all the amendments were withdrawn. And the Bill was passed by the majority of the House, wherein 326 members favoured the Motion and only one member Mohan Rawale [Bombay South Central] opposed it stating that there were political reasons behind the introduction of the Bill (LSD 2 June 1995: 369).

The deliberations during the discussion on the Bill show a concern for policy issues. These concerns were basically related with OBCs. Whether it was a question of punishment to officials who indulged in non-implementation of reservation policy or putting a check on adverse remarks in the CRs of SC/ST officials or even for that matter the fear of somebody going to the court against the Bill, all these related primarily to the Dalits. Thus it shows a prevalence of the representation of customary character among the legislation.

On the other hand, demands for amendments in the Bill in favour of SC/STs, while passing it were almost completely absent. One solitary example in favour of SC/STs was the amendment proposed by Ramvilas Paswan for promotions in the organisation, taking assistance

---

11 P.G. Narayanan [Gobichettipalayam], Ramvilas Paswan [Rosera], Anandi Charan Das [Jajpur] and Devandra Prasad Yadav [Jhanjharpur].

from the Government. This could have had a major impact on Dalit policy paradigm. Thus during the debate on the Bill, Enduring representation of specific character was present but it was more in favour of OBCs and almost neglected SC/STs.

Parliamentary Committee on the Welfare of SC/STs: Recommendations and the Policy Output

In the following discussion, an attempt has been made to examine the observations and the recommendations contained in the Reports and their impact on the policy output for Dalits. We shall also examine as to how far these Reports bridge the gaps left by the Lok Sabha for the development of Dalit policy paradigm.

Since the Parliament is pressed for time, it does not and cannot debate and discuss each and every matter that comes before it. To save time, several Committees are constituted by the House to look deeper into the questions as well as recommend to the Executive, measures to be taken under the given circumstances. Legislative committees are "meant to provide a balancing factor in a system that is otherwise geared to the hegemony of the Executive (*Parliamentary Committees in India* (*Preface*), Institute of Constitutional and Parliamentary Studies, New Delhi: 1973).

Accordingly, to save the time and resources of the Parliament, a Committee on the Welfare of SC/STs was set up in 1968 to consider: (i) the reports of Commissioner for SC/ST (now NCSCT), (ii) to report to both the Houses the action taken by the Government, (iii) to examine measures taken by the union government, (iv) to secure due representation and matters referred by the House, and (v) to report to both the Houses on the working of the Welfare measure regarding Dalits (Narayana 1980).

During the period 1985-95, the Committee produced 93 reports, where all but four were primarily concerned with the implementation aspects. Among the four, two were Action Taken Reports on the previous two prepared by the Committee. These were:

1. Reservation for Scheduled Castes and Scheduled Tribes in Private Sector (4th Report, 10th Lok Sabha 1991-92), and
2. Formulation Implementation and Monitoring of Reservation Policy (24th Report, 10th Lok Sabha 1993-94). The 53rd and 43rd Reports of the Committee respectively discussed the action taken by the Government on the above two reports.

Stating the reasons for coming out with the report on Reservations for SC/STs in Private Sector, mention was made, a) to examine the impact of new economic reforms, and b) study the lack of formal consideration by the Government on the issue.

The Minister of Welfare Ramvilas Paswan held discussions in 1990 with the concerned officials and took the view that reservations could be provided in private sector if the Article 46 was read with the Article 15(4).[12] Prior to this, the P.C. Mathew Committee on National Employment Service had also held that "any technical difficulty (to provide reservations in private sector to SC/STs) should be overcome by amending the Constitution. However the Cabinet on 19 July 1990 took a decision against such a move at that stage.

The demand for reservations in private sector by the Committee was not new, as the matter was examined previously also in the 41st Report, and the 5th and 18th Report by Sixth Lok Sabha. It was emphasised in the Reports that proportional representation should be provided to the SCs and STs in the private sector. These reports in particular recommended to make it compulsory in case of private institution who received any kind of assistance such as loans, land, and licences from the government.

The 18th Report specifically asked for enactment of a new legislation in this regard but the Ministry of Law retorted: "it was not possible under the law to impose such a condition", and that article 16 (4) permits reservation in jobs only with respect to services under the State and not under the private sector.

The Members of the 9th Lok Sabha Committee held discussions with various officials in Ministries. The then, Labour Secretary held that though legal opinion on the reservations in private sector was not favourable, even then "whatever has transpired since then (1983), the way constitutional law had developed, and based on the guidance of this committee, this issue would certainly be considered again". To the contrary, the Additional Secretary in the Deptt. of Industrial Development stated that in the changing scenario increasing

---

12 The State shall promote with special care the educational and economic interests of the weakers sections of the people, and, in particular, of the Scheduled Castes and the Scheduled Tribes, and shall protect them from social injustice and all forms of exploitation. It was added by the constitution (first Amendment) Act 1951 that says, "nothing in this article or in clause (2) of article 29 shall prevent the State from making any special provisions for the advancement of any socially and educationally backward classes of citizens or for the Schedule Castes and Schedule Tribes".

productivity will be the focus of industrial service and trading organisations. The focus should be to equip people rather than asking them (private sector) for reservation, which some of them are finding difficult to accept from the point of view of efficiency and productivity.

The Committee also learnt that the Ministry of Finance has proposed to impose a cut of Rs. 3500 crores on both plan and non-plan expenditure during 1991-92 and banned fresh recruitment in Government Departments, and public sector banks and undertakings due to financial constraints. A cut of Rs. 500 crores was also imposed on the annual budget outlay of Department of Rural Development. When the Ministry of Finance was suggested by the Committee Members not to impose cuts on various schemes/ programmes undertaken for socio-economic uplift of the SC/STs, the government replied that "this has to be seen in the overall context of the total available resources at the disposal of Central Government".

On the basis of above facts and figures, the Committee made six recommendations. These are as below:

(a) the impact of liberalisation of economy on poorer sections, particularly SC/STs has to be considered carefully.

(b) the second recommendation primarily narrated the recommendations of 4th and 5th Lok Sabha and Secretary in MW, etc.

(c) immediate measures need to be taken up, (a) to ensure reservation policy in employment to lower all new employment opportunities in private sectors, (b) to extend reservation policy in all such industrial service and trading organisations which receive any kind of assistance from the Government, (c) to ensure that retrenchment of staff due to new economic policy does not adversely affect the SC/ST employees, and (d) to take immediate steps to implement the above three measures in a time-bound framework.

(d) the allocations for welfare schemes in Central and State budgets should in no case be less than that of 1991-92 and grants-in-aid institutions should follow reservation policy in letter and spirit.[13] Making policy statements will not do, if needed even the Constitution could be amended for legislation in this regard.

---

13 The recommendation on "the allocations for Welfare activities should not be reduced was withdrawn by the Committee as these allocations did not reduce during 1992-93 and 1993-94 Budgets.

(e) need to review July 1990 Cabinet decision against reservations in private sectors.
(f) for amending the constitution, the Government should not rely on the legal advice given in 1983 but it must take into consideration the development of constitutional law since then.

The recommendations of the Committee need to be analysed in the light of the 53rd Action Taken Report on the issue. Action Taken Reports assess recommendations/ observations in terms of:

(a) those, accepted by Government,
(b) those, that the Committee does not want to pursue in the light of the replies,
(c) those, reiterated by the Committee,
(d) those, on which final replies were not received from the Government.

The first two observations were accepted by the Government, *i.e.* (i) the liberalisation process will reduce the Government activity and will affect Dalit population putting them in a helpless situation in the employment market unless adequate and immediate measures were adopted to correct the emerging imbalances, and (ii) previously the Committee, Cabinet, Ministry of Welfare etc. have also recommended in this regard.

The reply of the Government with regard to the major recommendations on the implementation of reservations in the private sector and the review of the Cabinet decision of July 1990 was not accepted by the Government on the pretext that the Attorney General of India to whom the matter was referred to by the Ministry of Law and Justice held that "legislation for reservation in private sector is constitutionally not in order". But the Committee reiterated the demand.

There has been no impact of the Committee's recommendations on the Dalit policy paradigm. The Government accepted only the observations of the Committee and not the recommendations for reservations in the private sector. The only output of the recommendations seems to be the absence of reduction in the budgetary allocations for welfare programmes *vis-à-vis* 1991-92 which is primarily a short-term concern. The administrative apparatus had become a hindrance in the policy formulation because the Additional Secretary in the Ministry of Industrial Development and Department of Personal (1980) and the Attorney General (1993) argued against such moves. Thus in spite of several developments since independence, the Committee's recommendation to have reservations in the private sector had no consequences on policy output of Dalits. Not only this, the Government also gave no assurance to come out with a legislation in future, leading to insignificance of PCWSCT.

On the notice given by Rajnath Sonkar Shastri [Saidpur] a Half-an-Hour discussion was held in the Lok Sabha on 'Reservation for SC/STs in DESU after Privatisation' (LSD 23 August 1993: 430-462). On the reports that the Government is contemplating for privatisation of DESU, the member raised two questions, while initiating the debate: (i) whether the Government contemplates to come out with a necessary amendment in the Constitution for reservations in private sector, and (ii) whether the Government had signed any agreement with the multinational corporations to safeguard constitutional provisions in jobs for Dalits.

While participating in the discussion, the four members made different observations. Santosh Kumar Gangwar [Bareiley] asked how, when power generation is in the hands of Government and distribution with the private sector, could the reservation policy be followed. Laxmi Narayan Pandeya [Mandsur] raised the issue of loss to DESU with the privatisation in general. Rasa Singh Rawat [Ajmer] wanted to know what assurances the Government took from the companies on reservation. Kalka Das [Karol Bagh] alleged that the Government is not taking the matter seriously.

Initially the Minister of Power and Energy N.K. P. Salve stated that if reservations can be implemented in private sector, "we shall definitely follow it'" (*Ibid*: 438). Further he said, "I do welcome your suggestion". "I personally stand for social emancipation and economic advancement of Backward Classes" (*Ibid*: 448). In the same breath he stated that there is no injunction which stipulates for providing reservation in private sector as there are no constitutional guarantees and the Article 335 categorically stipulates reservations only in the affairs of the Union and the State Governments. Regarding the agreement with the MNCs, the Minister remarked, "we have not made any agreement and whether I can stipulate or not, is not the issue in question" (*Ibid*: 460).

All this exposes the Government's concern to safeguard the interests of the SC/STs in the emerging economic scenario, where private sector is to play a more important role as compared to earlier times. Thus, the legislators raised the policy matters *vis-à-vis* Dalits but the Government's stand remains indifferent and even the assurances are not given.

Yet, another question that emerges on Dalit policy paradigm is, whether it would be extra-constitutional or against the Constitution to provide Dalit representation in private sector. Here it needs to be reaffirmed as stated by the Minister of Welfare in 53rd Action Taken Report that reservations could be made in private sector under Articles 46 read in conjunction with the Article 15(4). If the 73rd Amendment Act to give powers to *panchayats* can be implemented on the basis of the sole Article 40 of the Constitution under the Directive Principles of State Policy, then the question arises why it can not happen with regard to the representation of SC/STs in the private sector with the help of Articles 15(4) and 46 in which the former is part of fundamental rights, which are mandatory to be implemented on behalf of the State.

Another report on 'Formulation, Implementation and Monitoring of Reservation Policy', was prepared by the CWSCT in 1993-94. So far as formulation of reservation policy was concerned, the Committee was informed that six departments/ministries[14] were involved in the process. The Secretary in the Ministry of Personnel, Public Grievances and Pensions (DOPT) stated that special reservation for SC/STs in case of promotions comes under DOPT.

Some of the major recommendations of the Committee were:

(a) to develop an understanding with the Bank Unions for 50: 50 ratio for direct and promotional recruitments respectively
(b) relaxation in the period of qualifying service for SC/STs in case of promotions.
(c) to bring a proposal for removal of all restrictions limiting applicability of reservation orders and follow Supreme Court judgement in Syndicate Bank case for the departments ministries, PSU, etc.
(d) reservation in ad-hoc appointments
(e) reservation according to population as per the 1991 Census
(f) fulfil huge reserved quota in various departments
(g) best among SC/ST candidates to be selected
(h) in-service training at a massive level to wipe out the backlog, particularly in technical and quasi-technical services

---

14 (i) Department of Personnel and Training; (ii) Department of Public Enterprises, (iii) Banking Division of Ministry of Finance; (iv) Insurance Division of Ministry of Finance; (v) Ministry of Rural Development (vi) Ministry of Urban Development.

(i) setting-up pre-examination training centres at the district level particularly with reference to Special Recruitment Drive
(j) to hold special examination for SRDs
(k) supply of up-to-date statistics in various Departments/ Ministries and particularly in University Service, Judicial Service and Organised Private Sector
(l) reservation in allotment of Houses to government personnels
(m) making *Panchayati Raj* Act applicable to Schedule Areas immediately under para 5 (1) of the 5th Schedule.
(n) cooperating with the State Governments to monitor the administration of Scheduled Areas and under Article 339 (2)[15]
(o) to fix up income criteria of Rs. 11,000/- for beneficiaries of Integrated Rural Development Programme because the land capabilities vary from region to region.

A few recommendations of the Committee were accepted by the Government. These included:

(a) reservation in ad-hoc appointments
(b) maintaining and furnishing statistical information relating to SC/STs to the Committee
(c) special Recruitment Drive to fill up backlog under consideration
(d) legislation on Reservation for SC/STs under active consideration
(e) ban on dereservation.

In some of the cases, such as opening pre-examination centres, keeping information about the number of SC/STs, backlog in departments, etc., the Government maintained that the concerned department has been requested to take necessary action, and the Committee asked to be apprised of the result.

Two recommendations were withdrawn by the Committee in the light of Government reply. These were:

(a) relaxation in basic educational qualifications because it was not in consistence with article 335, and
(b) no reservations for the allotment of dwelling units because low income groups' interests are given preference in such cases.

---

15 The executive power of the Union shall extend to the giving of directions to a state as to the drawing up and execution of schemes specified in the direction to be essential for the welfare of the Scheduled Tribes in the State.

There were some areas of recommendations which the Government did not accept and the Committee reiterated those for action *viz*.:

(a) To increase the percentage of direct recruitment from 25 per cent to 50 per cent and negotiate with Bank Unions for the same.
(b) Relaxation in qualifying period of service for promotion may not be juxtaposed with Article 335 on the pretext of being inconsistent with it.
(c) To make applicable the Supreme Court judgement in Syndicate Bank case to all Ministries/Departments, Public Sector Undertakings, Public Sector Banks etc.
(d) To revise percentage of reservations as per the 1991 census.
(e) To enhance allotment of Government accommodation for SC/ST personnels.

Regarding the recommendation of extension of the *Panchayati Raj* Act, provisions to the Scheduled Areas, the Government was not able to provide any satisfactory reply but stated that the matter was in the pipeline for consideration with the Chief Ministers who have not been working in accordance with Article 339 (2). The Committee asked to bring to its notice the action taken by the Ministry of Welfare in this regard.

The Committee seems to have been successful to bridge some gaps left by the Lok Sabha on the floor of the House regarding the onslaught on reservation policy due to privatisation and liberalisation of the economy, and the need for relaxation to fulfill the reserved vacancies. The reports prepared by the Committee did not touch issues concerning the major chunk of Dalit population, *viz*., educational development, socio-economic upliftment, such as providing them lands or enhancing their capabilities through financial assistance.

Reservation in public sector does have the potential to have a major impact on the socio-economic and political development of Dalits but this is an aspect that does not touch majority of the Dalit population *i.e.*, to say, all the Dalits or the major chunk of Dalit population cannot be accommodated in public sector because even if hundred per cent jobs are reserved for them, only a small proportion of Dalit populace will be able to develop, and the rest will be left out without any consequence (Mandelsohn *et. al*., 1998). It is more relevant in the present circumstances, where private sector is controlling the economy at large and reservation as a safeguard for Dalits to secure jobs is declining due to its absence in private sector.

There were two important policy issues discussed by the 24th Report of the CWSCT. One related to providing reservations in ad-hoc appointments and the other for ban on dereservation.[16] Similarly there were two important aspects under the Government's consideration (a) special recruitment drive for filling up back log, and (b) new legislation on reservation. Another important aspect of 24th Report was the Government's pronouncement that the concerned Ministry/Department has been asked to take necessary action.

The most important recommendations which could have some consequences on Dalit Policy paradigm were not accepted by the Government, and the Committee reiterated those for reconsideration. Moreover, implementing the *Panchayati Raj* provisions in Scheduled Areas found no concrete and satisfactory reply from the Government.

The overall impression gained from Reports of CWCST appears to be that the Government is reluctant to accept major shifts in Dalit policy paradigm. The recommendations proposed by the CWCST hardly had positive responses from the Government. The recommendations which had the Government's consent are of minor consequence for Dalit policy paradigm and do not resemble any sort of shifts necessary under the present circumstances. The Government was found to be neither ready to launch effective socio-economic programmes on its own nor willing and able to pressurise the private sector to provide proper representation to Dalits.

Compensatory discrimination efforts or social justice programmes cannot be limited to education and public sector. Universalisation of education, healthcare, access to land and other property, and ensuring access to employment both in public and private sectors are necessary to strengthen safeguards. Moreover if the liberalisation process is to be successful, the private/corporate sector cannot remain an island of "upper" caste privilege, as argued by Omvedt (Omvedt 'Reservation in the Corporate Sector': *The Hindu*, 31 May 2001).

Summing Up

Policy perspectives by the legislators as discussed in the previous chapter shows their concern for strengthening existing institutional mechanisms and creating new ones for proper policy implementation.

16 The ban on dereservaton was addressed first by the Statement on 'Liberalisation of Orders for improving SC/ST Representation in Central government Posts/Services' on 19 April 1989 but dereservation could take place with the prior permission of the Ministry of Personnel.

They also termed present policies of the Government as inadequate, inefficient, and offered alternatives. Broadly, the policy issues the legislators had been concerned with were stringent laws to deal with atrocities, strengthening institutional mechanism of the Commission for SC/STs by providing it a constitutional status, shifting the Dalit subject from the MHA to the MW, amending land distribution mechanism to make it more efficient for Dalits, fulfilling backlogs in government jobs, framing law in the light of Mandal Commission judgement for reservations in promotions, and providing reservations in private sectors against the backdrop of liberalisation process, etc.

Policy proposals of the Government relate to atrocities, Commission for SC/STs, providing reservations to Buddhists converted from amongst Dalits, National Commission for *Safai Karamcharis*, and reservations in promotions. Regarding two major perspectives, one on land reforms and the other on reservations in private sectors, no policy proposal was forthcoming from the Government. Although in the 9th Lok Sabha, assurance was given to put this issue under the 9th Schedule of the Constitution and the PCWSCT also came out with a comprehensive report on private sector reservations, but the Government did little to respond positively on these issues.

The legislators' contributions to policy proposals of the Government could be put under two heads:

(a) representation of customary character
(b) representation of specific character

Whether Dalit or non-Dalit MPs, the representation of customary character was prevalent among the both, so was the case with representation of specific character.

A careful observation of representation of customary character is indicative of doubt among the representatives regarding the implementation of the legislations. During deliberations on almost all the five Bills, apprehensions were expressed on the implementation part of a legislation. The second observation relates to drifting away from the subject matter of the Bills, whether its a debate on NCSCT or NCSK, the interventions seldom attempted to strengthen these mechanism as institutions, rather these deliberated upon what functions they should perform and how the functions could be performed adequately and efficiently. Thirdly, while debating on a legislation, ancillary/related aspects were focussed more than the main/prime themes in the Bill. For instance, asking for special tribunal for SC/ST employees on the lines of Central Administrative Tribunal, while discussing NCSCT Bill, representation of Dalits in judiciary, while deliberating upon NCSK Bill, providing reservation in private sector and emphasis on OBC reservation during the discussion on the 77th Amendment Bill that was only for continuation of job reservations in promotions in government sector, etc. Thus representation of customary character indicates a lack of pin-pointed discussion on a particular Bill and this applies both to Dalit and non-Dalit MPs discussing Dalit policies.

On the representation of specific character, Dalit MPs have been equally active as compared to non-Dalits. While passing of PAA no amendment was introduced by Dalit MPs whereas a non-Dalit MP introduced eight amendments. Similarly in case of NCSCT Bill, two Dalit and one non-Dalit MP moved amendments, and during the SC Order Amendment Bill, two non-Dalits and one Dalit MP moved amendments, while no amendment was introduced while passing of NCSK Bill. It was during the 77th Amendment Bill that both the Dalits and non-Dalits were equally in favour of amendments.

A look at the policy proposals of the Government in terms of Bills and Statements makes it abundantly clear that the Government was more responsive during the 9th and 10th Lok Sabha as compared to 8th Lok Sabha. There had been only one Bill that was passed in the 8th Lok Sabha; it concerned the prevention of atrocities. No Policy Statement was made during 8th Lok Sabha. Hence, the view that the Lok Sabha has become more active towards Dalits in the post-Mandal period stands substantiated. This is further supplemented by the fact that all the four PCWSCT Reports on policies were prepared in the post-Mandal period.

Though the 9th and the 10th Lok Sabha discussed Dalit issues promptly but one major aspect of representation of specific character was that the emphasis was not on extending facilities but on bringing more groups within the framework of special safeguards. This is evident from the passing of the SC Order Bill in 1990, where major emphasis was to include Christian and Muslim converts. The same holds true for the 77th Amendment Bill, wherein OBCs inclusion in the promotional benefits was emphatically asked for.

It is to be noted that legislators have been more active on representation of specific character primarily on three occasions—one, during the 65th Amendment Bill, two while passing SC order Amendment Bill and three, while passing of the 77th Amendment Bill.

Analogy between policy perspectives during discussion on CSCT Reports and policy proposals by the Government reveal a nominal relationship between them. One of the aspects left untouched by the Bills has been covered by the Statement made on the Liberalisation of Orders to improve the Representation of Dalits in the Central Services.

Only the 9th Lok Sabha was responsive towards legislative deliberations as is evident from the fact that the 65th Amendment Bill was passed and many new clauses were added to the original Bill. Significantly at no other point of time the amendments introduced by the MPs were added to the original Bill.

Policy output of PCWSCT reports on Dalit policy paradigm has been to say the least, negligible. Although these reports were able to bridge the gap left by legislative debates on private sector reservations and fulfillment of backlogs, but here as well the Government's response has been both quite poor and muted. No substantive policy issue was tackled positively by the Government. It shows that PCWSCT may try to bridge the gaps left by legislative deliberations but the Government remains unaffected and unaltered on Dalit policy questions.

We may conclude thus that though the Lok Sabha does deliberate upon Dalit issues, it does so both poorly and inadequately. And the response of the Government remains negligible and muted. However, assurances are given for formulating policies in future. All this indicates that there has been no major shift in the Dalit policy paradigm and the focus only remains on strengthening mechanisms for implementing existing policies.

The Parliament seems to have been able to bring various Dalit issues on the agenda of the Government. It could be observed with regard to the perspectives adopted by the MPs on the reports of the CSCT and the Bills introduced by the Government. Nevertheless, in spite of deliberations and proposed amendments on the Bills the MPs failed to alter the themes contained in the legislations introduced by the regimes in power.

Neither the perspectives on CSCT reports, nor the deliberations on the Bills and even the PCWSCT would make the Government realise the need to provide representation to Dalits in the areas not covered by the present Dalit policy paradigm.

5

Attitude and Efforts in Parliament: The Question Hour

This chapter analyses the Lok Sabha Questions during the period of the study. For convenience sake, four years representing all the three Lok Sabhas, 8th, 9th and 10th – and two years each of pre-and-post-Mandal periods *viz.*, 1985, 1990, 1991 and 1995 have been chosen to find the attitude and effort of the Members regarding policies and programmes meant for Dalits. The prime emphasis of this chapter is on the Starred questions as only these have the potential to reveal the Enduring representation, which could initiate a discussion on a policy. This chapter seeks to establish that even during the discussion on Starred Questions, MPs hardly raised policy questions, Further, if and when such questions are raised, the discussion remains inconclusive and the Government easily ignores the Members' concern.

Apart from participating in debates on legislations, the MPs in Parliament make use of the Question Hour, to scrutinise the policies and programmes of the regime in power. The first hour of each working day of the Parliament is devoted to the interrogation of various ministries and departments regarding the status of Government schemes and policies. It is a significant and unquestionable right of the Members to know about any aspect of administration and government activity. The questions may or may not relate to pure policy concerns, but "these (questions) are the manifestations from which the nature and direction of policy is inferred" (Eulau 1978: 179). Hence, the Question Hour becomes an indirect instrument of policy development in the hands of the Members. If used skilfully, it becomes a powerful parliamentary weapon with the members. "A skilful and determined backbencher can use parliamentary question to extract much information or to conduct a campaign in favour of or against a particular policy". (Rush 1976:91).

A well accepted fact is that Members possess and utilise the instrument of Question Hour, for calling information on the Government's decisions, policies, and its performance. However, it remains subservient in the formulation of policies as the Question Hour is basically used either to elicit the necessary information or to prepare the ground for influencing decisions (Narayana 1980: 433). Though there are limitations to the Question Hour, the information provided by the Government can be used as a stick to beat the Government, and probe its performance on various issues. It also serves to alert the government, as the Members put forward the prevalent opinions in society, which then puts demands on the Government. Subsequently, it may help the Government to make up its mind to alter the existing policy. "This occasion is also used to express disagreement with government policy or to demonstrate how it has failed to achieve results" (Mathur *et. al.*, 1993: 87). It is not only the questioner but also other members who can join during a debate on the Starred question. Sometimes the interventions of the members keep multiplying, leading to a full-fledged discussion on a particular policy of the Government.

The oral questions during the Question Hour seek explanation with Members' intervention on the policy issues. The argument here is that legislative interrogation relate primarily to short-term Dalit aspects and thus having the Phenomenal and not the Enduring representation in its practice. During supplementaries too Enduring representation is almost absent, and even if some policy issues are raised, the Government does not respond satisfactorily.

Though thirty-seven Starred questions were asked during the four years, only eight questions were discussed in the House and the rest did not evoke legislators' reactions, in response to the Minister's reply. All these eight questions that were discussed, and the two other Starred questions which were policy questions but not discussed have been analysed here.

Sector-wise Parliamentary Questions

First, the total numbers of questions have been divided into three sectors, economic development, social upliftment, and miscellaneous. Economic development, primarily relates to the financial issues that have direct involvement with the development, whereas social upliftment relates to the issues of human resource development. The miscellaneous relate to those left uncovered by the previous two.

Economic development has been divided into four categories—

(1) job reservations

(2) aid/welfare schemes

(3) allotment of agencies like petrol pumps, LPG depots, etc., and,

(4) land distribution.

On the other hand social upliftment has seven divisions, *viz.*,

(1) atrocities,

(2) housing,

(3) health,

(4) scholarship,

(5) hostel facilities,

(6) training/coaching, and

(7) admission in educational institutions.

Under the miscellaneous, questions on Reports of Commissioner, Reports of Parliamentary Committee for the Welfare of SC/STs, etc., have been incorporated. Apart from the table on area-wise nature of questions, tables on Starred/Unstarred questions, pre-Mandal and post-Mandal questions, questions by ruling or Opposition Parties, questions by Dalits and non-Dalit-members have also been classified and analysed.

The sector-wise nature of questions in *Table 5.1* indicates that more than 50 per cent questions were asked regarding the economic

Table 5.1: Sector Wise Questions

		Number of Questions
I.	*Economic Development*	
	Job Sector	166
	Welfare Schemes Aid/Grants/Funds	66
	Allotment of Agencies	27
	Land Distribution	1
	Total	260
II.	*Social Upliftment*	
	Atrocities	20
	Housing	12
	Health	5
	Scholarship	18
	Hostel Facilities	9
	Training/Coaching for Education	9
	Admissions	18
	Total	91
III.	*Miscellaneous*	35
	Grand Total	386

Source: Lok Sabha Questions 1985,1990,1991 and 1995.

development of SC/STs. Within economic development, the service sector occupies the greatest concern of the MPs. The second major concern was related to the welfare schemes such as IRDP, TSP, SCP, etc. Next was the allotment of agencies to Dalits, *viz.*, petrol pumps, LPG depots, etc. The most astonishing aspect of the table is the negligence shown towards seeking information on land distribution, wherein only one (out of 386) question was asked. In contrast, when we look into the debates, we find that the Members have shown keen interest on the issues of land.

On the front of social upliftment, atrocities, scholarship to the Dalit students, and their admissions in various institutions occupy almost equal importance, followed by housing, hostel facilities, training/ coaching for education, and finally health. If we look at the concern for education (II-4, 5,6,7) within social upliftment, then more than fifty per cent (54) questions relate to it. Questions on 'miscellaneous' issues number merely thirty-five.

It shows that reservation in jobs remain the most significant issue in parliamentary questions with regard to Dalits. Consequently we can argue that the concern for economic development is quite higher than the concern of social upliftment and more precisely for human resource development. In the light of the social and economic pressures, which coincide with the liberalisation and globalisation where State will not be able to offer job reservations to Dalits, the emphasis of the MPs should have been on the development of human skills so that Dalits could compete in the new economic atmosphere.

Social Background of the MPs and the Lok Sabha Interrogations

To know the social background of the MPs who asked questions on Dalit issues, we divide the MPs into two categories, *i.e.* Dalits and non-Dalits. *Table 5.2* reveals the social background of the interrogators (MPs).

The table demonstrates that Dalits have been more curious and have information from the Government on economic development issues. They asked almost double the questions than the non-Dalits. There is a wide gap between the two. The question on land reforms was asked not by a Dalit but a non-Dalit, which is again an interesting part of the interrogation. On the 'miscellaneous' front also, there is a gap between the two. There does not appear to be much difference in the realm of interrogations pertaining to the issues of social upliftment among Dalit members and their counterparts. If Dalits asked forty-eight

Table 5.2: Social Background of MPs Asking Questions

		Dalits	*Non-Dalits*
I.	*Economic Development*		
	Service Sector	107	58
	Welfare Schemes/Aid/Grants/Funds	40	26
	Allotment of Agencies	20	7
	Land Distribution	0	1
	Total	167	93
II.	*Social Upliftment*		
	Atrocities	11	9
	Housing	7	5
	Health	1	4
	Scholarship	12	6
	Hostel Facilities	3	6
	Training/Coaching for Education	4	5
	Admissions	11	7
	Total	48	43
III.	*Miscellaneous*	22	13
	Grand Total	237	149

Source: Lok Sabha Questions 1985,1990,1991 and 1995.

questions, the non-Dalits did not lag behind and enquired about government schemes and policies on forty-two occasions.

On the 'miscellaneous' front, Dalits showed more concern than their counterparts. Although the gap between the two is not much in the realm of social development and miscellaneous issues, but in the sphere of economic development this gap becomes wider, pointing thereby towards a need for more economic development than social upliftment.

Periodwise Questions

The assertion among Dalits has been on the increase during the 1980s but the implementation of Mandal Commission Report by the V. P. Singh Government is seen as a breakthrough that gave rise to a more conscious assertion among the deprived groups in the Indian society. In the following *Table 5.3*, a classification has been made on the basis of pre-Mandal and post-Mandal periods *vis-a-vis* questions on Dalits.

Table No. 5.3: Periodwise Questions

		Pre-Mandal	*Post-Mandal*
I.	*Economic Development*		
	Service Sector	74	92
	Welfare Schemes/Aid/Grants/Funds	31	35
	Allotment of Agencies	10	17
	Land Distribution	0	1
	Total	115	145
II.	*Social Upliftment*		
	Atrocities	7	13
	Housing	3	9
	Health	1	4
	Scholarship	10	8
	Hostel Facilities	3	6
	Training/Coaching for Education	4	5
	Admissions	9	9
	Total	37	54
III.	*Miscellaneous*	21	14
	Grand Total	173	213

Source: Lok Sabha Questions 1985,1990,1991 and 1995

The period-wise classification of questions shows relatively more interrogations in the post-Mandal phase than in the pre-Mandal. The service sector again finds a major concern. It is revealing to note that the only question on land reforms was asked during the post-Mandal period. Overall, on the economic development front in the pre-Mandal phase, 115 questions were asked. And in the post-Mandal period, 145 questions were asked. The social upliftment sector has thirty-seven questions during the pre-Mandal and fifty-three questions in the post-Mandal period. Within the scope of the discussions on social upliftment, the questions on scholarship is reduced from ten in the pre-Mandal to eight in the post-Mandal phase. The issue of admissions in institutions have equal number of questions, *i.e.* nine during each period. However, whether it is atrocities, housing, health, hostel facilities, training/coaching for education, etc., the number of questions asked have increased progressively. It reflects that the human resource development aspect attracted the attention of the MPs, but if compressed to the total number of interrogations, the social concern seems to be quite low.

The questions on 'miscellaneous' items also registers a decline from twenty-one to fourteen showing a downward interest among members on these items. These questions show that concern for monitoring mechanism declined among members, or even the miscellaneous items that include interrogations regarding NCSCT and PCWSCT on SCT/STs. There is no doubt that during the post-Mandal phase, more questions were asked but the gap was not very high. If the former attracted 173 questions, the latter had 213, which is a mere increase of thirty-seven questions in the post-Mandal era. The table shows that there is not only progressive increase in the economic development but also social upliftment in the post-Mandal phase as compared to the earlier one.

Partywise Questions

The political parties are based on various ideological factors and usually opposition party members are considered to be more active as interrogators of the regime in power. *Table 5.4* shows a party wise-interrogation by the MPs.

Table No. 5.4: Partywise questions

		Ruling	*Opposition*
	Economic Development		
	Service Sector	84	82
	Welfare Schemes/Aid/Grants/Funds	26	40
	Allotment of Agencies	7	20
	Land Distribution	1	
	Total	118	142
II.	*Social Upliftment*		
	Atrocities	10	10
	Housing	5	7
	Health	2	3
	Scholarship	7	11
	Hostel Facilities	2	7
	Training/Coaching for Education	6	3
	Admissions	11	7
	Total	43	48
III	*Miscellaneous*	15	20
	Grand Total	176	210

Source: Lok Sabha Questions 1985,1990,1991 and 1995.

Here the categorisation is on the basis of questions asked by the ruling party and the opposition parties.[1] The table displays that Opposition members asked more questions than the ruling party members. On the economic development front, there are clear indications that opposition parties have been more interested on Dalit issues, and interrogated the Government 142 times as compared to only 118 times by the ruling party members.

On the question of social upliftment, both the opposition and the ruling party members asked almost equal number of questions, which were forty-seven and forty-three respectively. Atrocity-related questions were equally distributed with minor ups and downs in other categories. The miscellaneous questions also show more interest of the opposition than the ruling party.

Nature of Questions - Starred and Unstarred

Generally, the questions are divided into two groups–Starred and Unstarred. The former require a verbal reply from the Minister, whereas the latter is responded to in written form, and the information is debated in the House.

Table 5.5 shows the number of Starred and Unstarred questions asked by the MPs. It is quite obvious that the number of Starred questions is much lower than the Unstarred ones. It requires the Minister concerned to answer the questions orally which sometimes invite a full-fledged debate on a particular policy of the Government. Only thirty-seven Starred questions have been asked whereas the number of Unstarred questions is as high as 349. The maximum number of Starred questions are related to the service sector. However, surprisingly no starred questions were asked on land distribution, health, hostel, facilities and training/coaching for education. Another interesting aspect is the marginal difference between Starred questions on the economic development and social upliftment. As compared to the total of 260 questions on the former and ninety-one on the latter, the number of Starred questions is merely nineteen and fourteen respectively. This means the Lok Sabha deliberations showed more concern for the social upliftment agenda during Starred questions as compared to unstarred questions. The other four Starred questions were regarding miscellaneous items.

---

1 During the 8th and 10th Lok Sabha, Congress was the only ruling party whereas for the 9th Lok Sabha, National Front formed the Government with outside support from in the BJP, but the questions asked by the MPs from BJP have been put in the opposition party category due to its absence in the Government principally.

Table No. 5.5: Starred and Unstarred Questions

		Starred	*Unstarred*
I.	*Economic Development*		
	Service Sector	12	154
	Welfare Schemes/Aid/Grants/Funds	4	62
	Allotment of Agencies	3	24
	Land Distribution	0	1
	Total	*19*	*241*
II.	*Social Upliftment*		
	Atrocities	4	16
	Housing	3	9
	Health	0	5
	Scholarship	5	13
	Hostel Facilities	0	9
	Training/Coaching for Education	0	9
	Admissions	1	17
	Total	*13*	*78*
III.	*Miscellaneous*	5	30
	Grand Total	*37*	*349*

Source: Lok Sabha Questions 1985,1990,1991 and 1995.

Starred Questions and Dalit Policies

An analysis of the parliamentary Starred questions on Dalits between 1985-95 reflects that Phenomenal representation has a greater concern for obtaining information regarding the issues that varied from the number of SC/STs in various government departments, unemployed SC/STs, the filling up of reversed posts, the number of atrocities committed on Dalits, the educational status of Dalits, and the number of students benefited through scholarship, etc. A similar trend of Lok Sabha inquiries is shown by Mathur, *et. al.*, on drought, wherein the thrust is primarily on the questions of relief instead of looking into policy aspects (1993:107). Out of thirty seven such questions only eight relate to policy aspects and only six questions were not discussed. The latter related to education and representation in High Courts and Supreme Court.

It may be illustrated by a sample of questions relating to different aspects of Dalit policy paradigm where the MPs' interrogation sought nothing more than information contained in the annual reports of the concerned departments and ministries. Some instances are:

Satyanarayan Jatiya [Ujjain]

(a) the number of posts reserved for SC/STs for each class in each ministry of the Union Government, and
(b) the number of such posts that have been filled up and those lying vacant in each class as on January 31, 1991 (LSD 25 February 1991:73).

Kadambur M.R. Janardhanan [Tirunelveli]

(a) the number of persons appointed as IPS officers during the last three years–year-wise and state-wise,
(b) the number of percentage of persons belonging to SC/ST, year-wise, and
(c) the percentage of SC/ST candidates selected from rural and urban areas. (LSD 17 May 1990:29).

Bengali Singh [Hathras]

(a) the number of persons recruited in Central Industrial Security Force during the last three years, year-wise and state-wise;
(b) whether there is any special quota for recruitment of persons belonging to Scheduled Castes/Scheduled Tribes;
(c) if so, the number of persons belonging to SC/ST recruited during the above period;
(d) whether the prescribed reservation quota for SC/ST has been fulfilled; and
(e) if not, the reasons thereof. (LSD 24 May 1990:49).

Pius Tirkey [Alipurduars]

(a) the total number of stalls sanctioned to Scheduled Castes, Scheduled Tribes, handicapped, and ex-military men by the New Delhi Municipal Committee during each of the last three years, category-wise
(b) whether any priority is given to war-widows and riot victims;
(c) if so, the details thereof; and
(d) if not, the reasons thereof. (LSD 20 November 1991:46).

Mrityunjay Nayak [Phulbani] and Srikant Jena [Cuttack]

(a) the total number of petrol/diesel retail outlets and LPG agencies in the country, state-wise and Union-Territory-wise;
(b) the number out of these allotted to the persons belonging to scheduled Castes and Scheduled Tribes;

(c) whether the allotment made to SC/STs is in conformity with their reservation quota; and
(d) if not, the reasons thereof. (LSD 28 November 1991:36).

The answers to all these questions are almost in the same format. They catalogue the number of persons recruited in case of job reservations, the number of students provided with scholarships in the education sector and the number of persons allotted LPG agencies/petrol pumps, etc. There is no reflection on any policy either in the questions or during the answers by the Ministers. The questions are designed in such a way that information given by the Minister while replying to a question neither gives nor requires more than statistics available in the annual reports of the ministries of the concerned departments. No harsh facts about other socio-economic realities are contained in these replies. The overall impression conveyed here is of a ritualistic nature as reflected in the replies of the Unstarred questions. None of the above questions could invite supplementary enquiries by the members and generate a debate, which would subsequently culminate into a meaningful discussion. It shows an unanimous degree of satisfaction among MPs on the answers received. They seem to feel having fulfilled their duties towards those whom they represent in the House. The Ministers and the Government seemed happy and contented for not being watched too closely.

However, the above instances do not mean that Dalit issues are not at all discussed during the Question Hour. Sometimes policy issues are raised and clarifications sought by the MPs and it is followed by supplementaries. For instance:

K. Pradhani [Nowrangpur] asked

(a) whether a *Kutir Yojna* was started by the Union Government in the State of Orissa;
(b) if so the grants provided by the Union Government to the State Electricity Board through Rural Electrification Corporation Ltd. for the implementation of the scheme;
(c) whether it is proposed to provide certain concession to the beneficiaries, especially the SC/STs under the schemes.
(d) if so, the detail thereof . (LSD 9 December 1991:31-35).

Another question sought to know if the Union Government proposed to increase the area of peripheral development around the coal fields and projects taken by the Central Coal Field Ltd. (LSD 27 August 1991: 14-25).

Though these questions are related with developmental aspects but they generally seek information pertaining to the grants distributed by the Government or concessions provided to beneficiaries through various projects and schemes. In response to the first question of K. Pradhani, the Minister replied:

> The Rural Electrification Corporation provided in all, Rs. 167.591 lakhs to the Orissa State Electricity Board under the programme, for releasing 78,905 single point light connections. According to the available information, the State Electricity Board achieved the above target. The scheme was not continued after 31.3.1991 (LSD 9 December 1991:32).

The reply of the Government shows that the scheme was successful but was not continued. In spite of the discontinuation of such an important and successful basic developmental activity, the MPs, failed to impress upon the Government to restart the scheme that was to benefit the areas inhabited by the STs. It may not be wrong to conclude with this that (i) programmes which are successful in achieving the targets can also be withdrawn by the Government, and (ii) the peoples' representatives fail to rejuvenate schemes and programmes benefiting their constituents.

Responding to the second question, the Minister put the responsibility on the State Government for developing coal-field areas, though it was clearly mentioned in the question that Central Government authority, *i.e.* Central Coal Fields Ltd. monitors the development of the peripheral areas in and around the coal-fields. During a supplementary, the Minister just responded by saying that the Government plans to come out with a new rehabilitation policy. Here also none of the MPs bothered to ask about the details of the policy that was being proposed by the Government.

It indicates a peculiar contradiction in the Government's responses to the questions on SC/STs and their development. Whenever responsibility for failures needed to be owned, the Government clearly escaped its responsibilities and brought in the State Governments. Whenever new policies were to be formulated, it resumed the responsibility and promised to come out with a policy.

Next we address the questions on 'directives by the government' to check irregularities in terms of, (a) proper implementation of job reservations, and (b) misutilisation of funds for developmental programmes. Such questions are rarely asked and even if they are asked, the reply of the Minister is an obvious 'yes' as is revealed by the following two questions below:

Rajnath Sonbar Shastri [Saidpur] and Karia Munda [Khunti]

(a) whether the Government's directives regarding reservation of posts for SC/STs in Groups C&D posts including the pharmaceutical staff of Indian and Modern System of medicine under CGHS, both with regard to recruitment and promotions are being followed;
(b) if so, the details thereof, including the number of promotions made during the last two years; and
(c) the reasons for backlog, if any and the steps proposed to be taken to fill up the prescribed reserved quota (LSD 10 December 1991: 1-14).

Here the Minister responded that the directives of the Government were being followed but admitted the existence of backlog in various departments due to non-availability of candidates. But Members hardly asked why this was happening and what the Government planned to do in this regard. Another obvious aspect of the Government's response was, whenever the backlog has been fulfilled, by and large the credit was taken by the present regime, though the task sometimes was completed by the previous Government. It came out during a discussion on 10th December 1991. The following excerpts from the speech of Ram Vilas Paswan needs to be reproduced in this regard:

> These figures pertain to the period from January to October 1991. When 40 per cent candidates could be available... how is it that 15 per cent candidates were not available during a long period of 40 years? It means we made since efforts as a result of which we succeeded in filling 40 per cent quota... you have been requested to provide the figures of two years but you provide figures of ten months only and that too pertaining to the period when National Front Government was in power...the special recruitment drive we initiated, has been withdrawn by the present Government. That is why the figures of later period have not been provided (LSD 10 December 1991: 6-7).

In response to these remarks, the Minister of Health and Family Welfare (M.L. Fotedar) without confronting escaped the issues raised.

A controversy emerged on Dalit leadership that led to the adjournment of the House.[2]

A question on misutilisation of funds and the need for a committee to monitor the upliftment of SC/STs triggered a debate in the House where a vibrant discussion took place. The analysis of the Question and the reply of the Government needs critical illustration here as the Minister of that period was a vocal Dalit leader.

Gulab Chand Kataria [Udaipur] asked another set of questions

(a) whether governments are aware of the complaints that crores of rupees provided for the upliftment of *Adivasis* do not reach them; and

(b) whether governments propose to constitute a committee in each State to monitor the use of the money spent on the upliftment of Advisis (LSD 16 May 1990: 14-24).

Ramvilas Paswan as the Minister of Labour and Welfare responded positively to the first part of the question by saying "I believe that there is a lot of truth in the question raised by the member." He further pointed out that already, there are committees at various levels in the states to monitor and review the tribal development schemes and the State Governments have been asked to strengthen and make them more effective. The significant aspect of his reply was revelation of the fact that Tribal Sub-Plan (TSP) was meant towards infrastructural development in the Tribal areas, but the benefits do not directly and immediately reach them. But a working Group on Development of STs during the Eighth Five-Year Plan had identified this and recommended a significant shift from infrastructure development to family beneficiary oriented schemes, as only twenty per cent of the money was spent for the latter and eighty per cent was allocated to the former. It was said to be the prime reason for disenchantment over the misutilisation of funds which results in the lack of benefits to the tribals. Though the Monitoring Committees existed in the states, the Member asked whether the Government proposes to constitute a committee at the Centre. The Minister surprisingly answered that the "Ministry of Welfare does not have enough resources to monitor each and every thing". On the contrary he responded positively to the suggestion made by Ram Ganesh Kapse [Pune] to make arrangements in other states similar to the one prevalent in the State of Maharashtra, where District

---

2 The Minister remarked on the usefulness of installing Ambedkar's statues and a debate started on the politics, leaders, and intentions of the Governments in uplifting Dalit masses, leading to the adjournment of the House.

Planning and Development Committee look into the proper utilisation of funds under TSP. The Minister was quick enough to state that "...if there is any scope for a better arrangement, we shall implement that too". Similar was the response to, (a) the question of constituting Autonomous Councils as provided under the Constitution, and (b) on specific proposal looking at particular needs of the tribals to improve their economic standards. The Minister assured the members that the displacement of tribals would take place only after consulting them and by taking them into confidence. It was also stated that a sub-committee of the Cabinet was constituted to look into the question of rehabilitation. A new Forest Policy was also being formulated to cover all these aspects that affect the Tribal population in various parts of the country. This policy was meant to check the exploitation of Tribals and ensure their participation in the development projects related to them.

Absence of Discussion on the Starred Policy Questions

It is true that generally information seeking questions are asked by the MPs with regard to Dalits, but rare instances of questions on policies in various fields also show the concern . The policy questions are related with job reservations and atrocities on SC/STs. But they remotely focus attention on representation in untouched areas such as public schools, private enterprises, judiciary etc. For instance several changes have been taking place in the field of education for the last few years where private schools under non-governmental management have become increasingly important for imparting education. Not only the urban but also the rural areas have witnessed the influx of such schools. Questions related to this aspect was asked but no debate could be initiated owing to the irresponsive attitude of the Government. A Dalit MP raised the following policy question for reservation of seats in privately managed schools:

Ram Payare Panika [Robertsganj] enquired

(a) whether Governments have asked for reservation of seats in public schools for admission of children belonging to Scheduled Castes and Scheduled Tribes;
(b) if so, the number of seats so reserved and whether public schools have complied with those instructions;
(c) if not, whether Government have taken any action against such schools;
(d) if so, the details thereof; and
(e) if not, the reasons thereof (LSD 25 April 1985: 37).

Yet another policy question that was asked but not discussed in the House relates to the appointment of SC/STs as judges in Supreme Courts and High Courts.

A.K.A. Abdul Samad [Vellore] and K.D. Sultanpuri [Shimla] asked will the Minister of Law and Justice be pleased to state:

(a) the number of judges belonging to Scheduled Castes/Scheduled Tribes, backward classes and minority communities in the Supreme Court and the High Courts as on 1 January 1991, Court-wise and

(b) the steps taken by the government to provide adequate representation to these categories in these courts (LSD 22 February 1991: 26).

The absence of debate on the above policy questions makes us conclude that neither the Dalit MPs nor their counterparts were dynamic enough in their approach towards representation of Dalits in areas where reservations do not exist. There has been a significant change in the field of education in the last two decades and public schools became increasingly important for imparting education to the children of various groups. It is not only in urban but also in rural areas that public schools are occupying an important place in educating the people. The unresponsiveness and near apathy on the part of Dalit MPs, on a crucial area as education, shows how ignorant they remain of the emerging trends in the society. It seems that none of them could argue for equal representation in public schools and High Courts and Supreme Court[3] They seem to lack the vision to adopt a strategy wherein Dalits could also be asked to be accommodated in public schools . Moreover, they do not feel any importance of higher judiciary and perhaps its significance in the times of judicial activism—where Judiciary has come to occupy a third chamber *vis-a-vis* its place beside the Legislature.

Our analysis of the Starred questions show that though the questions on Dalit policies are rare but Government responses invite a debate on them in the Parliament. The discussion on the questions on reservations in jobs needs to be explained and analysed here.

---

3 The Minister denied of reservation in public schools in existence, and also pointed out that the Government had no plan to do so. There were only twelve judges in High Court and two in Supreme Court belonging to SC/STs.

Starred Questions and Job Reservation

With reference to the anti-reservation movement in some parts of the country in the early 1980s, a Statement was issued to review the reservation in jobs for SC/STs by the Prime Minister Rajiv Gandhi on 28 February 1985 to UNI that raised doubts among the political representatives *vis-a-vis* continuation of reservation policy. Under these circumstances, a clarification was sought by a member on the stand of the Government regarding the Statement issued.

Amar Roy Pradhan [Coochbehar] enquired

(a) whether the Government has decided to review the reservation policy in the country;
(b) if so, the details thereof; and
(c) if not, the reasons thereof (LSD 10 April 1985: 8-12).

Another policy question was asked when the Supreme Court verdict on Mandal Commission Report withdrew the reservations in promotions and it was made applicable to the Dalits as well. The Government had clarified in this regard on other occasions also, but in spite of that, various departments kept denying it on one pretext or the other. Subsequently a question on the continuation of reservation in promotions was asked by Shravan Kumar Patel [Jabalpur], who wished to know:

(a) whether the Government has taken or propose to take adequate steps for protecting the rights of the SC/ST incumbents services for reservation in promotions by way of amendment to the Constitution; and
(b) if so, the details thereof (LSD 4 May 1995: 18-21).

Both these question were related to policy concerns. Though the former inquiry was with respect to the overall reservation policy but the Minister of State for Home Affairs, Ramdulari Sinha in her reply confined herself only to political reservations in the Parliament and State Assemblies. In a supplementary, Som Nath Rath [Aska] wanted to know about the proposal on delimitation of the reserved constituencies due to increase in Dalit population. Responding to it, the Minister reaffirmed a decision of the National Development Council that the 1971 Census would be taken into account while deciding the matter. Referring to chapter 6, Item no. 31, page 196, Amar Roy Pradhan [Coochbeher] reminded the Minister that the NCSCT has suggested to evolve a scheme to attract the children of those SC/ST communities whose literacy rate was less than 50 per cent of the state average. He also asserted that by denying reservations to the SC/ST students, the States of Gujarat and Madhya Pradesh have violated the Article 29 (2) of the Constitution and wished to know what steps have been taken in this regard. But the Minister escaped by stating that he would ask for information from the State Governments.

In yet another supplementary, the Minister pointed out that so far as reservations in jobs and education are concerned, the Constitution is silent and no time-limit has been suggested. It was also emphasised that the Government does not consider it essential to evolve any sort of consensus in this regard and if at all a consensus was needed, it was in case of the OBCs.

In response to the question by Shravan Kumar Patel, the Minister of State for Welfare, K.V. Thangabalu of the Congress government, reversed his stand on the need to protect the reservations in promotions for SC/STs and stated the need to evolve a consensus on the issue. He informed that a meeting of all political parties had been convened.

Once again, the issue of growth in Dalit population was raised and a demand was put to the government to increase the reservation quota. However, without mentioning about the strategy and a plan to realise it, the usual reply was reiterated that 'the Government is committed to the welfare of SC/STs and it is under consideration'.

It shows a change in the stance of the Government, because while protecting the interests of Dalits in 1985, no need was felt to generate consensus with respect to reservations for SC/STs.

One of the most vocal Dalit MPs, Ramvilas Paswan [Rosera] contemplated upon the attitude of the Government and repetition of its replies, he wanted to know why the NCSCT was not consulted on the issue.[4] In another supplementary it was inquired whether any proposal for a new legislation on the number of posts reserved for SC/STs and lying vacant in various departments and ministries, was under consideration. But the Minister was non-committal and put the responsibility on the DOPT regarding the 1800 reserved vacancies lying unfulfilled in various departments.

Starred Questions on Atrocities

To stop atrocities on Dalits has been one of the most debated and discussed aspect with regard to safeguards against adverse

4 It had been made mandatory under the new Act to keep the Commission acquainted and informed on issues which relate to Dalit Policy.

discrimination during our study.[5] Though four Starred Questions were asked for this purpose, here two of those discussed by the 10th Lok Sabha are analysed.

Mukul B. Wasnik [Buldana] enquired regarding

(a) the number of cases of atrocities on Scheduled Castes and Scheduled Tribes which were taken up by the National Commission for SC/STs upto March 31, 1991;
(b) whether the governments have received the recommendations made by the commission for SC/STs to curb the rising trend of atrocities on SCs & STc;
(c) it so, the details thereof; and
(d) the reaction of the Government thereto (LSD 19 August 1991:11-17).

Vijay Raghvan [Palakkad] and Shravan Kumar Patel [Jabalpur], similarly wished to know

(a) the measures discussed in the two day Chief Minister Conference held last month in New Delhi to prevent atrocities on Scheduled Castes and Scheduled Tribes;
(b) whether any state government has taken steps to implement the proposals of the Conference; and
(c) If so, the details thereof (LSD 25 November 1991: 20-33).

The first question directly deals with the policy because the NCSCT functions as a monitoring body, not only for compensatory discrimination but also against adverse discrimination. It goes into the complexities of atrocities by visiting the place of atrocity and recommends the Government ways and means to curb them. And the Government is supposed to respond to its recommendations under the new act. The second question complements the first as a special conference of Chief Ministers was called by the Central Government, since maintenance of law and order is a State-subject.

In response to both these questions, Statements were laid on the Table of the House and the recommendations of the NCSCT and the decisions of the Chief Ministers Conference were said to have been communicated to the States and Union Territories for action. Although the recommendations of the NCSCT and the decisions of the Chief

---

5 The atrocities were discussed four times under the Rule 193, once under Adjournment Motion and also when the PAA 1989 was passed by the Parliament.

Ministers Conference, both dealt with the implementation aspect of the existing laws, the former were exclusive in nature, whereas the latter included other areas, like fulfilling the reserved quota in job appointments, building houses and distributing surplus land under land ceiling laws. The common issues addressed by them comprised identifying areas of high incidence of atrocities, establishing special courts which made local officers responsible to visit the place of crime as early as possible, entrusting investigation to state-level agencies such as Vigilance Bureau, Anti-Corruption Branch, etc. Thus NCSCT's recommendations dealt primarily with atrocities and specific remedies to contain them, but the Chief Minister's Conference dealt with the problem loosely by addressing the digressive issue of extra-atrocity remedies.

During supplementaries a few more policy questions were raised, *viz.*, (a) the constitution of the NCSCT, and (b) its monitoring powers and interventions in policy-making. Regarding the former, Ramvilas Paswan [Rosera] inquired when the Government would be able to constitute the NCSCT so that it could function according to the new powers vested in it. The Minister stated that it would be done by the last week of September 1991. When Malini Bhattacharya wanted to know about the monitoring powers of the present Commission, she was given the reply that it would have vast powers such as to summon any person or document connected with any incident of atrocity. But regarding the Commission's monitoring powers and its role in policy making, the Speaker intervened and pointed out that big policy matters are not discussed during Question Hour. Regarding the supplementary by Anna Joshi [Pune] question on the special courts exclusively dealing with atrocity cases, the responsibility was again put on state governments, though it was assured that information about negligence would be dealt with by the Home Ministry.

Interestingly, on the question by Chanderjeet Yadav [Azamgarh] for providing arms licences to SC/STs and doing away with the clause of property, the Minister denied to comment by saying that it generates animosity and that he was against any kind of violence.

Responding to the question on the Chief Ministers Conference, it was reiterated by the Minister of Welfare Sitaram Kesri that the PAA 1989 was adequate enough to deal with the officers violating and ignoring their duties and if at all some modifications were needed the basis could be the experience gained after its implementation. But he was unable to provide data on the officers prosecuted under the Act.

When a supplementary by Ramvilas Paswan on the existence of Special Courts to settle Dalit disputes and whether they are functioning in Andhra Pradesh was asked (due to the *Tsundur* incident), the Minister confirmed their existence and proper functioning. But it was refuted by the Member because no case was initiated against the culprits involved in the *Tsundur* incidence of 1991, which forced the Minister to assure that he will collect the progress report from the concerned government.

Mukul B. Wasnik [Buldana] in yet another supplementary wanted to know about the number of officials prosecuted during the period under PAA. But the Minister had no information. Malini Bhattacharya [Jadavpur] inquired about the discussion of the recent rape of tribal women by Jawans of Assam Rifles and the response by the Minister was that no individual case was discussed in it.

Ramvilas Paswan [Rosera] and Buta Singh [Jalore] bringing the backlog issue at the fag end of the session inquired about the strategy being adopted by the Government to fulfil the backlog of one lakh vacancies in various departments within the stipulated four months time. But the Minister denied to divulge any strategy in this regard and reaffirmed his position to do it by 31 March 1992.

Summing Up

The concerns raised during the Question Hour show the main emphasis to be on economic developmental issues, particularly on jobs in the public sectors, and the welfare schemes for Dalits. The issue of land distribution, which has a major impact on a sizeable Dalit population did not merit any concern by the MPs. The issue of social upliftment of the Dalits, did find some mention but here too atrocities against them attracted more attention than housing, health facilities, scholarships, admission, etc.

A comparison between Dalit and non-Dalit MPs, reveals more inquiries by the former. Similar is the case with pre-and-post-Mandal period wherein 173 questions were asked in the former and 213 questions in the latter period. So far as party-wise questions are concerned, the opposition had been more active. Opposition Members asked 210 questions as against the 176 questions put forth by the ruling party Members.

Though the number of Unstarred questions was more than the Starred questions, but the emphasis of Starred questions was mainly on social upliftment, in comparison to Unstarred questions which emphasised on aspects of economic development. However, there was no question on health, hostel facilities, and training and coaching for education under social development concerns.

Majority of the Starred questions reflected on Phenomenal representation. It sought information on the number of SC/STs being given scholarship in education, the number of persons allotted LPG agencies, petrol pumps, the number of atrocities committed on Dalits etc. Such questions failed to elicit specific information except the one contained in various reports of the NCSCT. They mentioned no harsh facts of the matter except showing how marginal improvements were made as compared to previous years. Moreover, the reply of Government to these questions remained at best, stereotypical.

No supplementary questions were asked on most of the Starred questions. As stated in the beginning, out of the thirty-seven Starred Questions, only eight questions could evoke debate, the rest passed off unnoticed by the MPs after the Minister's response. Generating a discussion and turning it into a meaningful debate remained a distant reality. Thus, MPs were overwhelmingly satisfied with the replies, showing a sense of satisfaction, for having raised the concerns of the masses merely by asking a few questions.

The eight starred questions discussed by the legislators point to a similar trend of Phenomenal representation in the following areas: beneficiaries of the schemes, increasing the area of peripheral development around the coal-fields, directives issued by the Government and their compliance with regard to the backlog in jobs, complaining about the misutilisation of funds meant for SC/STs, and the number of cases taken up by the NCSCT on atrocities against Dalits, etc.

Even during supplementaries, MPs did not pursue the schemes which have benefited Dalits and had seen a considerable success rate as was in the case of *Kutir Yojna* in Orissa. In the case of yet another supplementary question relating to the development of peripheral areas in and around the coal fields, and on the rehabilitation policy, the Members were satisfied with the Minister's response that the Government would come out with a new rehabilitation policy in case of tribals. They failed to probe further as to what were the basic components and themes of the policy. Based on these questions a peculiar contradiction can be seen with regard to the implementation of schemes and programmes, *i.e.*, the Central Government at times dodged the issue by bringing the state governments in, and whenever new policies needed formulation, it took up the responsibility without laying out the essential components of such a policy. Either it escaped addressing the issue or it did half -heatedly.

Regarding the misutilisation of funds particularly in the tribal areas, and need to constitute committees at the Central level, the Minister referred to 'non-availability of resources to monitor each and everything. None of the Members thought it proper to raise the issue through supplementaries. On the displacement of tribals, the Government once again tried to satisfy the House by saying that they were formulating a new forest policy to check the exploitation of the tribals.

The questions on the review of reservation policy and reservations in promotions are the major policy questions asked by the Members. These have been discussed and debated by the Lok Sabha. But the fact of the matter is that both these questions were asked by non-Dalit legislators. Replying to the former, the Minister categorically mentioned that there was no question of reviewing the reservation policy but at the same time he did not commit to increase the quota with the rise in the Dalits' population. Subsequently, he asserted that the Constitution was silent on the time-limit with regard to reservation in jobs and education. As far as political reservations in the Lok Sabha and State Assemblies were concerned, it was pointed out that the Government did not want to drop it.

With regard to promotions in reservations, the Minister reiterated that the Government is committed to the welfare of SC/STs. But he abstained from divulging any information about the steps being taken. There was a supplementary on the proposal for a new legislation to fulfil the backlog of vacancies, but the Minister again evaded the responsibility and stated it was under the purview of DOPT to look into these matters.

Questions with regard to atrocities were purely related to implementation and its failures. These asked the Government for information on the follow-ups of the recommendations of the NCSCT Reports to curb the atrocities. The information provided by the Minister mentioned about the number of atrocities. It was told that the report of the NCSCT had been forwarded to the state governments and an assurance was given regarding finances for compensation to the victims. The two supplementaries by Ramvilas Paswan and Malini Bhattacharya were nothing more than regretting the non-implementation of the 65th Amendment Act to constitute the NCSCT and to know the powers conferred on it respectively. In reply to the supplementary about continuing violence in spite of PAA, the Minister offered no further policy amendments and the Members were contented with the answer.

Two policy inquiries were made under Starred questions about, (a) reservation in admission in public schools, and (b) representation of SC/STs as judges in Supreme Court and High Courts. Once again no discussion was initiated by the MPs on the reply of the Minister who admitted poor representation of Dalits in the Supreme Court and the High Courts as Judges and non-existence of reservation in public schools.

Our argument thus holds forth the view that the problem lies in the legislators hardly raising demands on adequate representation of Dalits in the areas untouched by the Dalit policy paradigm. Even if such demands are remotely raised, there is a definite lack of pursuance by them.

The substantive concerns of the legislators during Question Hour largely show the importance attached to the question of Phenomenal representation, where the implementation of safeguards remains of paramount importance. Demands are seldom in the direction of strengthening the implementation mechanism or formulating new policies. Even rarely if there are demands to strengthen the implementation agencies and clamour for new policies to uplift the Dalits, these are not pursued vigorously. The Government's response on the enquiries remains stereotypical. The replies of the Ministers whether or not to come out with new proposals is not an issue which is discussed and debated further. Thus legislators seem to have been generally contented with the replies and even if sometimes they remain unsatisfied they did not pursue their dissatisfaction to force the Minister to take proactive policy measures.

6

Voices in the Lok Sabha
A Socio-Political Profile of the MPs

Political systems generally claim to be democratic in one or the other sense of the term. Democracy entails participation in politics and in Parliamentary democracy, participation in Parliament signifies involvement of people's representatives in the decision-making process. In this sense any voluntary action, successful or abortive, episodic or continuous, that is intended to influence the choice of public policies and the administration of public affairs, indicates political participation (Weiner 1971: 212).

Participation in the legislative process is a conscious choice of the legislators. It is clearly reflected in the way a representative develops a perspective towards an issue and responds to the policies of the government, as already examined in the previous three chapters of this study. Participation involves an active involvement of the legislator in the legislative process, where not only legislations are initiated but "legislative viscosity" in terms of amendment, delay, or even rejection of executive proposals is demonstrated (Blondel 1970).

Besides, a sense of accountability that leads to participation is the corner-stone of any democratic government and in a parliamentary system it works at two levels :1) Executive's accountability towards the Legislature, and 2) legislators accountability to the constituents. A feeling of accountability on the part of legislators impels them to participation. At the same time, behind this accountability there could be an incentive to get re-elected. This is defined as 'electoral incentives' (Scully 1997). Various other factors like social background, political affiliation, involvement in civil rights movements, etc., may also influence the participation of a legislator in the legislative process with particular reference to Dalits.

In the present chapter, the focus is on the socio-political background of the MPs, who frequently participated during discussion or interrogation of Dalit issues, in the Lok Sabha. To outline the frequency of participation, the participants have been divided into two kinds, (i) those who participated upto two times, and (ii) those who participated more than twice. We shall deal in detail with only those legislators who either asked questions or participated in the debate more than twice during the period 1985-95. An MP may have participated in one Lok Sabha or in all the three during the 8th, 9th and 10th Lok Sabha.

The socio-political background of these Members has been divided into five categories: (i) social background in terms of Dalit and Non-Dalit, (ii) educational qualification in terms of below matric, matric, graduate, post-graduate and doctorate, (iii) party affiliation, (iv) involvement in socio-political activities, (either exclusively in social sphere or exclusively in political sphere or both in social as well as in political arena or none), and (v) previous experience in the legislatures either in the Parliament or in the State Assembly, or none.

Participation of Dalit MPs on Dalit matters is often necessitated due to their similar social background, and on account of their election from 'reserved constituencies'. But the question, why non-Dalit MPs participate, becomes a formidable question that needs concrete explanation.

We argue that the majority of those who frequently participate in the legislative process on Dalit matters are educated, socio-politically active, and are experienced hands in the Legislature. However, non-Dalits participation apart from other factors, is primarily influenced by electoral calculations because majority of their constituencies comprise a large number of Dalits who obviously play an important and decisive role in the victory or defeat of the non-Dalit candidates due to their numerical strength.

As has been stated earlier, legislators have two occasions to participate in the legislative process—Question Hour and debate and discussion on various Bills, Resolutions, etc. The *Table 6.1* below classifies the participation of MPs in terms of those who participated upto two times and those participated for three or more times.

The table reveals that there is a gap among those who participated upto two times and those who did so for three times or more. However, this gap is quite reasonable both in the case of Question Hour and debate and discussion on Bills, Resolutions, etc.

Below, we concentrate only on those legislators, who have been quite active and participated for more than two times on Dalit issues in the House.

Table No. 6.1: Frequency of Participation of the MPs in Lok Sabha

Occasion	*Frequency*	
	Those who participated upto two times	*Those who participated for three or more times*
Question Hour	55	39
Debate and Discussion on Bills, Resolutions etc.	50	37
Total	*105*	*76*

Source: Who's Who 1987, '90 & '92 Lok Sabha Secretariat, New Delhi.

Socio-Political Background of the Active Participants

Various social groups have representation in the Lok Sabha. For convenience sake, we divided these groups into two parts: Dalits and non-Dalits. The categorisation of social background is an indicator that would enable us to examine which of the two groups participate more on Dalit issues. The total number of MPs participating quite frequently as shown in Table 6.1 was seventy six, and six[1] of them were common during Question Hour and Debates. Thus, we are left with 70 MPs. So far as social background is concerned the participation of Dalit MPs was greater as compared to non-Dalits, because of seventy MPs, fifty were Dalits, while the non-Dalits comprised merely twenty. This is obvious because for Dalits there is special representation in the form of reserved constituencies, specifically designed to provide adequate representation to them, so that they can raise their voice against the discriminatory attitude of the society against the Dalits, and intervene while policies specially on Dalits are being formulated in the form of legislations in the Lok Sabha. Such special representation from reserved constituencies enable as well, the redressal of Dalit populations' grievances through their special representatives.

Party Affiliation of the Participants

Political parties function as vehicles of political mobilisation, and create enthusiasm among the voters as well as make the electoral process participative. The nature of political parties decides the efficiency and sustainability of the democratic system. The contestants in the electoral fray usually have political affiliation that largely

1 Two MPs were from General Constituencies and the rest four from the Reserved Constituencies.

indicates their inclination towards a particular political organisation and subsequently their support to its ideology. Political parties can broadly be divided into three categories—leftist, rightist, and centrist. The centrist parties may have a socialist outlook as was the case of Janta Dal during the late 1980s and early 1990s. The Congress has been usually seen as a centrist party which does not cater to the extremist ideas of either the left or the right. The Bhartiya Janta Party is considered to be a rightist party, while the Communist parties are seen as leftist. The following *Table 6.2* shows the party affiliation of the MPs participating actively on Dalit matters.

Table No. 6.2: Party-Affiliation of the Participants

Party	*Dalits*	*Non Dalits*	*Total*	*Percentage*
Congress-1	28	10	38	54.28
Bhartiya Janta Party	6	4	10	14.29
Janta Dal	11	3	14	20.00
Bahujan Samaj Party	1	0	1	01.43
Communist Parties (Revolutionary Social Party, CP1, CP1 (M) Forward Block)	3	3	6	08.57
Others	1	0	2	01.42
Total	*50*	*20*	*70*	*100.00*

Source: Who's Who 1987, '90 & '92 Lok Sabha Secretariat, New Delhi.

Majority of the MPs, whether Dalits or non-Dalits, belonged to the Congress Party as per the table. Second comes the Janta Dal, while the Bhartiya Janta Party MPs stand at third position. The Congress was in power during the 8th and 10th Lok Sabha, whereas Janta Dal formed the government in the 9th Lok Sabha. The table shows that the ruling party MPs are more active than their counterparts. The BSP, which is considered to be a party of the Dalits, was not much participative in the Lok Sabha. Though it had six MPs during this period, only one of them was active in the Lok Sabha. It surprisingly shows a lack of interest in a party dominated by Dalits while participating in the Parliament, though the BSP had been very vocal outside the Parliament. In various public meetings, the party has countered and defended its stand on not being an active participant by arguing that since their views have little impact on the ruling class which holds power, it is thus better not to limit one's engagement merely to the participation in the Lok Sabha. It argued for preparing public opinion outside the arena of Parliament.[2]

Educational Background of the MPs

Education is considered to be an important factor to understand the complexities of social and political systems. The MPs communicate the grievances of their constituents to the Government. If the representative is illiterate, then it becomes a bit difficult for him or her to respond properly to the demands and grievances of the electorate on the one hand, and to understand the complex issues of administration and governance on the other. To ascertain the educational background of the MPs participating on Dalit issues, their level of education has been classified into five categories, *i.e.*, below-matric, matriculate, graduate, post-graduate, and doctorate. The following *Table 6.3* exhibits the educational background of the MPs.

Table No. 6.3: Educational Profile of the Participants[3]

Level of Education	*Dalits*	*Non-Dalits*	*Total*	*Percentage*
Under-matric	4	3	7	10.29
Matriculate	11	1	12	17.64
Graduate	23	9	32	47.06
Post-Graduate	11	3	14	20.58
Doctorates	0	3	3	04.42
Total	*48*	*20*	*68*	*100.00*

Source: Who is Who 1987, 1990 and 1992 Lok Sabha Secretariat, New Delhi.

The table clearly indicates that the majority of the MPs were well-educated and very few of them were either highly or poorly educated. Of the total sixty-eight, the number of those having education between matriculation and post-graduation stood at fifty-eight. There were only three MPs with Doctorate, but none Dalit. Majority of the MPs in both the social categories were graduates. Importantly, it shows that whereas education made Dalits MPs vocal and participative, simultaneously it

---

2 The researcher came to know of the BSP on two occasions - first during a debate on a 'No Confidence Motion' in 1998 in the Lok Sabha on Television and, secondly, during a personal interaction with Mr. Kanshi Ram, the BSP President .

3 Educational profile of two MPs was not available.

imparts sensitivity among the non-Dalit MPs to participate on Dalit matters in the Lok Sabha.

Involvement of the MPs in Socio-Political Activities

Participation is not an isolated phenomenon. It is influenced by several social, economic, and cultural factors which fall under the concept of political socialisation. Political socialisation is an inescapable process. An individual is socialised throughout his/her life, and accordingly forms political perceptions. Political perceptions are the consequences of the way s/he is socialised politically. "Individuals are socialised into polities on the basis of experiences in given groups and environments, who actively judge the environment and select experience" (Hymen 1972: 133). Whether the MPs participating on Dalit issues have been socially and politically involved in various activities, needs to be probed here.

The *Table 6.4* shows that the majority of the MPs, whether Dalit or non-Dalit, were involved in socio-political activities. It means they have been participating not only in electoral politics but also in social activities which were perhaps geared towards the welfare of marginalised sections of the society. Some of the MPs have also been either socially or politically involved in various activities and the number of socially active members was higher by more than two times (10:4) to those involved only in political activities. The table shows non-involvement of merely ten MPs in the socio-political or social activities. We can thus draw the inference that those who are socially sensitive make their political involvement visible in the Lok Sabha on Dalit policies.

Table 6.4: Involvement in Socio-Political Activities of the Participants

Nature of activities	*Dalits*	*Non-Dalits*	*Total*	*Percentage*
Social	10	6	16	23.52
Political	4	3	7	10.29
Social and Political	26	9	35	51.48
None	8	2	10	14.70
Total	48	20	68	100

Source: Who is Who 1987, '90 and '92 Lok Sabha Secretariat, New Delhi.

Past Experience of the MPs as Legislators

Participation and articulation to an extent depends on the previous experience of the legislator in the Legislature, though sometimes new entrants may also participate actively in legislative deliberations. It is experience which can bring a sophisticated and proper understanding of the issues. *Table 6.5* illustrates the previous experience of the participating legislators in the Legislature. Their experiences have been categorised at two levels—either in Parliament or State Legislatures, and those who had no past experience as legislators.

Table No. 6.5: Previous Experience of the Participant as Legislator

Legislature	*Dalits*	*Non-Dalits*	*Total*	*Percentage*
Parliament	32	11	43	63.23
State Assembly	7	5	12	17.65
None	9	4	13	19.12
Total	48	20	68	100

Source: Who's Who 1987, '90 and '92 Lok Sabha Secretariat, New Delhi.

The table reveals that the majority of the MPs who participate in legislative deliberations on Dalit issues are old hands in the Parliament. Those having no experience on the one hand and those who had been Members of State Assemblies were almost in equal numbers. We can thus conclude that the majority of those who participated in Lok Sabha on Dalit issues have been Members of either Parliament or of State Legislatures.

Why Non-Dalits Participate on Dalit Issues?

We were curious to examine why non-Dalit MPs participate on Dalit issues in the Lok Sabha. An urge was felt to know that whether it is electoral compulsions, party stand or a sympathetic attitude that makes them active on Dalit issues in the Lok Sabha. It was found that majority of them raise issues or participate in, on Dalit issues due to the existence of a sizeable population of SC/STs in their constituencies. Though the population of Dalits in the areas lying in their constituencies varied from 10 per cent to 42 per cent but a majority of these had 20 to 42 per cent SC/ST population.[4] Thus, the electoral compulsions are important, and the underlying cause for non-Dalit MPs' participation during Lok Sabha debates on Dalit issues. For the

4 See Annexure II.

rest, the explanation could be principally a pro-Dalit stand of their parties because majority of them belonged to either a communist party such as CPI, CPI(M), or centrist party like Congress.

Summing Up

The socio-political profile of the MPs participating on Dalit issues reveals that majority of the participants were from SC/STs categories. Secondly, majority of them belonged to the Congress party which has been in power during the 8th and the 10th Lok Sabhas. It indicates that the ruling party MPs are more active than the MPs from opposition parties. Even the MPs from a party whose leadership comes from Dalits, *i.e.*, the BSP were not active during debates in the Lok Sabha. Thirdly, majority of the participants are well qualified. It shows that if education makes the Dalit MPs vocal and participative then it also instills sensitivity among non-Dalit MPs, who get involved on Dalit issues in the Lok Sabha. Fourthly, the participating MPs usually have a history of their involvement in the social and political activities and they have been socially sensitive towards the marginalised sections. Fifthly, the MPs who have already been Members of Parliament or Members of State Legislatures are more participative and concerned on Dalit issues. Finally, we found that the majority of the non-Dalits participating on Dalit matters are from the constituencies, which have a sizeable SC/ST population. It means that the non-Dalit MPs are influenced primarily by electoral compulsions apart from some other factors.

7

Conclusion

The present study is primarily concerned with the contribution of Dalit MPs, to the formulation and influencing of public policies for the upliftment of Dalits. We have chosen to study their role in the Parliament. Even though various studies have shown that the role of Parliament in policy formulation remains quite limited, nevertheless its significance in the overall process of policy formulation cannot be altogether ignored. The legislators are supposed to put forward the grievances and demands of those, whom they represent, and one cannot completely ignore the fact that some of them do raise their voice on the floor of the House. It is a different matter that only a small section of them do it consistently, a few others reluctantly, and the rest may just either support or oppose, actively or passively, those who consistently raise their voices.

Our study regarding the role of the Lok Sabha in policy formulation for Dalits reveals: (i) Dalit issues are not only discussed but legislations are also passed for them in response to the discussions, and (ii) both the Dalit and non-Dalit MPs participate during the debate and discussion. Though Dalit issues are debated and discussed in Lok Sabha but its involvement merely modifies or extends existing Dalit policy paradigm. It hardly enabled alteration or shift in the paradigm as per the demand of times and circumstances.

An analysis of the recommendations of CSCT and NCSCT affirms that their reports address various issues on Dalits, which can be utilised by the MPs in impressing upon the Government to formulate policies to uplift the Dalit masses as per the prevailing and emerging trends.

One of the important findings of the study is the prevalence of gaps at various levels, *viz.*, (i) between the reports of the Commissioner and the Commission and the perspectives adopted by the MPs, and (ii) between the perspectives adopted by the MPs on these reports and the Minister's response to the reports, wherein even the assurances were not provided by the Government. There was hardly any response with regard to framing new policies that are required in the present circumstances. Thus, we can say that the Government has two policies with regard to Dalits, one to formulate policies, and two not to formulate policies and the later over-shadows the previous one.

The MPs used various rules under which Dalit issues were discussed in the Lok Sabha but their major emphasis had been on immediate concerns and primarily on the atrocities. In spite of atrocities having been discussed five times, there was no check on them. So the issue of efficient governance and sensitisation of civil society was raised at last, where the transformation of caste system was emphasised and it was argued that without abrogating the caste atrocities cannot be stopped.

Whether it was Motion, Rule 193, or Adjournment Motion, or amendments on Bills, every time the MPs withdrew their proposals, giving a free hand to the Government to pursue its own proposals on Dalits. Even while passing legislations, MPs' recommendations for amendments were not included in the Bills. The MPs seemed to be merely satisfied with the assurances given by the Government.

Thus, it is obvious that the Government handles the proposals of the MPs on Dalit issues in a rather casual manner and even the Dalit MPs fail to impress upon the Government to consider their proposals, seriously, and diligently.

The number of non-Dalit MPs frequently participating on Dalit matters was lesser in comparison to Dalit MPs, but the quality of participation in terms of arguments and perspectives of Dalit MPs differs little, when compared with the non-Dalit MPs.

Deliberations by the legislators during discussion on the reports of the Commissioner and the Commission revealed articulations for increasing, (i) the funds for welfare activities, (ii) vacancies in various departments and fulfilling them, and (iii) scholarships for students, etc. Another significant aspect points to the fact that while in 1985 the concerns were for raising scholarships, funds, and reserved vacancies, in 1994 the focus shifted to delay in scholarship and non-fulfillment of existing reserved vacancies. Constituency concerns even with regard to short-term objectives were absent. The legislators seldom bothered about the lack of funds for developmental activities *vis-à-vis* Dalits in their constituencies, and hardly raised the issue of atrocities in their areas, in spite of the fact that MPs from states having atrocity-prone areas were present.

Though Members were primarily concerned with short-term objectives, the long-term policy objectives received no less attention. Before the conferment of constitutional status to the CSCT, they kept raising this issue during the 1985 discussion. However, constitutional status of 1990 also did not satisfy them and they pushed for the Commission to be strengthened with adequate budget and staff for its proper functioning. Another aspect for the proper implementation of safeguards was related to the constitution of a separate ministry for SC/STs or to bring Dalit subject under the MHA. With regard to containing atrocities, the legislators were not happy with the PCRA, and felt the need for a more stringent act to punish the guilty for atrocities against Dalits and special courts with Dalit personnels in atrocity-prone areas, etc. Legislation of laws on land reforms to enable proper distribution of land to the landless Dalits, was another area of concern of the MPs.

With regard to compensatory discrimination they argued for a Special Recruitment Drive to fulfill the backlog in government jobs. In 1992, the Mandal Commission judgement on the withdrawal of SC/ST reservations in promotions attracted their attention. They earnestly took up the matter during the 1994 discussion on the Commissioner's reports. However, the MPs raised the issue of adverse impact of the liberalisation process on Dalits and asked the Government to come out with the necessary Bill to safeguard Dalit interests.

While replying to the debate on the Motions on reports, the Government was able to satisfy the Members of following a coherent policy towards the Dalit problem. In a 1985 reply to the Motion, the Minister of Welfare convinced the Members with regard to the existence of review committees at the state, district and *Taluqa* levels for the welfare of these groups. Members were also informed that the Ministry of Welfare was already working as a nodal agency so that polices are implemented. None of the two ministers who replied the Debate in 1985 satisfactorily addressed the question of constitutional status to the Commission. It was merely reiterated in a cliched manner, that the matter would be looked into.

One of the issues raised by a majority of the MPs relates to the question of punishment to the officers involved in non-implementation of policies meant for Dalits. The Ministers neither told what is being done nor promised to come out with sufficient concrete measures or a policy to check the conduct of the officials *vis-à-vis* Dalits. The responsibility was put on the state governments. Facts and figures were merely reeled out with regard to various schemes and allocation of funds for them. Such presentations by the Government were undertaken to merely dilute the attention of the MPs while replying to the Motion, in 1994. But the Government was unable to provide figures for those erring officials who were responsible for non-implementation of backlog and the welfare schemes meant for Dalits.

Several policy issues like the need for legislation to ensure reservations in promotions, representation in private sector, promotion of scavengers to group 'D' services, providing share to tribals in newly created assets, and reviewing the ongoing projects in tribal areas were ignored by the Government. Also the constitution of the Commission to report on the Administration of Scheduled Areas and welfare of STs in the States were ignored by the Government. Even though some Members reminded the Minister in-charge of these issues, the latter preferred to reel off statistics, while ignoring the policy aspects.

The Government neither in 1985 nor in 1994 was able to satisfy the MPs who raised the issue of punishment to officers who did not implement the policies meant for Dalit upliftment. They wanted some assurance as state governments were not paying heed to orders and guidelines issued by the Central Government. But on both the occasions, the Ministers reiterated that they will look in to it and had asked for clarification from the states. The discussion on the Reports of the Commissioner and the Commission reveal that Dalit policies are indeed deliberated upon by the Lok Sabha. But the legislators' emphasis is more often on strengthening the mechanism of policy implementation rather than pursuing representation of Dalits in 'untouched areas' such as private sectors, Supreme Court, and High Courts, etc. One of the important issues raised by the Commissioner's reports was to constitute a Commission to report on the administration of the Scheduled Areas and the Welfare of STs under Article 339, but the MPs failed to mention it during the debates. Though some questions on education were asked, the issue of effectively providing the SC/STs with better educational facilities and thus making them self-reliant failed to find mention in the debates. Thus, there have been some gaps between the recommendations of the CSCT and the perspectives adopted by the MPs. At the same time only occasional demands are made for such provisions but not pursued by, and the MPs are more or less satisfied with the replies of the Ministers.

In many circumstances, the need to formulate policies in the arena 'untouched areas' was usually ignored. Assurance for a time-bound programme for these to materialise remained a far cry. Even with regard to reservations in Central services other ministeries were roped in to say that it does not come within the purview of Ministry of Welfare. When the legislators reminded the Government of its role of co-ordination to safeguard the Dalit interests, the ministers respond in a cliched manner, that "orders in specific matters can be issued", or "the matter will be looked into."

The reports of the Commissioner and the Commission for SC/STs, show that they provided sufficient feedback to the MPs and the Government to formulate policies in view of the emerging scenario. These recommendations were made not only to strengthen but also to alter the existing Dalit policy paradigm. Though the major emphasis on the reports of the commission has been on compensatory discrimination *i.e.* reservations in jobs and education, but the prime emphasis of the Commissioner's reports was on the proper distribution of land to the SCs and to protect the land rights of the STs, because majority of them, it was argued, depend on land for their livelihood. This observation gets strengthened when we relate the remarks of Mandalsohn and Vicziany (1998) who argue that even if 100 per cent quota meant for Dalits is fulfilled in jobs even then merely two per cent of them would be able to come up in life. But MPs, especially the Dalit MPs, who should have utilised the reports to alter the policy paradigm on Dalits have miserably failed to discharge their duties and obligations effectively and conscientiously.

We also found that the constitutional status granted to the CSCT did not help much because the discussion on its reports did not take place in time. And the MPs did not raise the question of absence of discussion on the fresh reports.

Thus policy perspectives by the legislators show concern for strengthening existing institutional mechanisms and creating new ones for proper policy implementation. They also termed present policies of the government as inadequate, and inefficient and offered alternatives. Broadly, the policy issues the legislators have been concerned with are: stringent law to deal with atrocities, strengthening institutional mechanism of the Commission for SC/STs by providing it constitutional status, shifting the Dalit subject from the MHA to the MW, ensuring efficient land distribution for Dalits, fulfilling the backlog in government jobs, legislating in the light of Mandal Commission judgement for reservations in promotions, and providing reservations in private sectors in the event of liberalisation process, etc.

Policy proposals of the Government relate to atrocities, constitutional status for SC/STs, reservations to Buddhist converts, constitution of National Commission for *Safai Karamcharis*, and reservations in promotions. Regarding two major perspectives, one on land reforms and the other on reservations in private sector, no policy proposal came forth from the Government. Though in the 9th Lok Sabha, assurance was given to put this issue on land reforms under the 9th Schedule of the Constitution, but no legislation was introduced in this regard. The PCWSCT came out with a comprehensive report on private sector reservations. However the Government did not respond positively on the issue.

Legislators not only participated on policy proposals of the Government but also asked for amendments on the proposals. We have observed that the MPs were dissatisfied with implementation of the policies during deliberations on all the five Bills. They usually drifted away from the subject matter of the Bills, be it a debate on NCSCT or NCSK, and the interventions do not reflect on strengthening these mechanisms as institutions. Significantly, ancillary and related aspects were focussed more than the main themes of the Bill. For instance, asking for special tribunal for SC/ST employees on the lines of Central Administrative Tribunal while discussing NCSCT Bill, representation of Dalits in judiciary while deliberating upon NCSK Bill and providing reservation in private sector and emphasis on OBC reservation during discussion on the 77th Amendment Bill. Thus the deliberations were tangent and went off target, and were devoid of focussed discussion on a particular Bill; this applies both to Dalit and non-Dalit MPs.

The MPs have been less active during proposing amendments to a Bill. In the case of Prevention of Atrocities Bill, no amendment was introduced by Dalit MPs whereas a non-Dalit MP introduced eight amendments. While passing the NCSCT Bill, two Dalit and one non-Dalit MP moved amendments. During the SC order Amendment Bill two non-Dalit and one Dalit MP moved amendments; no amendment was however, introduced, while passing of NCSK Bill. It was during the 77th Amendment Bill that the Dalit and non-Dalit MPs were equally active for amendments.

If we look at the policy proposals of the Government in terms of Bills and Statements, it can be shown that the Government was more responsive during the 9th and 10th Lok Sabha as compared to the 8th Lok Sabha. There had been only one Bill that was passed in the 8th Lok Sabha, and it related to the prevention of atrocities against Dalits. No policy statement was made during the 8th Lok Sabha. Our hypothesis that the Lok Sabha has become more active towards Dalits in the post-

Mandal period stands vindicated. Even all the four PCWSCT Reports on policies were prepared in the post-Mandal period.

Legislators have been more active on three occasions - one, during NCSCT Bill, two, while passing SC order Amendment Bill, and three, while passing the 77th Amendment Bill.

Though MPs were more active in the post-Mandal period for amendments in the Bills, but these amendments were not to strengthen the themes contained in them but rather for extending facilities to bring more groups within the framework of special safeguards. While passing the SC Order Bill in 1990, the major emphasis was to include Christian and Muslim converts in the SC list. Similarly, it was the inclusion of OBCs in the promotional benefits that was the focus of the 77th Amendment Bill.

So far as responsiveness of the regimes in power in concerned, V.P. Singh Government was more responsive towards legislative deliberations as could be seen, when the NCSCT Bill was passed and many new clauses were added to the original Bill. At no other point of time the amendments introduced by the MPs were added to the original Bill.

Even the PCWSCT Reports had minor impact on Dalit policy paradigm. Although the reports were able to bridge some of the gaps left by legislative debates, *e.g.* on private sector reservations and fulfillment of backlog (regarding which two separate Reports were prepared), but the Government's response to these reports was both poor and muted. No substantive policy issue raised and recommended by the Committee was tackled positively by the Government. It shows that PCWSCT may have tried to bridge the gaps left by legislative deliberations but the Government remained unaffected and unaltered on Dalit policy questions.

Thus, the role of Lok Sabha and especially of Dalit MPs in the process of policy formulation to alter Dalit policy paradigm remains insignificant. For instance, if the Prevention of Atrocities Act was passed, it was merely a modification of the Protection of Civil Rights Act, and if the 65th Amendment was passed, it was an extension of powers of the already existing Commission for SC/STs. Yet again, establishing the National Commission of *Safai Karamcharis* was extension of the National Scheme for Elimination of Scavenging and Disposal of Night Soil. Moreover, four Acts were passed for the extension of facilities to few other communities by bringing them into the SC/STs list. And it had little or no impact on the safeguards for

Dalits as such but favoured a few more deprived sections, with reservation benefits. Above all, the 77th Amendment Bill was nothing but continuation of the previous facility of reservation in promotions, that was withdrawn by the Supreme Court by the Mandal Commission verdict.

In spite of frequent commission of atrocities during the period of our study, not even once the MPs moved a 'No Confidence Motion' against the Government. It also indicates the apathy of both, the Government and the Parliament towards Dalit issues. Quite surprisingly, no proper discussion took place on the burning issue of privatisation and liberalisation that was taking place in the country. Only once, a half-an-hour discussion on the subject was held, and as usual the Minister kept assuring the MPs that "we are committed to the welfare of SC/STs" but did not mention how the rights of SC/STs employees will be protected after the privatisation of Delhi Electricity Supply Undertaking (DESU).

The concerns raised during Question Hour show the major emphasis to be on economic developmental aspects, particularly on jobs in the public sector, and welfare schemes. The question of land distribution which has an adverse impact on the major chunk of Dalit population did not merit the concern of the MPs. The issue of social upliftment found some mention but here too atrocities attracted more attention than education, housing, health facilities, etc.

There was no significant difference between the inquiries on the Starred and Unstarred questions. Even the Starred questions could not elicit specific information except the one contained in the various reports of the NCSCT. No harsh facts were produced except showing how marginal improvements were made as compared to previous years. Moreover, the reply of Government to these questions was always cliched and stereotypical.

During the supplementaries as well, the MPs did not raise policy issues. They could not even pursuade the Government to continue the schemes which had benefited Dalits and had shown a considerable success as was in the case of *Kutir Yojna* in Orissa. In another supplementary question on development of peripheral areas in and around the coal-fields, and on the rehabilitation policy, the Members were satisfied with the Minister's response that the Government would come out with a fresh rehabilitation poiicy for the tribals. They did not quiz the government, as to what were the basic components of the policy being proposed.

Based on the analysis of Question Hour, a peculiar contradiction can be seen with regard to the implementation of schemes and programmes. The Central Government escapes its responsibilities by bringing the state governments in, and whenever new policies need to be formulated, it takes up the responsibility.

The questions on the review of reservation policy and reservations in promotions have been the major policy questions asked by the Members. Both these questions were also asked by non-Dalit legislators.

Questions on atrocities were purely on implementation failures which asked the Government for follow-up, after recommending the state governments to check them. The information provided by the Minister mentioned merely the number of atrocities committed, rather than the measures adopted to curtail them.

Two policy inquiries were made under Starred questions, namely; (a) reservation in admission in public schools, and (b) representation of SC/STs as judges in Supreme Courts and High Courts. But no discussion was initiated by the MPs on the reply of the Minister who admitted the prevalence of poor representation of Dalits in the Supreme and the High Courts, and non-existence of reservations in public schools.

Our argument thus holds forth the view, that the legislators hardly raise demands on adequate representation of Dalits in the areas untouched by the original Dalit policy paradigm. Even if such demands are remotely raised, there is a lack of pursuance by them.

The substantive concerns of the legislators during the Question Hour largely show prevalence of phenomenal representation, where implementation of safeguards assumes importance. The demands are seldom in the direction to strengthen the implementation mechanism, nor formulate new policies. Even if rarely there are demands to strengthen the implementation agencies, and for new policies to uplift the Dalits, these are not pursued vigorously. The replies of the ministers, whether or not to come out with new proposals, is not an issue which is discussed and debated further. Thus, the legislators seem to be generally content with the replies and even if sometimes they remain dissatisfied, they do not pursue their dissatisfaction to force the Minister to take proactive policy measures.

The socio-political profile of the MPs participating on Dalit issues reveal that the majority of the participants are from SC/STs categories, and belonged to the Congress Party. Even the MPs from a party whose leadership comes from Dalits were not active during debates in the Lok Sabha. Majority of the participants are well qualified, showing that education makes the Dalit MPs vocal and participative, and brings sensitivity among non-Dalits, who are thus involved on Dalit issues in the Lok Sabha. The participating MPs usually had a history of their involvement in the social and political activities and they were socially sensitive towards the marginalised sections. Previous experience also made the participants more participative and concerned with the Dalit issues. However, our belief is that the participation of the non-Dalits was more due to electoral compulsions.

Our analysis reveals that the MPs are neither committed to their Dalit constituents nor do they play a role in policy shifts for the broader Dalit interests. They remain confined to the issues of implementation and thus there is no policy change in the Dalit policy paradigm due to Parliament's involvement in the policy-making process. The impact of recommendations of the NCSCT and MP's deliberations is limited to development and minor modification of prevalent policies.

In the light of the above analysis, it is being recommended that the Parliament and especially the Dalit representatives in it need to impress upon the Government to formulate policies in the areas where they have no legal claims, such as public schools, judges in Supreme Court and High Courts, and above all in the private sector, and proper implementation of land reforms. A regular discussion on the reports of NCSCT should ensue so that the MPs are aware of the present Dalit conditions and pressurise the Government to formulate policies accordingly. The MPs are expected not only to protest against the Government's attitude of neglecting their opinions but also to walk out of the House to register their resentment. The question Hour and discussion on Starred questions in particular is also required not merely on the question of policy implementation but for policy formulation as well. The PCWSCST should be made more policy-oriented so that it can also help in strengthening the demands in favour of policy shifts.

We have observed that the atrocities against Dalits are being discussed time and again with hardly any effective check on their commission. In this regard, there is a need to fix responsibility on the concerned administrative apparatus, and if no change takes place, then the Chief Ministers of the respective states need to be made accountable, and if need arises, Article 356 should be imposed on the errant state. Measures should also be taken to sensitise the society against prevalent attitudes, through mass media and people egged to cherish civil society initiatives.

Thus, we have been able to assess: (i) what Dalit parliamentarians do in the Lok Sabha, (ii) how do they put Dalit issues on policy agenda, and (iii) what is the reaction of the Government to their proposals. However, questions like why Dalit MPs behave in a particular fashion, and why the Government ignores alteration of Dalit policy paradigm need to be analysed. There is neither a lack of interest as shown during the deliberations, nor dearth of information on Dalit issues, as NCSCT reports would suggest. Therefore, the question as to why policy shifts do not take place needs to be examined. One explanation for Dalit MPs not being able to pursue a radical agenda relates to the structural limitations of their representation through joint electorates. But, whether rigidities of the party leadership also influence their behaviour in a particular manner needs to be looked into by further research. Future researches can examine the validity of joint electorates as the reason for lack of Dalit MPs' inability to pursue the agenda of radical changes in the policies for Dalit masses.

We are convinced that the Lok Sabha being the representative body of the whole Indian society can put the need for social transformation on the national agenda by looking at the Dalit question as a central problem of Indian social and political system to be tackled with efficient and responsive governance and civil society initiatives.

Appendix I

Active MPs on the Dalit Matters

S.No.	*Name of the MP*	*Constituency*	*Category*	*Party*	*Education*	*Nature of Organisation*	*Previous Experience*
(1)	*(2)*	*(3)*	*(4)*	*(5)*	*(6)*	*(7)*	*(8)*
1.	Ramashray P. Singh	Jahanabad	OT	CPI	UM	P	LA
2.	Arvind Netam	Kanker	ST	Cong.	G	No	Y
3.	Anadi Charan Das	Jajpur	SC	Cong.	M	P	Y
4.	Amar Roy Pradhan	Coochbehar	SC	FB	M	PS	Y
5.	Uttam Rathod	Hingoli	OT	Cong.	G	S	Y
6.	Ganga Ram	Firozabad	SC	Cong.	G	S	M
7.	Ram Bahdur Singh	Maharajgang	OT	JD	G	PS	LA
8.	R.P. Suman	Akbarpur	SC	Cong.	G	PS	N
9.	Virdhi Chander Jain	Barmer	OT	Cong.	G	S	Y
10.	Ram Swaroop Ram	Gaya	SC	Cong.	G	S	Y
11.	Bapu Lal Malviya	Shajapur	SC	Cong.	G	S	LA
12.	Manikrao Hodlya Gavit	Nandurbar	ST	Cong.	M	P	Y
13.	K.D. Sultan Puri	Shimla	SC	Cong.	UM	PS	Y
14.	Ram Ratan Ram	Hajipur	SC	Cong.	G	S	LA
15.	Ram Payare Panika	Robertsganj	SC	Cong.	G	PS	Y
16.	Kammodilal Jatav	Morena	SC	Cong.	UM	P	LA
17.	Manku Ram Sodi	Bastar	ST	Cong.	M	No	LA
18.	K.S. Rao	Machilipatnama	OT	Cong.	G	S	N
19.	Harish Rawat	Almora	OT	Cong.	M	PS	Y
20.	Syed Shahaduddin	Kishanganj	OT	Janta	G	P	N
21.	G.S. Rajhans	Jhanjharpur	OT	Cong.	D	PS	N
22.	Sunder Singh	Phillaur	SC	Cong.	NA	NA	NA

Contd.

(1)	*(2)*	*(3)*	*(4)*	*(5)*	*(6)*	*(7)*	*(8)*
23.	Phulrenu Guha	Contai	OT	Cong.	D	PS	Y
24.	Mamta Bannerjee	Jadavpur	OT	Cong.	D	PS	N
25.	Mayawati	Bijor	SC	BSP	G	PS	N
26.	R.N. Rakesh	Chail	SC	Cong.	G	PS	Y
27.	Khemchanbhai Somabhai Chandra	Patan	SC	JD	G	PS	Y
28.	Ratilal Kalidas Verma	Dhanduka	ST	BJP	G	PS	No
29.	Kalka Das	Karol Bagh	SC	BJP	G	S	No
30.	Jagpal Singh	Hardwar	SC	Cong.	G	PS	Y
31.	Prem Pradip	Nawada	SC	CPM	G	PS	No
32.	Ram Sajiwan	Banda	OT	CPI	G	PS	LA
33.	Hari Bhau Shankar Mahale	Malegoan	ST	JD	UM	No	Y
34.	Satyanarayan Jatia	Ujjain	SC	BJP	G	PS	Y
35.	Keyur Bhushan	Raipur	OT	Cong.	UM	PS	Y
36.	Chintamani Jena	Balasore	OT	Cong.	UM	S	Y
37.	Chhedi Paswan	Sasaram	SC	JD	PG	PS	Y
38.	Lalaram Ken	Bayana	SC	Cong.	M	S	Y
39.	Banwari lal Bairwa	Tonk	SC	Cong.	G	PS	Y
40.	Chinta Mohan	Tirupati	SC	TDP	G	No	No
41.	Narsinh Makwana	Dhandhuka	SC	Cong.	UM	PS	Y
42.	M.R. Halder	Mathurapur	SC	Cong.	PG	S	LA
43.	R.P. Das	Krishnagar	OT	CPM	PG	PS	Y
44.	Bangali Singh	Hathras	OT	JD	G	S	LA
45.	Chhavi Ram Agral	Morena	OT	BJP	G	PS	Y
46.	Ramji Lal Suman	Firozabad	SC	JD	G	No	No
47.	Het Ram	Sirsa	SC	JD	PG	PS	Y
48.	Than Singh Yatav	Bayana	SC	BJP	G	PS	No
49.	Kusuma K. Murthy	Amlapuram	SC	Cong.	PG	PS	Y
50.	Gopal Pacherwal	Tonk	SC	JD	M	PS	LA
51.	Bhagwan Das	Nawada	SC	NA	NA	NA	NA
52.	Ramnarain Berwa	Tonk	SC	BJP	G	P	No
53.	Rajnath Sonkarshastri	Saidpur	SC	JD	PG	PS	Y
54.	Mrutyunjaya Nayak	Phulbani	SC	Cong.	PG	PS	Y
55.	Govind Chander Munda	Keonjhar	ST	JD	M	NO	Y
56.	Mukul B. Wasnik	Buldana	SC	Cong	PG	PS	Y
57.	Bhagey Gobardhen	Mayur Bhanj	SC	JD	PG	PS	Y

Contd.

(1)	*(2)*	*(3)*	*(4)*	*(5)*	*(6)*	*(7)*	*(8)*
58.	K. Pradhani	Nowrangpur	ST	Cong.	M	No	Y
59.	Koddikunnil Suresh	Adoor	SC	Cong.	G	S	Y
60.	A.K. Patel	Mehsana	OT	BJP	PG	P	Y
61.	Phool Chand Verma	Shajapur	SC	Cong.	G	S	Y
62.	Shravan Kumar Patel	Jabalpur	OT	Cong.	G	S	LA
63.	Ramvilas Paswan	Rosera	SC	JD	PG	PS	Y
64.	Pius Tirkey	Alipurduars	SC	RSP	M	NO	Y
65.	Lalit Oran	Lohardaga	ST	BJP	M	PS	LA
66.	N.J. Rathva	Chhota Udaipur	ST	Cong.	PG	S	Y
67.	Khelan Ram Jangde	Bilaspur	OT	BJP	G	NO	Y
68.	Gabhaji Mangaji Takore	Kapadvanj	OT	BJP	M	NO	Y
69.	Chitubhai Gamit	Mandvi	ST	Cong.	G	PS	Y
70.	P. Vallal Peruman	Chidambaram	SC	Cong.	PG	PS	Y

SC Scheduled Castes
ST Scheduled Tribes
OT Others (Non-SC/ST)
BJP Bhartiya Janta Party
Cong. Congress (I)
JD Janta Dal
CPI Communist Party of India
P Political
NA Not Available
Y Member of Parliament
NO None
LA Member of Legislative Assembly
CPM Community Party of India (Marxists)

PG Post Graduate
G Graduate
M Matric
UM Under Matric
D Doctorate
PS Political Social
S Social
TDP Telgu Deshan Party
RSP Revolutionary Socialist Party
BSP Bhahujan Samaj Party

Appendix II

Population of SC/STs in the Constituencies of Active Non-Dalit MPs

Constituency	*Total*	*SC*	*ST*	*Percentage of Dalits*
Machilipatanam	3698833	613230	91767	19.00
Jhanjharpur	2832024	363687	597	12.80
Jahanabad	1174900	216083	238	18.40
Kishanganj	984107	65157	34830	10.16
Mehsana	2937810	263655	10907	9.34
Kapadvang	4801812	553846	42574	12.60
Morena	1710574	340241	95216	25.45
Jabalpur	2649962	339912	474466	30.73
Bilaspur	3793566	687221	873741	41.15
Raipur	3908042	563577	714027	32.67
Hingoli	2117035	233323	111470	16.29
Balasore	2802417	555069	197992	26.87
Barmer	1435222	225324	84232	21.57
Hathrus	3295982	758308	127	23.01
Maharajganj	1676378	325270	2691	19.56
Almora	8636617	184237	2739	22.35
Banda	1862139	432884	43	23.25
Krishnagar	3852097	1117506	90525	31.36
Contai	8331912	1361828	689636	24.62
Jadarpur	3729644	588907	10090	16.00

Source: Census/1991 of India, Final Population, Table SC/ST.

Appendix III

Parliamentary Acts on SC/STs 1985-95

Bill No. 93-F of 1987

The Constitution (Fifty-Seventh Amendment) Bill, 1987 (as passed by The Houses of Parliament)

A bill further to amend the Constitution of India.

Be it enacted by Parliament in the Thirty-eighth Year of the Republic of India as follow:

1. (a) This Act may be called the Constitution (Fifty-seventh Amendment) Act, 1987.

   (b) It shall come into force on such date as the Central Government may, by notification in the Official gazette, appoint.

2. (a) In article 332 of the Constitution, after clause (3), the following clause shall be inserted, namely:

   (b) Notwithstanding anything contained in clause (3), until the taking effect, under article 170, of the re-adjustment, on the basis of the first census after the year 2000 of the number of seats in the Legislative assemblies of the States of Arunachal Pradesh, Meghalaya, Mizoram and Nagaland, the seats which shall be reserved for the Scheduled tribes in the Legislative Assembly of any such State shall be,-

      (i) if all the seats in the Legislative Assembly of such State in existence on the date of coming into force of the Constitution (Fifty-seventh Amendment) Act, 1987 (hereafter in this clause referred to as the existing Assemble) are held by members of the scheduled Tribes, all the seats except one

      (ii) in any other case, such number of seats as bears to the total number of seats a proportion not less than the number (as on the said date) of members belonging to the

Scheduled tribes in the existing Assembly bears to the total number of seats in the existing Assembly."

3. The amendment made to article 332 of the Constitution by sub-section (1) shall not affect any representation in the Legislative Assembly of the State of Meghalaya or the Legislative Assembly of the State of Mizoram or the Legislative Assembly of the State of Nagaland until the dissolution of the Legislative Assembly of the State of Arunachal Pradesh or the Legislative Assembly of the State of Meghalaya or the Legislative Assembly of the State of Mizoram or the Legislative Assembly of the State of Nagaland existing at the commencement of this Act.

Bill No. 104-F of 1987

The constitution (scheduled tribes) order (amendment) bill, 1987 (As Passed by the Houses of Parliament)

A bill to provide for the inclusion of certain tribes in the list of Scheduled

Tribes specified in relation to the State of Meghalaya.

BE it enacted by Parliament in the Thirty-eighth year of the Republic of India as follows:-

1. (1) This Act may be called the Constitution (Scheduled Tribes) order (Amendment) Act, 1987.
   (2) It shall be deemed to have come into force on the 19th day of September, 1987.
2. In the Scheduled to the Constitution (Scheduled Tribes) Order, 1950 (hereinafter referred to as the principal Order), in "Part XI.– *Meghalaya"*, after item 14, the following items shall be inserted, namely:

   "15. Boro Kacharis, 16. Koch, 17. Raba, Rava".
3. (1) The Constitution (Scheduled Tribes) Order (Amendment) Ordinance, 1987, is hereby repealed.
   (2) Notwithstanding such repeal, anything done or any action taken under the principal Order, as amended by the said ordinance, shall be deemed to have been done or taken under the principal Order, as amended by this Act.

The Scheduled Castes and the Scheduled Tribes (Prevention of Atrocities) Act, 1989.

Act No. 33 of 1989 (11th September, 1989)

An Act to prevent the commission of offences of atrocities against the members of the Scheduled Castes and the scheduled Tribes, to provide for Special Courts for the trial of such offences and for the relief and rehabilitation of the victims of such offences and for matters connected therewith or incidental thereto.

Be it enacted by Parliament in the Fortieth Year of the Republic of India as follows:

Chapter I

Preliminary

1. Short title, extent and commencement.
   - (a) This Act may be called the Scheduled Castes and the Scheduled Tribes (Prevention of Atrocities) Act, 1989.
   - (b) (2) It extends to the whole of India except the State of Jammu and Kashmir.
   - (c) (3) It shall come into force on such date[1] as the Central government may, by notification in the Official Gazette, appoint.
2. Definition
   - (d) In this Act, unless the context otherwise requires,-
   - (e) "atrocity" means an offence punishable under section 3;
   - (f) "code" means the Code of Criminal Procedure, 1973 (2 of 1974);
   - (g) "scheduled Castes and Scheduled tribes" shall have the meanings assigned to them respectively under clause (24) and clause (25) of article 366 of the Constitution;
   - (h) "special Court" means a Court of Session specified as a Special Court in section 14;
   - (i) "special Public Prosecutor" means a public Prosecutor specified as a Special Public prosecutor or an advocate referred to in section 15;
   - (j) words and expressions used but not defined in this Act and defined in the Code or the Indian Penal Code (45 of 1860) shall have the meanings assigned to them respectively in the Code, or as the case may be, in the Indian Penal Code.

3. Any reference in this Act to any enactment or any provision thereof shall, in relation to an area in which such enactment or such provision is not in force, be construed as a reference to the corresponding law, if any, in force in that area.

Chapter II

Offences of atrocities

1. Punishments for offences of atrocities: (1) Whoever, not being a member of a scheduled Caste or a Scheduled tribes...
   (a) forces member of a Scheduled Caste or a Scheduled Tribe to drink or eat any inedible or obnoxious substance;
   (b) acts with intent to cause injury, insult or annoyance to any member of a Scheduled Caste or a scheduled tribe by dumping excreta, waste matter, careasses or any other obnoxious substance in his premises or neighbourhood.
   (c) forcibly removes clothes from the person of a member of a Scheduled Caste or a Scheduled tribe or parades him naked or with painted face or body or commits any similar act which is derogatory to human dignity;
   (d) wrongfully occupies or cultivates any land owned by, or allotted to, or notified by any competent authority to be allotted to, a member of a Scheduled Caste or a Scheduled tribe or gets the land allotted to him transferred;
   (e) wrongfully dispossesses a member of a Scheduled Caste or a Scheduled Tribe form his land or premises or interferes with the enjoyment of his rights over any land, premises or water;
   (f) compels or entices a member of a Scheduled Caste or a Scheduled Tribe to do '*begar*' or other similar forms of forces or bonded labour other than any compulsory service for public purposes imposed by Government;
   (g) forces or intimidates a member of a Scheduled Caste or a Scheduled Tribe not to vote or to vote to a particular candidate or to vote in a manner other than that provided by law;
   (h) institutes false, malicious or vexatious suit or criminal or other legal proceedings against a member of a Scheduled Caste or a Scheduled Tribe;
   (i) gives, any false or frivolous information to any public servant and thereby causes such public servant to use his lawful power to the injury or annoyance of a member of a Scheduled Caste or a Scheduled tribes;

(j) intentionally insults or intimidates with intent to humiliate a member of a Scheduled Caste or a Scheduled Tribe in any place within public view;

(k) assaults or uses force to any woman belonging to a Scheduled Caste or a Scheduled tribe with intent to dishonour or outrage her modesty;

(l) being in a position to dominate the will of a woman belonging to a Scheduled Caste or a Scheduled Tribe and uses that position to exploit her sexually to which she would not have otherwise agreed;

(m) corrupt or fouls the water of any spring, reservoir or any other source ordinarily used by members of the Scheduled Castes or the scheduled Tribes so as to render it less fit for the purpose for which it is ordinarily used;

(n) denies a member of a scheduled Caste or a Scheduled tribes any customary right of passage to a place of public resort or obstructs such member so as to prevent him from using or having access to a place of public resort to which other members of public or any section thereof have a right to use or access to;

(o) forces or causes a member of a scheduled Caste or a scheduled Tribe to leave his house, village or other place of residence.

(p) shall be punishable with imprisonment for a term which shall not be less than six months but which may extend to five years and with fine.

2. Whoever, not being a member of a SC or ST,

(a) gives or fabricates false evidence intending thereby to cause, or knowing it to be likely that he will there by cause, any member of a Scheduled Caste or a Scheduled Tribe to be convicted of an offence which is capital by the law for the being in force shall be punished with imprisonment for life and with fine; and if an innocent member of a Scheduled Caste or a Scheduled Tribe be convicted and executed in consequence of such false or fabricated evidence, the person who gives or fabricates such false evidence, shall be punished with death;

(b) gives or fabricates false evidence intending thereby to cause or knowing it to be likely that he will thereby cause, any member of a Scheduled Caste or a Scheduled Tribe to be convicted of an offence which is not capital but punishable with imprisonment for a term of seven years or upwards, shall be punishable with imprisonment for a term which shall not be less than six months but which may extend to seven years or upwards and with fine;

(c) commits mischief by fire or any explosive substance intending to cause, or knowing it to be likely that he will thereby cause damage to any property belonging to a member of a Scheduled Caste or Scheduled Tribe, shall be punishable with imprisonment for a term which shall not be less than six months but which may extend to seven years and with fine;

(d) commits mischief by fire or any explosive substance intending to cause or knowing it to be likely that he will thereby cause destruction of any building which is ordinarily used as a place of worship or as a place for human dwelling or as a place for custody of the property by a member of a Scheduled Caste or a Scheduled Tribe, shall be punishable with imprisonment for life and with fine;

(e) commits any offence under the Indian Penal Code (45 of 1860) punishable with imprisonment for a term of ten years or more against a person or property on the ground that such person is a member of a scheduled Caste or a Scheduled Tribe or such property belongs to such member, shall be punishable with imprisonment for life and with fine;

(f) knowingly or having reason to believe that an offence has been committed under this Chapter, causes any evidence of the commission of that offence to disappear with the intention of screening the offender from legal punishment, or with that intention gives any information respecting the offence which he knows or believes to be false, shall be punishable with the punishment provided for that offence; or

(g) being a public servant, commits any offence under this section, shall be punishable with imprisonment for a term which shall not be less than one year but which may extend to the punishment provided for that offence.

3. Punishment for neglect of duties–whoever, being a public servant but not being a member of a Scheduled Caste or a Scheduled Tribe, wilfully neglects his duties required to be performed by him under this Act, shall be punishable with imprisonment for a term with shall not be less than six months but which may extend to one year.

4. Enhanced punishment for subsequent conviction—whoever, having already been convicted of an offence under this Chapter is convicted for the second offence or any offence subsequent to the

second offence, shall be punishable with imprisonment for a term which shall not be less than one year but which may extend to the punishment provided for that offence.

5. Application of certain provision of the Indian penal Code– Subject to the other provisions of this Act, the provisions of section 34, Chapter III, Chapter IV, Chapter V, Chapter VA, section 149 and Chapter XXIII of the India Penal Code (45 of 1860), shall so far as may be, apply for the purposes of this Act as they apply for the purposes of the Indian Penal Code.

6. Forfeiture of property of certain persons.:

   (a) Where a person has been convicted of any offence punishable under this Chapter, the Special Court may, in addition to awarding any punishment, by order in writing, declare that any property, movable or immovable or both, belonging to the person, which has been used for the commission of that offence shall stand forfeited to Government.

   (b) Where any person is accused of any offence under this Chapter, it shall be open to the Special Court trying him to pass an order that all or any of the properties, movable or immovable or both, belonging to him, shall, during the period of such trial, be attached, and where trial ends in conviction, the property so attached shall be liable to forfeiture to the extent it is required for the purpose of realisation of any fine imposed under this Chapter.

7. Presumption as to offence—In a prosecution for an offence under this Chapter, if it is proved that:

   (a) the accused rendered any financial assistance to a person accused of, or reasonably suspected of committing, an offence under this Chapter, the Special Court shall presume unless the contrary is proved, that such person had abetted the offence;

   (b) a group of persons committed an offence under this Chapter if it is proved that the offence committed was a sequel to any existing dispute regarding lands or any other matter, it shall be presumed that the offence was committed in furthermore of the common intention or in prosecution of the common object.

8. Conferment of Power.

   (a) Notwithstanding anything contained in the Code or in any other provision of this Act, the State Government may, if it consider it necessary or expedient so to do–

(i) for the prevention of and for coping with any offence under this Act, or

(ii) for any case or class or group of cases under this Act, in any district or part thereof, confer, by notification in the Official gazette, on any officer of the State Government, the powers exercisable by a police officer under the Code in such district to part thereof or, as the case may be for such case or class or group of cases, and in particular, the powers of arrest, investigation and prosecution of persons before any Special Court.

(b) All officers of police and all other officers of Government shall assist the officer referred to in sub-section (1) in the execution of the provision of this Act or any rule, scheme or order made thereunder.

(c) The provisions of the Code shall, so far as may be, apply to the exercise of the powers by an officer under sub-section (1).

Chapter III

Externment

1. Removal of person likely to commit offence.

(a) Where the Special Court is satisfied, upon a complaint or a police report that a person is likely to commit an offence under Chapter II of this Act in any area included in "Scheduled Areas " or ' tribal areas' as referred to in article 244 of the Constitution, it may, by order in writing direct such person to remove himself beyond the limits of such area, by such route and within such time as may be specified in the order, and not to return to that area from which he was directed to remove himself for such period, not exceeding two years, as may be specified in the order.

(b) The Special Court shall, along with the order under sub-section (1), communicate to the person directed under that sub-section the grounds on which such order has been made.

(c) The Special Court may revoke or modify the order made under sub-section (1), for the reasons to be recorded in writing, on the representation made by the person against whom such order has been made or by any other person on his behalf within thirty days from the date of the order.

2. Procedure on failure of person to remove himself from area and enter thereon after removal.

(a) If a person to whom a direction has been issued under section 10 to remove himself from any area–

(i) fails to remove himself as directed; or

(ii) having so removed himself enters such area within the period specified in the order, Otherwise than with the permission in writing of the Special Court under sub-section (2), the Special Court may cause him to be arrested and removed in police custody to such place outside such area as the Special Court may specify.

(b) The Special Court may, by order in writing, permit any person in respect of whom an order under section 10 has been made, to return to the area from which he was directed to remove himself for such temporary period and subject to such conditions as may be specified in such order and may require him to execute a bond with or without surety for the due observation of the conditions imposed.

(c) The Special Court may at any time revoke any such permission.

(d) Any person who, with such permission, returns to the area from which he was directed to remove himself shall observe the conditions imposed, and at the expiry of the temporary period for which he was permitted to return, or on the revocation of such permission before the expiry of such temporary period, shall remove himself outside such area and shall not return thereto within the unexpired portion, specified under section 10 without a fresh permission.

(e) If a person fails to observe any of the conditions imposed or to remove himself accordingly or having so removed himself enters or returns to such area without fresh permission the Special Court may cause him to be arrested and removed in police custody to such place outside such area as the Special Court may specify.

3. Taking measurements and photographs, etc, of persons against whom order under section 10 is made.

(a) Every person against whom an order has been made under section 10 shall, if so required by the Special Court, allow his measurements and photographs to be taken by police officer.

(b) If any person referred to in sub-section (1), when required to allow his measurements or photographs to be taken resists or refuses to allow his taking of such measurements or photographs, it shall be lawful to use all necessary means to secure the taking thereof.

(c) Resistance to or refusal to allow the taking of measurements or photographs under sub-section (2) shall be deemed to be an offence under section 186 of the Indian Penal Code (45 of 1860).

(d) Where an order under section 10 is revoked, all measurements and photographs including negative) taken under sub-section (20 shall be destroyed or made over to the person against whom such order is made.

4. Penalty for non-compliance of order under section 10.– Any person contravening an order of the Special Court made under section to shall be punishable with imprisonment for a term which may extend to one year and with fine.

Chapter IV

Special Courts

1. Special Court—For the purpose of providing for speedy trial, the State Government shall, with the concurrence of the Chief Justice of High Court, by notification in the Official Gazette, specify for each district a Court of Session to be a special court to by the offences under this Act.
2. Special public Prosecutor - for every special court the State Government shall, by notification in the Official Gazette, specify a Public Prosecutor or appoint an advocate who has been in practice as an advocate for not less than seven years, as a Special Public Prosecutor for the purpose of conducting cases in that Court.

Chapter V

Miscellaneous

1. Power of State Government to impose collective fine.– The provisions of section 10A of the Protection of Civil Rights Act, 1955 (22 of 1955) shall, so far as may be, apply for the purposes of imposition and realisation of collective fine and for all other matters connected therewith under this Act.
2. Preventive action to be taken by law and order machinery.

   (a) A District Magistrate or a Sub-divisional Magistrate or any other Executive Magistrate or any police officer not below the rank of a Deputy Superintendent of Police may, on receiving information and after such inquiry as he may think necessary, has reason to believe that a person or a group of persons not belonging to the Scheduled Castes or the Scheduled Tribes, residing in or frequenting any place within the local limits of his jurisdiction is likely to commit an offence or has threatened to commit any offence under this Act and is of the opinion that there is sufficient ground for proceeding, declare such an area to be an area prone to atrocities and take necessary action for keeping the peace and good behaviour and maintenance of public order an tranquillity and may take preventive action.

(b) The provision of Chapters VIII, X and XI of the Code shall, so far as may be, apply for the purposes of sub-section (1).

(c) The State Government may, by notification in the Official Gazette, make one or more schemes specifying the manner in which the officers referred to in sub-section (1) shall take appropriate action specified in such scheme or schemes to prevent atrocities and to restore the feeling of security amongst the members of the Scheduled Castes and the Scheduled Tribes.

3. Section 438 of the Code not to apply to persons committing an offence under the Act.– Nothing in section 483 of the Code shall apply in relation to any case involving the arrest of any person on an accusation of having committed an offence under this Act.

4. Section 360 of the code of the provisions of the Probation of Offender Act not to apply to persons guilty of an offence under the Act - The provisions of section 360 of the code and the provisions of the Probation of Offenders Act, 1958 (20 of 1958) shall not apply to any person above the age of eighteen years who is guilty of having committed an offence under this Act.

5. Act to override other laws—Save as otherwise provided in this Act, the provisions of this Act shall have effect notwithstanding anything inconsistent therewith contained in any other law for the time being in force or any custom or usage or any instrument having effect by virtue of any such law.21. Duty of Government to ensure effective implementation of the Act.–

(a) Subject to such rule as the Central Government may make in this behalf, the State Government shall take such measures as may be necessary for the effective implementation of this Act. (2) In particular, and without prejudice to the generality of the foregoing provision, such measures, may include:

(i) the provision for adequate facilities including legal aid, to the persons subjected to atrocities to enable them to avail themselves of justice;

(ii) the provision for travelling and maintenance expenses to witnesses, including the victims of atrocities, during investigation and trail of offences under this Act;(iii) the provision for the economic and social rehabilitation of the victims of the atrocities;

(iii) the appointment of officers for initiating or exercising supervision over prosecutions for the contravention of the provisions of this Act;(v) the setting up of committees at such appropriate levels as the State Government may think fit to assist that Government in formulation or implementation of such measures;(vi) provision for a periodic survey of the working of the provisions of this Act with a view to suggesting measures for the better implementation of the provisions of this Act;

(iv) the identification of the area where the members of the Scheduled Castes and the Scheduled Tribes are likely to be subjected to atrocities and adoption of such measures so as to ensure safety for such members.

The Central Government shall take such steps as may be necessary to co-ordinate the measures taken by the State Governments under sub-section (1).

The Central Government shall, every years, place on the table of each House of Parliament a report on the measures taken by itself and by the State Governments in pursuance of the provisions of this section.

6. Protection of action taken in good faith.– No suit, prosecution or other legal proceedings shall lie against the Central Government or against the State Government or any officer or authority of GOVERNMENT or any other person for anything which is in good faith done or intended to be done under this Act.

7. Power to make rules.

(a) The Central Government may, by notification in the Official Gazette, make rules for carrying out the purposes of this Act.

(b) Every rule made under this Act shall be laid, as soon as may be after it is made, before each House of Parliament, while it is in session for a total period of thirty days which may be comprised in one session or in two or more successive sessions, and if, before the expiry of the session immediately following the session or the successive sessions aforesaid, both Houses agree in making any modification in the rule or both

Houses agree that the rule should not be made, the rule shall thereafter have effect only in such modified form or be of no effect, as the case may be; so, however, that any such modification or amendment shall be without prejudice to the validity of anything previously done under that rule.

Bill No. 98-F of 1990

The Constitution (Sixty-Fifth Amendment) Bill, 1990 (As Passed by the Houses of Parliament)

A Bill Further to amend the constitution of India.

Be it enacted by Parliament in the Forty-first year of the Republic of India as follow:-

1. (a) This Act may be called the Constitution (Sixty-fifth Amendment) Act, 1990.

   (b) It shall come into force on such date as the Central Government may, by notification in the Official gazette, appoint.

2. In article 338 of the Constitution,-

   (a) For the marginal heading, the following marginal heading shall be substituted, namely:—"National Commission for Scheduled Castes and Scheduled Tribes.";

   For clauses (1) and (2), the following clauses shall be substituted, namely:-

   (i) "There shall be a Commission for the Scheduled Castes and Scheduled Tribes to be known as the National Commission for the Scheduled Castes and Scheduled Tribes.

   (ii) Subject to the provisions of any law made in this behalf by Parliament, the Commission shall consist of a Chairperson, Vice-Chairperson and five other Members and the Conditions of service and tenure of office of the Chairperson, Vice-Chairperson and other Member so appointed shall be such as the President may by rule determine.

   (iii) The Chairperson, Vice-Chairperson and other Member of the Commission shall be appointed by the President by warrant under his hand and seal.

   (iv) The Commission shall have the power to regulate its own procedure.

   (v) It shall be the duty of the Commission

(c) To investigate and monitor all matters relating to the safeguards provided for the Scheduled Castes and Scheduled Tribes under this Constitution or under any other law for the time being in force or under any order of the Government and to evaluate the working of such safeguards;

(d) To inquire into specific complaints with respect to the deprivation of rights and safeguards of the Scheduled Castes and Scheduled Tribes;

(e) To participate and advise on the planning process of socio-economic development of the Scheduled Castes and Scheduled Tribes and to evaluate the progress of their development under the Union and any State;

(f) To present to the President, annually and at such other times as the Commission may deem fit, reports upon the working of those safeguards;

(g) To make in such reports recommendations as to the measures that should be taken by the Union or any State for the effective implementation of those safeguards and other measures for the protection, welfare and socio-economic development of the scheduled Castes and Scheduled Tribes; and

(h) To discharge such other functions in relation to the protection, welfare and development and advancement of the Scheduled Castes and Scheduled Tribes as the President may, subject to the provision of any law made by Parliament, by rule specify.

3. The President shall cause all such report to be laid before each House of Parliament along with a memorandum explaining the action taken or proposed to be taken on the recommendations relating to the Union and the reasons for the non-acceptance, if any, of any of such recommendations.

4. Where any such report, or any part thereof, relates to any matter with which any State government is concerned a copy of such report shall be forwarded to the Governor of the State who shall cause it to be laid before the Legislature of the State along with a memorandum explaining the action taken or proposed to be taken on the recommendations relating to the State and the reasons for the non-acceptance, if any, of any of such recommendations.

5. The Commission shall, while investigating any matter referred to in sub-clause (a) or inquiring into any complaint referred to in sub-clause (b) of clause (5), have all the powers of a civil court trying a suit and in particular in respect of the following matters, namely:

(a) summoning and enforcing the attendance of any person from any part of India examining him on oath;
(b) requiring the discovery and production of any document;
(c) receiving evidence on affidavits;
(d) requisitioning any public records or copy thereof from any court of office;
(e) issuing commissions for the examination of witnesses and document;
(f) any other matter which the President may, by rule, determine.

6. The Union and every State Government shall consult the Commission on all major policy matters affecting Scheduled castes and Scheduled Tribes." (c) existing clause (3) shall be renumbered as clause (10).

Bill No. 111 of 1991

The Constitution (Scheduled Tribes) Order (Second Amendment) Bill, 1991

A bill to provide for the inclusion of certain tribes in the list of Scheduled Tribes specified in relation to the State of Karnataka.

Be it enacted by parliament in the Forty-second Year of the Republic of India as follows:-

1. (a) This Act may be called the Constitution (Scheduled Tribes) Order (Second Amendment) Act, 1991.
   (b) (It shall be deemed to have come into on the 19th day of April, 1991.
2. In the Schedule to the Constitution (Scheduled Tribes) order, 1950, in "Part VI. Karnataka", in item 38, the following shall be inserted at the end namely: "Naik, Nayak, Beda, Bedar and Valmiki".

Bill No. 56 of 1993

The National Commission for *Safai Karamcharis* Bill, 1993

A bill to constitute a National Commission for *Safai Karamcharis* and to provide for matters connected therewith or incidental thereto.

Be it enacted by Parliament in the Forty-fourth Year of the Republic of India as follows:

Chapter I

Preliminary

1. (a) This Act may be called the National Commission for *Safai Karamcharis Act*, 1993.

(b) It extends to the whole of India except the State of Jammu and Kashmir.

(c) It shall come into force on such date as the Central Government 10 May, by notification in the Official Gazette, appoint.

(d) It shall cease to have effect after the 31st day of March, 1997, except as respects things done or omitted to be done before such, and upon such section 6 of the General Clauses Act, 1897, shall apply as if this Act had then been repealed by a Central Act.

2. In this Act, unless the context otherwise requires:

(a) "Chairperson" means the Chairperson of the Commission;

(b) "Commission" means the National Commission for *Safai Karamcharis* constituted under section 3;

(c) "Member" means a Member of the Commission;

(d) "Prescribed" means prescribed by rules made under this Act;

(e) "*Safai Karamchari*" means a person engaged in or employed for manually carrying human excreta;

(f) "Vice-Chairperson" means the Vice-Chairperson of the Commission.

Chapter II
The National Commission for *Safai Karamcharis*

3. (1) The Central Government shall, by notification in the Official Gazette, constitute a body to be known as the National Commission for *Safai Karamcharis* to exercise the powers conferred on, and to perform the functions, assigned to, it under this Act.

(b) The Commission shall consist of -

(i) a Chairperson;

(ii) a Vice-Chairperson;

(iii) Five Members;

To be nominated, from amongst the persons of eminence connected with the socio-economic development and Welfare of *Safai Karamcharis*, by the Central Government;

Provided that at least one of the Members shall be a woman.

4. (a) The Chairperson, Vice-Chairperson and every Member shall hold office for such period not exceeding three years as may be specified by the Central Government in this behalf or up to 31st day of March, 1997, whichever is earlier.

(b) The Chairperson, Vice-Chairperson or a Member may, by notice in writing, addressed to the Central Government, resign from the office of Chairperson, Vice-Chairperson, or as the case may be, of the Member at any time.

(c) The Central Government shall remove a person from the office of Chairperson, Vice-Chairperson or a Member if that person-

(d) becomes an undercharged insolvent;

(e) is convicted and sentenced to imprisonment for an offence which, in the opinion of the Central Government, involves moral turpitude;

(f) becomes of unsound mind and stands so declared by a competent court;

(g) Refuses to act or becomes incapable of acting;

(h) is, without obtaining leave of absence from the commission, absent from three consecutive meetings of the Commission; or

(i) in the opinion of the Central Government has so abused the position of Chairperson, Vice-Chairperson or Member as to render that person's continuance in office detrimental to the public interest;

Provided that no person shall be removed under this clause until that person has been given a reasonable opportunity of being heard in the matter. (4) A vacancy caused under sub-section (2) or sub-section (3) or otherwise shall be filled by fresh nomination and a person so nominated shall hold office for the unexpired period of the term for which his predecessor in office would have held office if such vacancy had not arisen.

5. The salaries and allowances payable to and other terms and conditions of service of the Chairperson, Vice-Chairperson and Members shall be such as may be prescribed.

   (a) The Central Government shall provide the Commission with such officers and employees as may be necessary for the efficient performance of the functions of the Commission under this Act.

   (b) The salaries and allowances payable to, and other terms and conditions of service of, the officers and other employees appointed for the purpose of the Commission shall be such as may be prescribed.

6. No act or proceeding of the Commission shall be questioned or shall be invalid on the ground merely of the existence of any vacancy or defect in the constitution of the Commission.

7. (a) The Commission shall meet as and when necessary and shall meet at such time and place as the Chairperson may think fit.
   (b) The Commission shall regulate its own procedure.
   (c) All orders and decisions of the Commission shall be authenticated by the Chairperson or any other officer of the Commission duly authorised by the Chairperson in his behalf.

Chapter III
Functions and Powers of the Commission

8. (a) The Commission shall perform all or any of the following functions, namely:-
   (b) recommend to the Central Government specific programmes of action towards elimination of inequalities in status, facilities and opportunities for *Safai Karamcharis* under a time-bound action plan;
   (c) study and evaluate the implementation of the programmes and schemes relating to the social and economic rehabilitation of *Safai Karamcharis* and make recommendations to the Central Government and State Governments for better co-ordination and implementation of such programmes and schemes;
   (d) investigate specific grievances and take *suo moto* notice of matters relating to non-implementation of;
      (i) programmes or schemes in respect of any group of *Safai Karamcharis*;
      (ii) decisions, guidelines or instructions, aimed at mitigating the hardship of *Safai Karamcharis*;
      (iii) the provisions of any law in its application to *Safai Karamcharis*;

   And take up such matters with the concerned authorities or with the Central or State government;
   (e) make periodical reports to the Central and State Governments on any matter concerning *Safai Karamcharis*, taking into account any difficulties or disabilities being encountered by *Safai Karamcharis*;
   (f) any other matter which may be referred to it by the Central Government.

9. In the discharge of its functions under sub-section (1), the Commission shall have power to call for information with respect to any matter specified in that sub-section from any Government or local or other authority.

Chapter IV
Miscellaneous

1. The Chairperson, Vice-Chairperson, Members, officers and other employees of the Commission shall be deemed to be public servants within the meaning of section 21 of the Indian Penal Code.
2. The Central Government shall consult the Commission on all major policy matter affecting *Safai Karamcharis*.
3. The Commission shall prepare in such form and at such time for each financial year as may be prescribed its annual report giving a full account of its activities during the previous financial year and forward a copy thereof to the Central government.
4. (a) The Central Government shall cause the annual report to be laid before each House of Parliament along with the memorandum explaining the action taken or proposed to be taken on the recommendations contained therein in so far as they relate to the Central Government and the reasons for non-acceptance, if any, of any such recommendation.

   (e) Where the said report or any part thereof relates to any matter with which a State Government is concerned, a copy of such report shall be forwarded to the Governor of the State who shall cause it to be laid before the Legislature of the State along with a memorandum explaining the action taken or proposed to be taken on the recommendations relating to the State and the reasons for the non-acceptance, if any, of any such recommendation or part.
5. The Commission may, by general or special order, delegate to the Chairperson, Vice-Chairperson or any Member or to any officer of the Commission subject to such conditions and limitations, if any, as may be specified therein, such of is powers and duties, under this Act as if may deem fit.
6. No suit, prosecution or other legal proceeding shall lie against the Central Government, Commission, Chairperson, Vice-Chairperson, Members or any officer or other employees of the Commission for anything which is in good faith done or intended to be done under this Act.
7. (a) The Central Government may, by notification in the Official Gazette, make rules for carrying out the provision of this Act.

(b) In particular, and without prejudice to the generality of the foregoing power, such rules may provide for all or any of the following matters, namely:
   (i) Salaries and allowances payable to, and the other terms and conditions of service of, the Chairperson, Vice-Chairperson and Members under sub-section (5) of section 4 and of officers and other employees of he Commission under sub-section (2) of sections 5;
   (ii) The form in, and the time at, which the annual report shall be prepared under section 11.
   (iii) Any other matter which is required to be or may be or may be, prescribed.

(c) Every rule made under this Act shall be laid, as soon as may be after it is made, before each house of Parliament, while it is in session for a total period of thirty days which may be comprised in one session or in two or more successive sessions, and if, before the expiry of the session immediately following the session or the successive sessions aforesaid, both Houses agree in making any modification in the rule or both Houses agree that the rule should not be made, the rule shall thereafter have effect only in such modified form or be of no effect as the case may be; so, however, that any such modification or annulment shall be without prejudice to the validity anything previously done under that rule.

Bill No. 43-F of 1995
The Constitution (Seventy-Seventh Amendment) Bill, 1995
(as passed by the Houses of Parliament)

A bill further to Amend the Constitution of India.

Be it enacted by Parliament in the Forty-sixth year of the Republic of India as follows:

1. This Act may be called the Constitution (Seventy-seventh Amendment) Act, 1995.
2. In article 16 of the constitution after clause (4); the following clause shall be inserted, namely:
3. Nothing in this article shall prevent the State from making any provision for reservation in matters of promotion to any class or classes of posts in the services under the State in favour of the Scheduled Castes and the Scheduled Tribes which, in the opinion of the States, are not adequately represented in the services under the State."

Bibliography

Primary Sources

Reports

Parliamentary Committee on the Welfare of SC & ST 1969, 1st Report
Parliamentary Committee on the Welfare of SC & ST 1970, 6th Report.
Parliamentary Committee on the Welfare of SC & ST, 1993, 24th Report.
Parliamentary Committee on the Welfare of SC & ST, 1993, 27th Report.
Parliamentary Committee on the Welfare of SC & ST, 1995, 45th Report.
Parliamentary Committee on the Welfare of SC & ST, 1995, 53rd Report.
Report of the Commissioner for SC & ST 1977-78
Report of the Commissioner for SC & ST 1979-81
Report of the National Commission for SC & ST 1992-93
Report of the National Commission for SC & ST 1993-94
Report of the National Commission for SC & ST 1994-95
Report of the National Commission for SC & ST Special Report 1997-98
Census of India, 1991. Final Population for SC & ST, Table 2
India Constitutional Reforms, Report of the Franchise Committee (Southborough Committee). Calcutta: Government Printing office, 1919.
India Round Table Conference (Second Session) 7 September -1 December 1931 .
India Quarterly Register, 1923.
India Quarterly Register, 1930. *All India Depressed Classes Conference,* Vol. II.
Government of India, Report of the Commission on Untouchability, Economic and Educational Development of Scheduled Castes and Connected Documents, Department of Social Welfare, 1969.
Proceedings of Federal Structure and Minorities Committee, Indian Round Table Conference (Second Session), 7th September-1st December, 1931.
Proceedings of Sub-Committee, Vol. 11, Sub-committee No. 111 (Minorities), Indian Round Table Conference 1930-31.
Report of First Backward Class Commission Report, 1955.
Report on Indian Constitutional Reform, 1918.
Report on Reforms Enquiry Committee, 1924.
Government of India, Census 1951, West Bengal, The Tribes and Castes of West Bengal.
Government of India, Report of Commissioner, National Commission Report, 1979-81.
Lok Sabha Debates (LSD), 1985 - 95, Lok Sabha Secretariat, New Delhi.

Secondary Sources

Books, Journals and Periodicals

Ahir, D.C. 1977. *Selected Speeches of Dr. B.R. Ambedkar 1927-51*, Delhi: Blumoon.
____ 1991. *The Legacy of Dr. Ambedkar*. Delhi: B.R. Publishing Corp.
Ahmed, K. 1978. "Towards Equality: Consequences of Protective Discrimination". *Economic and Political Weekly*, January 14:69-76.
Ajay, G. and Vijay, G. 2000. "Civil Society, State and Social Movements", *Economic and Political Weekly,* March 18:1035-36.

Ambedkar, B. R. 1977. *What Congress and Gandhi Have Done to the Untouchables*? .Lahore: Classics.

Austin, Granville 1966. *The Indian Constitution: Cornerstone of a Nation*, Oxford: Clarendon Press.

____ 1985. *The Indian Constitution: Cornerstone of a Nation*, Bombay: Oxford University Press.

Bajpai, Rochana, 2000. "Constituent Assembly Debates and Minority Rights", *Economic and Political Weekly*, May 27:1837-45.

Basu, D. D. 1995. *Introduction to the Constitution of India*. 17th edition, New Delhi: Pretice-Hall of India.

Baxi, Upendra 1984. "Legislative Reservation for Social Justice: Some Thoughts on India's Unique Experiment'" in R. Goldman and A. J. Wilson (eds) *From Independence to Statehood*, London: Frances Printer:210-24.

Berkman, Michael 1994. "State Legislators in Congress: Strategic Politicians, Professional Legislatures and the Party Nexus", *American Journal of Political Science* 38:1025-55.

Berreman, Gerald 1960. "Caste in India and the United States', *American Journal of Sociology*, 66: 120-27.

____ 1979. *Caste and Other Inequalities*, Meerut: Folklore Institute.

Beteille, Andre 1969, *Caste:Old and New*. New Delhi: Oxford University Press.

____ 1999. "Empowerment, Background and Context", *Economic and Political Weekly*, March 6-13, 589-597.

Bhandari, M. K. 1993. *Basic Structure of the Indian Constitution: A Critical Reconsideration*, New Delhi: Deep and Deep.

Bharathi, M. and Rao, R.S. 1999. "Linking Development to Displacement". *Economic and Political Weekly*, July 10:1955-56.

Bhatt, Anil 1975. *Caste, Class, and Politics*, Delhi: Manohar.

Birch, A.H. 1971. *Representation*, London: Pall Mall.

Blondel, Jean 1970. "Legislative Behaviour: Some Steps Towards a Comparative Measurement" *Government and Opposition*, 5: 67-85.

Bokil, Milind 1996. "Privativization of the Commons for the Poor: Emergence of New Agrarian Issues", *Economic and Political Weekly*, August 17: 2254-61.

Cadell, Sir Patrick 1938. *History of the Bombay Army*. London: Longmans Green.

Canon, David T. 1999. "Electoral System and the representation of Minority Interests in Legislatures", *Legislative Studies Quarterly*, XXIV:331-85.

Chalm, K.S. 1999. *Economic Reforms and Missing Safety Nets*, Mumbai: Vikas Adhyayan Kendra.

Chandra, Ramesh 1999. "Rehabilitation of Scavengers", *Economic and Political Weekly*, September 11:2635-36.

Chandu, Subha Rao & Francis, D. 2000. *Development of Weaker Sections*, Jaipur: Rawat.

Chatterjee, S. K. 1996. *The Scheduled Castes in India*, Vol. 1, New Delhi: Gyan Publishing House.

____ 1998. *The Scheduled Castes in India*, New Delhi: Gyan Publishing House.

Chauhan, D. N. S. and Chopra, S. L. 1969. "A Comparative Study of Socio-Economic Background of the Members of the Lok Sabha Elected from the Reserved and General Constituencies" *Journal of Constitutional and Parliamentary Studies* (Delhi) Vol. III (2).

Chitnis, S.M. 1972. "Education for Equality: Case of the Scheduled Castes", *Economic and Political Weekly*, Special No.

Cohen, Percy S. 1979 *Modern Social Theory*, London: Morrison and Gibb.

Cohen, Stephan P. 1969 "The Untouchable Soldier - Caste Politics and the Indian Army" (Asbor), *Journal of Asian Studies*, Vol. 28.(3): 453-68.

Connoly, William 1991. *Identity/Difference: Democratic Negotiations Political Paradox, Ithaca,* New York: Cornell University Press.

Dangle, Arjun 1992. *Poisoned Bread*, New Delhi: Orient Longman.

De Grazia, Alfred 1968. "Theory of Representation" in Sills, Daniel (ed.) *International Encyclopedia of Social Sciences*, vol. XIII.

Deliege, Robert 1992. "Replication and Consensus: Untouchability, Caste and Ideology in India" Man (n.s.) 27:155-73.

____ 1992. *The World of the 'Untouchables': Paraiyars of Tamil Nadu*, Delhi: Oxford University Press.

____ 1999. *The Untouchables of India,* Oxford: Berg.

Dumont, Louis 1979 *Homo Hierarchus*, London: Weindenfield and Necolson.

Duskin, Lelah 1961. "Removal of Disabilities", *Economic and Political Weekly*, November:1695-1709.

____ 1961. "Special Treatment Policy", *Economic and Political Weekly*, October:1965-66.

____ 1961, "The Backward Classes', Special Treatment Policy "Economic and Political Weekly, 13, 1665, 68, 95, 1705, 1727-38, 1979" Backward Class Benefits and Social Class in India a 1920-1970 *Economic and Political Weekly*, 14 April.

____ 1972. "Scheduled Caste Politics" In Michael Mahar (ed) *The Untouchables in Contemporary India*, Tucson: University of Arizona Press.

Dworkin, Ronald 1977. *Taking Rights Seriously*, Cambridge, Massachusetts: Harvard University Press.

Easton, David 1957. "An Approach to the Analysis of Political Systems," *World Politics,* Vol. No.9.

Eligie, Robert 1995. *Political leadership in Liberal Democracies,* Houndmills: Macmillan Press.

Elwin, Verrier 1959. A Philosophy of NEFA, Shillong: NEFA Administration.

Eulau, H. 1962. "The Legislator as Representative: Representational Roles" in Wahalke *et. al. The Legislative System: Explorations in Legislative Behaviour*, New York: John Wiky and Sons.

____ and Wahlke, John C. 1978. *The Politics of Representation*, California: Sage.

Freeman, J. 1979. *Untouchable: An Indian Life History*, London: Allen and Unwin.

Gaikwad, S.L. 1999. *Protection Discrimination Policy and Social Change,* New Delhi: Rawat, 1996.

Gawarguru, G.N. 1986. "The Party Politics in Reserved Constituencies: A Case Study of Pandarpur Parliamentary Reserved Constituency for Scheduled Castes in Maharashtra", Unpublished Ph.D. Thesis, CPS/SSS, Jawaharlal Nehru University, New Delhi.

Ghosh, P. K. 1932. *The Constitution of India: How it has been Framed,* Calcutta: The World Press Syndicate.

Ghurye, G. S. 1963. *The Scheduled Tribes,* Bombay : Popular Prakashan.

____ 1990. *Caste and Race in India*, Bombay: Popular Prakashan.

Gifford, D.J. and Salter, John 1996. *How to Understand an Act of Parliament*, London: Cavendish.

Glanter, Marc 1984. *Competing Equalities- Law and Backward Classes in India*, Delhi: Oxford University Press.

Gore, M.S. 1993. *The Social Context of an Ideology: Ambedkar's Political and Social Thoughts*, New Delhi: Sage Publications.

Government of India (GOI) 1992. *Ambedkar and Social Justice*, Vol. II New Delhi: Ministry of Information and Broadcasting.

Griffith, J.A.G. 1974. *Parliamentary Scrutiny of Government Bill*, Oxford: George Allan and Unwin.

Gupta, S. K. 1985. *The Scheduled Castes in Modern Indian Poultices,* New Delhi: Munshiram Manoharlal Publications.

Gupta, S.P. 1995. "Economic Reform and Its Impact on Poor", *Economic and Political Weekly*, June 3: 1295-1320.

Guru, Gopal 1986. "Political Reservation for th Scheduled Castes: A Politics of Reformism", in R. G. Singh (ed.) *The Depressed Classes in India,* New Delhi: B. R. Publishing Corp: 81-89.

Guttsman, W. 1964. The British Political Elite, London: Mac Gibbon and Kee.

Harris, John 2001. "Globalisation and World's Poor Institutions Inequality and Justice", *Economic and Political Weekly,* June 9: 2034-57.

Hofferbert, Richard I. 1966. "The Relationship Between Public Policy and Some Structural and Environmental Variables", *American Political Science Review,* 60:73-82.

Hoffman, Carl and Reed, John 1981. "When is Imbalance Not discrimination?" In Walter Block and Michael Walker (eds) *Discrimination, Affirmative Action and Equal Opportunity*, Vancouver: The Fraser Institute.

Howlett, Michel and Ramesh, M. 1995. *Studying Public Policy*, Toronto: Oxford University Press.

Human Right Watch, 1999. *Broken People*, New York.

Hyman, Herbert H. 1972. *Political Socialisation* (Indian Edition), New Delhi: The Free Press.

Ilaiah, Kancha, 1996, *Why I am Not a Hindu*, Calcutta: Samya.

Ingram, Helen and Mann, Dean (eds.) 1980. *Why Policies Succeed or Fail*, Beverly Hills: Sage Publications.

Jain, Meenakshi, 1990. "A Myth the British Created" *India Express*, 5th October.

Jain, R. B. 1983 "Parliament and Policy in India", *Indian Journal of Public Administration* July-September:559-89.

____ 1985. "Electronics Policy and Indian Parliament", *Indian Journal of Public Administration* April-June:239-74.

James, P. A. and Srinivas Reddy 1979. "Commission for Scheduled Castes and Scheduled Tribes". *Economic and Political Weekly,* 30 June:1100-03.

Jordon, A. G. and Richardson, J. J. 1987. *British Polities and Policy Process,* London: Allen & Unwin.

Joshi, Barbara R. 1982. *Democracy in Search of Equality: Untouchable Politics and Indian Social Change.* Delhi: Hindustan Publishers.

Kananaikil, J. 1982. *Scheduled Castes in the Constituent Assembly*, New Delhi: Indian Social Institute.

Kashyap, Subhas C. 1992. (ed) *Reforming the Constitution*, New Delhi: UBS Publishers and Distributors Ltd.

____ 1987. *The Parliament and the Executive*, (Monograph Series -1), New Delhi: Parliament Secretariat.

____ 1992. *Our Parliament.* New Delhi: NBT, 2nd Ed.

Keer, Dhananjay 1962. *Dr. Ambedkar: Life and Mission* (Second Edition), Bombay: Popular Prakashan.

Kothari, Rajni. 1988. "Integration and Exclusion in Indian Politics", *Economic and Political Weekly*, XXIII (43), 22 October: 2223-29.

____ 1997. "Rise of the Dalits and the Renewed Debate on Caste", in Partha Chaterjee (ed) *State and Politics in India*, New Delhi: Oxford,

Krishnan, P. S. 1993. "Untouchability and Atrocities", *Social Action*, Vol. 43, October-December:412-426.

Kuppuswamy 1979. *Social Change in India*, Sahibabad: Vikas.

Larrdis, 2000. "Members of the Twelfth Lok Sabha- A Socio-Economic Profile", *The Journal of Parliamentary Information,* Vol. XLVI March Lok Sabha Secretariat 67-89.

Lascher Jr., Edward L.1996. "Assessing Legislative Deliberation: A Preface to Empirical Analysis", *Legislative Studies Quarterly*, Vol.XXI, November : 501-19.

Lathe, A. B. 1924. *Memories of His Highness Shri. Chhattrapati Maharaja of Kolhapur*, Vol. 11, Bombay: Publication not mentioned.

Lowi, T.J. 1994. "American Business, Public Policy, Case Studies and Political Theory", *World Politics*, 16:677-93.

Lynch, Owen. M. 1969. *The Politics of Untouchability- Social Mobility and Social Change in a City of India*, New York: Columbia University Press.

Maestar, Cherie 2000. "Professional Legislatures and Ambitions Politicians: Policy Responsiveness of State Institutions" *Legislative Studies Quarterly*, Vol.XXV, November 4:663-90.

Margech, James 1981. *The Anatomy of Power*, London: Allen.

Marsh, Ian 1986. *Policy-Making in a Three Party System: Committees, Coalitions and Parliament*, London: Methuen.

Massey, James 1990. "Christian Dalits in India: An Analysis", *Religion and Society*, XXXVII(3), September : 40-53.

Mathur, Kuldeep 2000. "Governance and Alternative Sources of Policy Advice: The Case of India", (unpublished paper).

____ and Neerja Jayal 1993. *Drought Policy and Politics in India,* New Delhi: Sage.

____ 1997. *Policy Studies: An Emerging Area of Concern,* Guntur: Indian Political Science Association.

Mendelsohn, Oliver and Vicziany, Marica 1988. "The Untouchables Forty Years On", Paper presented at the Conference, *India Forty Years On*, The University of Sydney, Sydney, Australia, May 18-20.

____ 1998. *The Untouchables: Subordination, Poverty, and the State in Modern India,* Cambridge: Cambridge University Press.

Michael, S.M. 1999. *Dalits in Modern India*, New Delhi: Vistar.

Michells, J.M. 1969. *Political Analysis and Public Policy: An Introduction to Political Science*, New Delhi: Thomson Press.

Moffatt, Michael 1979. *An Untouchable Community in South India*, Princeton: Princeton University Press.

Moon, Vasant 1979. *Dr. Babasaheb Ambedkar Writings and Speeches*, Vol.1, Govt. of Maharashtra, Mumbai: Education Department.

____ 1989. *Dr. Babasaheb Ambedkar Writings and Speeches*, Vol.5, Govt. of Maharashtra, Mumbai: Education Department.

____ 1990. *Dr. Babasaheb Ambedkar Writings and Speeches*, Vol.9, Govt. of Maharashtra, Mumbai: Education Department.

____ 1991. Dr. Babasaheb Ambedkar Writings and Speeches, Vol.10, Govt. of Maharashtra, Mumbai: Education Department.

Morris-Jones W. H. 1957. *Parliament in India*, London: Longmans.

Mungekar. B. L. 2001. "Globalisation and the Dalits", *The Radical Humanist* April 9-10.

Nagraj, R. 2000. "Indian Economy Since 1980 Virtuous Growth or Polarisation", *Economic and Political Weekly*, August 5, 2831-39.

Narayana, G. 1978. "Social Background of Scheduled Castes Lok Sabha Members: 1962-71", Economic and Political Weekly: 1603-7.

____ 1980. "Rule Making for Schedule Caste: Analysis of Lok Sabha Debates 1962-71", *Economic and Political Weekly,* September 16: 433-440.

Natraj, V. K. 1999. "Reservations Seeking New Perspectives", *Economic and Political Weekly*, August 21-28, 2384-5.

Nayyar, Deepak 1998. "Economic Development and Political Democracy: Economics and Politics in Independent India", *Economic and Political Weekly*, December 5:3121-31.

Nayyar, Dhiraj 2000. "Alleviating Poverty: Role of Good Governance and Constitutional Reform", *Economic and Political Weekly,* October 2000, 3739-42.

Nesiah, Devanesan 1997. *Discrimination with Reason: The Policy of Reservations in the United States, India and Malaysia,* Delhi: Oxford University Press.

Nicholas, Mansergh 1970. *The Transfer of Power*, vol. II No. 58 London: His Majesty's Stationary Office.

Norton, Philip 1984. Parliament and Policy in Britain: The House of Commons as a policy Influencer", *Teaching Politics*, 13: 198-202.

____ 1993. *Does Parliament Matter*? Harvester, Wheat Sheaf: Hartfordshire.

Omprakash, S. 1989. *Development of the Weaker Sections: Problems, Policies and Issues*, New Delhi: Uppal Publishing House.

Omvedt, Gail 1976. *Cultural Revolt in a Colonial Society: The Non-Brahmin Movement in Western India, 1873 to 1930.* Poona: Scientific Socialist Education Trust.

____ 1994. *Dalits and the Democratic Revolution: Dr. Ambedkar and the Dalit Movement in Colonial India,* New Delhi: Sage Publications.

____ 2001 Reservation in Corporate Sector, *The Hindu,* May 31.

____ 2001. "Reservation in the Corporate Sector" *The Hindu*, June 1.

Oomen, T. K. 1984. "Sources of Depravation and Styles of Protests: The Case of Dalits in India" *Contributions to Indian Sociology,* (NS) 18 pp 45-61.

Pathak, Bindeshwar 1991. *Road to Freedom: A Sociological Study on the abolition of Scavenging in India,* Delhi: Motilal Banarsidas Publishers

Pathy, Jagannath 1997. "Scheduled Tribes and Broken Promises" in Bhattacharjee, Ajit (ed) *Social Justice and Indian Constitution,* Shimla: Indian Institute of Advanced Studies.

Phule, Jotiba 1991. *Mahatma Phule Samagra Vangmaya (MPSV)*, Edited by Yeshwant Dinaker Phadke, Mumbai: Maharashtra Rajya Sahitya ani Sanskriti Mandal.

Poister, Theodore H. 1978. *Public Programme Analysis*, Baltimore: Md. University Park Press.

Polsby, Nelson 1975. "Legislatures" in Fred Greenstein and Nelson Polsby (ed), *Handbook of Political Science,* Reading MA: Addison Wesley.

Rahman A. and Haritash, Nirmal 1985. *The Role of Parliament in The Formulation of National Science And Technology Policy*, New Delhi: NISTADS.

Rajashekhar, C. 1993. *Social Revolution and the Indian Constitution: Inter-relationship Between Fundamental Rights and Directive Principles,* New Delhi: Deep and Deep.

Ram, Nandu 1989. "Prevention of Atrocities Act Studying Atrocities on Dalits: Some Theoretical- Methodological Explanations", Unpublished Paper.

____ 1995. *Beyond Ambedkar,* Delhi: Har-Anand.

Rai, V.K. 1999. "In Search of New Balance - Caste, Region and Community in Uttar Pradesh" Economic and Political Weekly, August 21-28:2400-08.

Rao, M.S.A. 1984. *Social Movements in India*, in 2 volumes, New Delhi: Manohar Publications.

Rao, Shiva 1967. *The Framing of India's Constitution*, Vol. 11, New Delhi: Indian Institute of Public Administration.

Richardson, J. J. and Jordon, A. G. 1979. *Governing Under Pressure: The Policy Process in a Post Parliamentary Democracy*, Oxford: Basil Blackwell.

Robertson, Alexander 1938. *The Mahar Folk.* Calcutta: YMCA Publishing House.

Roy Burman, B.K. 1977. "The Problem of Untouchables", in Romesh Thapar (ed) *Tribe, Caste and Religion in India*, Delhi: Macmillan.

Rubinoff, Arthur G. 1995. "India's New Subject-Based Parliamentary Standing Committees", *Asian Survey,* Vol, 36 July-September:722-40.

Rush, Michel 1976. *Parliament and the Public*, New York: Longman.

Saberwal, Satish 1972. "The Reserved Constituency - Candidates and Consequences", *Economic and Political Weekly*, Vol.7.

____ 2000. "Constitutional Ideas and Political Practices", *Economic and Political Weekly*, March 11:885-87.

Sachidanand 1977. *Harijan Elite,* Faridabad: Thomson India Limited.

Saksena, H.S. 1981. *Safeguards for Scheduled Castes and Tribes: Founding Fathers Views*, New Delhi: Uppal Publishing House.

Sanyal, Annapurna 1991. *Scheduled Castes And Scheduled Tribes in Indian Polities*, Calcutta: Minerva.

Sapru, R.K. 1998. *Public Policy: Formulation Implementation and Evaluation*, New Delhi: Sterling.

Sathe, Dhanmanjiri 1999. "Economic Development and Political Democracy", *Economic and Political Weekly*, April 3:839-40.

Scully, Roger M. 1997. "Policy Influence and Participation in European Parliament", *Legislative Studies Quarterly*, XXII May:233-52.

Sen, Amartya 1981. *Poverty and Famines: An Essay in Entitlement and Deprivation*, Oxford: Clarendon Press.

Shakdher, S. L. 1977. *Glimpses of the Working of Parliament*, New Delhi: Metropolitan.

Sharma, B. D. 1994. *Dalits Betrayed*, New Delhi: Har-Anand.

Sharma, Devindra 2001. "A Critique of 'Leses and Olive' View of Globalization", *The Hindu,* May 29.

Sheth, D.L. 1987. "Reservation Policy Revisited" *Economic and Political Weekly*, Bombay. November 14: 1957-62.

Singer, Milton 1958. "Traditional India: Structure and Change", *Journal of American Folklore*. 71: 191-205.

Singh, R.G. 1986. *The Depressed Class in India*, New Delhi: B.R. Publishing Corporation.

Sinha, R. K. 1986. *Alienation Among Scheduled Castes,* Delhi: Manas Publications.

Sivaramayya, B. 1984. "Affirmative Action: The Scheduled Castes and the Scheduled Tribes", In *International Perspectives on Affirmative Action*, USA: Rockfeller Foundation.

Solomon, Gerald B.H. and Donald R. Wolfensberger 1994. "The Decline of Deliberative Democracy in the House and Proposals for Reform", *Harward Journal on Legislation*, 31:321-70.

Sowell, Thomas 1987. *A Conflict of Visions: Ideological Origins of Political Struggles*, New York: Quill William Morrow.

Stephans, Wilk and Wright, Maurice (ed) 1987. *Comparing Government Industry Relations: States: Section and Networks*, Oxford: Clarendon.

Subbarao, G. C. Venkata 1982. *Legislative Powers in Indian Constitutional Law,* Hyderabad: Law Academy.

Sundaram K. 2001. "Employment-Unemployment Situation in the Nineties Some Results form NSS. 55th Round Survey", *Economic and Political Weekly*. March 17, (931-940).

Surya, Prakash A. 1995. *What Ails Indian Parliament*? New Delhi:Harper Collins Publishers.

Swain, Carol M. 1993. *Black Faces, Black Interests: The Representation of African Americans in Congress*, Cambridge MA: Harward University Press.

Tendulkar, Suresh D. and Jain, L.R. 1995. "Economic Reforms and Poverty", *Economic and Political Weekly*, June 10 : 1373-76.

Thekaekara, Marcel 2001. Annihilating Caste, *The Hindu*, June 10.

Thorat, S.K. 1992. *Dalit Reality: An Analysis from Economic Perspective*, Madras: The Gurukul Institute.

Trivedi, Harshad R. 1996. *Scheduled Caste Quest for Land and Social Equality*, New Delhi: Concept

Vaidyanathan 2001. "Poverty and Development Politics", *Economic and Political Weekly*, August :1807-22.

Verma, Vidhu 1999. "Colonialism and Libeation: Ambedkar's Quest for Distributive Justice", *Economic and Political Weekly*, September 25:2804-10.

Wahlke, John C. 1978. "The Legislative and the Political System", in Eulau, Heinz and Wahlke, John C. (ed) 1978. *The Politics of Representation*, California: Sage: 151-75.

Wasby, Stephen 1986. "Indian Compensatory Discrimination" and American "Affirmative Action", Some Parallels - A Review of Galanter's Competing Equalities", *Law & Policy*, Vol. 8, No. 3. July.

Waterman, Peter 1993, *Some Propositions on Globalisation, Civil Society, Solidarity*, The Hague: Institute of Social Sciences.

Weber, Ronald E. 1999. "The Quality of State Legislative Representation: A Critical Assessment", *The Journal of Politics*, 61:609-27.

Webster, John C.B. 1994. *The Dalit Christians: A History*, Delhi, ISPCK.

Weiner, Myron 1971. "Political Participation: Crisis of Political Process" in Leonard Binder (ed) *Crisis and Sequence in Political Development*, Princeton: Princeton University Press.

Xaxa, Virginius. 1999. "Transformation of Tribes in India: Terms of Discourse", *Economic and Political Weekly*, June 12:1519-24.

Yadav, Yogendra 1999. "Electoral Politics in the Time of Change India's Third Electoral System, 1989-99", August 21-28, 1999, *EPW* 2393-99

Young, Iris M. 1993. "Justice and Communicative Democracy" in Roger S. Gotlieb (ed) *Radical Philosophy: Tradition, Counter-Tradition, Politics*, Philadelphia: Temple University Press.

Zaidi, A. M. and S. G. Zaidi 1987. *The Encyclopaedia of the Indian National Congress*, 1916-20, Vol. 7, New Delhi: S. Chand & Company.

____ 1987. *The Encyclopaedia of the Indian National Congress*, Vol, 9, New Delhi: S. Chand & Company.

Zelliot, Eleanor 1972. "Gandhi and Ambedkar: A Study in Leadership", In M. Mahar (ed.), *The Untouchables in Contemporary India*, Tucson: University of Arizona Press.

____ 1992. *From Untouchable to Dalit: Essays on the Ambedkar Movement*, Delhi: Manohar.